ADVAN

Surpris

In this true, modern-day love story, Jay and Julie live the principle that destiny is not a matter of chance but a willingness to choose who you must become to make your relationship all it can be.

—**Anthony Robbins**
Entrepreneur, author, and peak-performance strategist

This is one of the most personal and enlightening books I have ever read on affairs and healing from betrayal. This book is a dialogue one couple had over a long time period, and it gives the reader insight on what the processes of honesty, transparency, forgiveness, and rebuilding trust are all about. This is a great book and I learned a lot from it. I recommend everyone read it.

—**John M. Gottman, PhD**
Author of *The Seven Principles for Making Marriage Work*
and founder of The Gottman Relationship Institute

Every once in a while I come across a book that grabs my attention and stands out. *Surprised by Love* is riveting in that it reads like a classic novel yet is a true story told with boldness and compassion. It is invaluable and the authors write from the heart. Practical and wise with many useful insights, this book is a must-read for every couple who wants to have a happy, fulfilling relationship as well as for every marital therapist who works with couples. I plan on using it in my teaching!

—**Cloé Madanes**
World-renowned teacher/author; founder of Strategic Marital
Therapy, The Tony Robbins-Cloé Madanes Center for Strategic
Intervention

Wow! What a story. Jay and Julie have written an important book that will help and heal many couples. The authors' willingness to be transparent and expose it *all*, though difficult to read at times, is a gift for those who have suffered through the betrayal of an affair and those who want to understand it.

—**Arielle Ford**
Best-selling author of *Soulmate Secret*

Surprised by Love is tangible proof that love is stronger than betrayal or even the death of a marriage. This amazing story portrays how a woman's fierce and unconditional love and a man's willingness to evolve restored their broken marriage and helped them create spiritual and emotional healing in the process. Jay and Julie's story provides not only hope for every couple but marriage truths that are truly revelational.

>—**Richard Exley, DD**
>**Pastor; author of *Intimate Moments for Couples***

I have long been aware of the work of Dr. Jay Ferraro. Now he goes far beyond new ideas and innovative approaches to help transform executives and their teams, as he shines a light on one of the most tragic and damaging aspects of our modern society. Bravely, he and his wife tell the truth about infidelity—their own story of coping with and overcoming it. If you're investing your life in a relationship, you should at least invest a few hours in reading this amazing book so you can get a roadmap and avoid the pitfalls.

>—**Jim Stovall**
>**Author of *The Ultimate Gift***

Remarkable! *Surprised by Love* is a brilliant read for anyone contemplating being in or recovering from an affair or simply avoiding one—I was captivated and read it in a night. This gift of a book challenges those who simply want to know the solution to their problems. Through Jay and Julie's story, we ride the emotional roller coaster, we reconnect to our own most vulnerable parts, and we ask our own questions. Ultimately, we are more aware of our own tender humanity by listening to two profound voices triumphing over the same excruciating experience. As you live the journey with them, you will feel the tension, experience the pull, see the humanness in both, and feel the pain while becoming the wiser for having traveled with Jay and Julie through their powerful story.

>—**Camille Preston, PhD, PCC**
>**Psychologist, executive coach, and best-selling author**
>**AIM Leadership, LLC: www.aimleadership.com**

In a world of "relationship advice" that is immensely wide and woefully shallow, *Surprised by Love* is a buoy in the morass of relationship "mis-advice" propagated by well-intentioned pop-psychologists and relational gurus who have done little to turn the rising tides of today's relational devastation. Authors Jay and Julie embark on a heart-wrenching narrative of two individuals awakened to the all-too-common void of "intimacy lost" and the epic struggle to recapture their relationship, themselves, and one another. *Surprised by Love* is an honest and vulnerable descent into the vicis-situdes of intimacy and isolation. It grants passage to the secret world of two individuals besieged with the struggle to confront the erosion of intimacy and reclaim the love that surprised them in the beginning.

—Dr. Brian R. Epperson, PhD
Founder and CEO, Human Performance Advisors
Co-founder of Blended Love, a non-profit endeavoring to
mitigate the negative effects of divorce on children

Surprised by love? You will be when you read Jay and Julie's incredible story. Hurting from an act of infidelity and think it's all over? You might think otherwise after reading this book. Jay and Julie's brutal honesty in telling of hurt, anger, frustration, righteousness, and ultimate betrayal from both the "his" and "her" sides will answer the question everyone has: *why?* Why did I do this? Why did they do that? There's no right or wrong; there's no villain or victim. There are just two people, losing their way, experi-encing pain and anguish to an incredible level but, through their journey, finding each other again, stronger—because one refused to stop loving. A book for those who have experienced infidelity as well as for those who haven't, *Surprised by Love* is proof that love really can overcome everything. Thank you, Jay and Julie. Sharing your story will change what stories are possible for many.

—Keiron McCammon
Co-founder, Kaboodle.com

Surprised by Love is an important book for many reasons. As a clinician, what struck me was the raw authenticity of it. While many people have affairs, very few are willing to talk about them publically. Even fewer people, especially when they're licensed clinicians, will tell you the truth about *their own affair*, teach you how and why it happened, and more importantly, show you how to repair your marriage and design a new relationship when an affair happens to you. Dr. Jay and Julie have given us a rare gift by allowing us to peer into the sometimes shadowy but certainly transformative journey of their life from marriage, infidelity, and divorce to a new relationship. Read this book! It could change your life.

—**Leslie Masters, MD**
The Masters Clinic; Drlesliemasters.com

As a marital and family therapist who has worked with couples and their relationships for over twenty years, I can enthusiastically say that Dr. Jay and Julie have given you an amazing gift—the truth about why infidelity happens and what to do if it does. Their amazing story reminds us about the power of love and the possibility of the human spirit to overcome even the most painful relational adversity. You will be moved, bothered, soothed, and provoked by the raw honesty of this remarkable true-life love story, and I trust, changed by it. I will certainly be recommending *Surprised by Love* to clients and professionals alike.

—**Stuart Holderness, PhD**
Drstuartholderness.com

The truth about love is that it is not easy! The emotional spark that brings two people together can be simple, yet the emotions that bind one to another are not easy. In this unique book, Jay and Julie offer us a probing exposé on an all-too-common problem in our relationships—betrayal. Every chapter teaches us through bold exposition that, no matter what circumstances a couple finds themselves in, the seeds of intimacy are not born from emotional tides of attraction, but rather from a bold and courageous act of patience, time, attention, and personal development. I have known Jay and Julie for more than a decade and have had a front-row seat to their show of life. What they share through their story are the real, hard lessons for lasting *truth* and *love*.

—**Jeffrey L. Magee, PhD, PDM, CSP, CMC**
Founder, Jeff Magee International

Our relationship with our spouse is the most important thing in our life, and it takes special care and attention to keep a marriage strong, exciting, and emotionally satisfying. *Surprised by Love* offers you the truth about what's happening in modern relationships, why they fail, and more importantly, how one couple changed their destiny by refusing to be another divorce statistic. Dr. Jay and Julie invite us into their very intimate journey, in all its ugliness and beauty, by giving us access to sensible, effective, provocative, and extremely insightful truths based on their very real and painful love affair. Through it, we are inspired and taught by their pain and transformation. Your marriage will be changed by reading their story, and I'm confident it will help you and your spouse work through times of trouble and rediscover the joy of shared passions, hopes, and happiness that marriage can offer.

—Dr. Chris Wright, PhD
Licensed psychologist; www.reliantlive.com

As a clinician with more than thirty years of experience, I believe *Surprised by Love* will help couples heal their own relationships. This penetratingly compelling story, told by a real couple (one of them a trained psychologist) surviving a real relationship tragedy, leads readers to "look in the mirror" and challenge themselves to become authentic in relating to their partner. As you walk Jay and Julie's incredible journey, you will be transformed by the authenticity and truths within it. The result will revolutionize your relationship! I plan to incorporate this book in my clinical practice with couples and in my teaching and supervision of clinicians who must understand the truth about infidelity. I appreciate the contribution this book makes to the therapy field and am excited about the possibilities for all the people seeking happy, healthy relationships whose lives will be touched through its message.

—Dr. Carol Dillard, PhD
Licensed marriage and family therapist

Surprised by LOVE

One Couple's Journey from Infidelity to True Love

DR JAY AND
JULIE KENT-FERRARO

FRANKLIN GREEN
PUBLISHING
www.franklingreenpublishing.com

Surprised by Love: One Couple's Journey from Infidelity to True Love

Published by Franklin Green Publishing
P.O. Box 2828
Brentwood, TN 37024

EAN: 978-1-936487-03-5
Printed in the United States of America

Contact information:
    Web site: www.surprisedbylove.com
             www.drjayandjulie.com
    Phone: 877.944.7025

To my wife, Julie…

*You complete me in ways I am only now beginning to understand
and appreciate the power of. Thank you, my bride, for mentoring
me in the art of love and for the gift of second chances. I am
eternally indebted to your grace and will spend the rest of my life
becoming a man worthy of you. You are my true soul mate.*

Jay

To Jay…

*It has been said, "If you love something, set it free; if it comes back, it
was and always will be yours. If it never returns, it was never yours to
begin with."* Thank you for your love, strength, and courage. You are
an amazing gift to me. I am so proud of the man you are today and am
blessed to be by your side. Thank you for believing in us. I love you.*

Julie

---

* Richard Bach, http://quotationsbook.com/quote/46300/.

CONTENTS

FOREWORD

I LOVE THIS BOOK! No matter what you accomplish in your life, you're not going to be happy if you're not happy in your marriage. We suffer most in our lives from failed or failing relationships. Marital strife, infidelity, separation, and divorce are at the top of the list in terms of struggling with pain. On the other hand, nothing compares to the joy and happiness of a loving and fulfilling intimate relationship.

This rare book is the inspiring true story of two intelligent, kind, and loving people who fell in love, got married, fell out of love, and got divorced. Amazingly, they rediscovered their love for each other and remarried.

I guarantee this book will give you a higher level of understanding of what it takes not only to save your marriage but to take it to a higher level of love and happiness than you ever thought possible. Through this book, you will be able to envision possibilities that you never thought were available to you.

With amazing courage, Jay and Julie take you on their journey from infidelity to love. Page by page, they each give you their version of the events that took them from being the perfect couple—with three beautiful children, a lovely home where Julie could afford to be a stay-at-home mom, and Jay's successful career—to estrangement, resentment, alienation, and Jay's infidelity that culminated in their divorce. Yet true love never dies, and after the divorce, they were surprised to discover how deeply they still loved each other.

The book is unique, not only because Julie and Jay open their hearts to you fearlessly, but because they each give you their own version of what was happening and what they were thinking and feeling. There isn't an attempt to put a spin on their story. On the contrary, each lets you into the innermost secrets of their version of reality.

Jay and Julie are great writers and the book reads like a novel, reminiscent of Harold Pinter's play *Betrayal*. The book demonstrates that no matter how troubled a marriage may be, it can be saved, and love and happiness can be rediscovered.

I invite you to join Julie and Jay in their journey of transformation that will transform your life as well.

—Cloé Madanes
August 8, 2010
La Jolla, California

Cloé Madanes is a world-renowned teacher of marriage and family therapy. She is the author of seven books that are classics in the field, the latest of which is *Relationship Breakthrough*. She is the president of the Robbins-Madanes Center for Strategic Intervention (www.robbinsmadanestraining.com).

ACKNOWLEDGMENTS

To Drs. John and Julie Gottman:

Thank you for showing us that love is both an art and a science and for teaching us how to do both much better. Your guidance and wisdom have been the pathway to restoring a family legacy almost lost.

To Tony and Sage Robbins:

Your bold stand for what is possible in love and relationships was a gateway without which our transformation might not have been fulfilled. Thank you for your uncompromising stand that served as an example for us all to be more than the limitations we so easily accept.

To You, Our Readers:

Thank you for the courage to pick up this book! We pray that our lives and the pain that has instructed us will be meaningful to you and touch your life in a significant way. It is our hearts' desire that sharing our story will change lives as it inspires hope and possibility to transform individuals, couples, and families by opening up choices not available before— and that, in so doing, families touched by infidelity and divorce will take control of their destinies.

LIFE ON THE RUN

Julie

"Jay, are you having an affair?" I asked.

"Where'd you get a crazy idea like that?" he said as he shook his head in denial.

Tall, dark, and handsome in his orange polo shirt and stylish jeans, he looked like a winner. Why then, did I sense we were on the verge of great loss?

It was a warm, sunny day that felt cold and cloudy. I'd driven Jay in his sparkling white Escalade to the Tulsa airport. On that first Thursday of September, all that had been bright and shiny in our marriage seemed to have turned dark and tawdry. Lately, Jay had been sneaky, defensive, and on edge—even aggressive and hostile at times. He'd found fault with me and had shown no patience with our children, ages two, six, and seven.

At the airport, planes took off and landed. My mind whirled with misgivings. I felt nauseated and clammy even though I knew we appeared to be the perfect, upwardly mobile couple as we stood together on the sidewalk.

"I've been so worried about you. About *us*," I said. "I've been walking on eggshells around you for weeks." I could hardly believe my own words.

"Julie, I'm tired. I'm working fifteen-hour days to support you and the kids. What more do you want?"

"I want you."

He stepped away.

Clutching his arm, I forced him to stay. "I gave you several chances last week to come clean about what's going on."

From the moment Jay told me he would be flying to Orlando, I had started watching the phone records closely. In six years, he had never visited his son Keaton in Orlando more than once every three months. He had just been there a month ago.

"Nothing's going on."

"I investigated you. I know you're staying at the Villa Suites in Room 314."

"You're spying on me? You don't trust me?" He looked angry and indignant.

"I want to. But well, your issues—"

"Stop it. These suspicions are your issues, not mine."

"Jay, I contacted a PI and set up surveillance."

"You what?"

I let go of his arm in the face of his fury, but I held my own. My marriage was at stake. "All I have to do to push the trigger is give her my credit card number."

"I can't believe you'd do that." He leaned close. "How could you be so selfish?"

"Me?" I felt defensive when I wanted to feel angry.

"You don't want me to see Keaton, do you? You want our children to come first."

"I've always been supportive of your son." I'd tried so hard to blend the child of his first marriage into our family, but I got little appreciation for my efforts.

"Forget the PI," he said.

Jay pulled me into his arms and held me close, but I didn't feel happiness, only fear and sadness.

"Everything is fine. We're okay," he said.

"I don't want to call the PI." My tears spilled onto his shirt as I felt his strong hands stroke my back. The gesture was meant to be comforting. "I love you."

"You know you can trust me. I love you, too."

"I feel dirty even thinking about this."

I wanted to believe in Jay. Surely this was about the stress of his career change from psychologist to consultant. He was doing well and on the road a lot. I was lonely, but I'd focused on our children. Still, I worried about another woman. I needed more reassurance. We had three kids to think about.

"Julie, let it go. You're tired and stressed. We both are. You're not thinking clearly."

"I guess not."

Loosening his arms from around me, Jay looked into my eyes. "I've got to catch my flight," he said. And then he was gone.

As I drove away from the airport that day, I felt more alone than I ever had in my life. But I desperately wanted to accept his words.

So I chose to trust. I chose to believe. I chose to love.

Jay

Julie was upset. Over the past several months, I'd become keenly aware of her suspicions. Now, once again I recognized all the signs—the tone of her voice, the tears in her eyes, her desperate, cloying need for reassurance. She was alarmingly close to discovering the truth.

My mind raced. Would she really hire a PI? Clearly she was warning me and at the same time giving me the benefit of the doubt. She knew in her heart and mind that I was involved with someone and was doing things I had no business doing as a married man. She wouldn't have called a PI otherwise.

What did she expect? She wanted to be a trophy wife and live the good life. I was her ticket. But she'd made an emotional prison of our marriage. I'd married her with hope in my heart, but I'd paid a high price that left me resentful, alienated, and lonely. I was entitled to get what I wanted any way that suited me.

Intoxicated with the excitement of my current life, I was living a jet-set lifestyle. As I traveled around the country, I was consumed with being important, making money, and creating a name and a brand. Especially thrilling for me was my success in having an illicit affair while giving the appearance of leading a normal family life. It was an adrenaline rush that offered a soothing contradiction to my soul-death existence with Julie.

By now my life in two worlds had become almost normal. I was surprised Julie hadn't caught on before. My ability to live a family life and simultaneously engage in an affair without remorse was alarming. *Almost.* My dark side actually relished living so well in such complexity.

On the move, I gave people only the pieces of me that I chose to offer. I remained emotionally aloof and disconnected, yet physically present when it mattered. I maintained an illusion of intimacy that allowed me to be perceived as a good guy in the areas where I needed to be considered responsible.

That fateful day I felt like I had dodged a bullet, but I was willing to take the risk. In fact, I was emboldened by it. I almost dared Julie to stop playing games because in my heart I knew she knew. Most of all, I was angry that my gig was likely up, which put at risk the house of cards I'd so carefully built. I feared I was about to experience a significant loss of power and control over my worlds.

Deep down, a small part of me had grown weary of the lies, the duplicity, the compartmentalized existence, and the loss of character and integrity. That part of me wanted to be found out, wanted Julie to put an end to my lies. But a bigger part of me refused to give up the adrenaline rush or the promise of what my fantasy world offered me.

I prepared to do battle for it.

Julie

When Jay returned from Florida, I noticed on his work laptop that someone named Dayanara had been checking her email from his computer. Shocked and alarmed by the intrusion, I confronted Jay. He insisted that Dayanara was a friend who lived in Orlando and that she was simply checking the emails for business information. I found this behavior odd because certain emails had been read, deleted, opened, and forwarded. It was something a business alliance would never do. Nevertheless, I chose to trust and believe in my husband.

Then Jay again flew on a Thursday to see Keaton in Orlando, despite the fact that it meant he would miss another family event. On Friday, our daughters were cheering with the high school cheerleaders at a football game and then performing in the halftime show. Naturally, our girls wanted Jay to be there.

It was a cold, drizzly night, October 13 to be exact, and I'll never forget the horrible feeling I had in the pit of my stomach. I was stressed beyond belief and convinced I was half-crazy. Because I was beginning not to trust anyone, I walked back and forth behind the football bleachers as I tried to reach Jay by phone. Every now and then I popped up to the stands so that the girls would think I was watching them cheer.

I couldn't reach Jay all evening.

After the game, we returned home and I put my daughters to bed. I attempted to eat something, but I was so worried, all I could do was pace. Finally, Jay's ex-wife called me.

"Julie, Keaton and I haven't heard from Jay," Cindy said. "Is he or isn't he coming to town? Keaton is worried."

I started to shake all over as my fears came alive. "I haven't been able to reach him tonight. Did his flight arrive?"

"Yes."

"Was there an accident? Did you call the hospitals?"

"I hate to tell you, but I doubt if he's in trouble," Cindy said with sympathy in her voice.

"Wh— What do you mean?"

"I suspect his frequent trips to Florida are not all about Keaton. In fact, Keaton knows Jay has a girlfriend. He even had dinner with them."

"What? I don't believe it."

"Let me get him. He'll tell you."

While I waited for Keaton, I continued pacing the floor. By then I was shaking so badly, I could hardly hold the phone. Still, I had to know the truth.

"Julie, it's true," Keaton said a few moments later. "Dad took me to dinner with his friend. A girl."

I didn't say goodbye, just slammed the phone down, all manners forgotten. Then I quickly dialed Jay again and left another message for him to call me back. By that point, I felt so sick to my stomach, I had to lie down.

When Jay finally called that night, his voice sounded cool and composed. "What's up? Can't I go to dinner without you hounding me?"

"Cindy left me a message, something about dinner and a girl." I'd learned to be cautious, so I didn't let Jay know that I'd spoken to them.

"I was at a great Italian restaurant, phone off. You know how it is."

"What about Keaton and this girl?"

"We're just friends. I deserve a couple of friends in my life; nothing wrong with that. I thought Keaton would like to meet her."

"That's not the point. I doubt if it's the right message to send your children."

"Julie, back off. Give me some space. Privacy. I'm working hard, setting up business acquaintances. I can't be trying to explain every time I have lunch or dinner."

"Okay." I pushed the fear down in my stomach. "I understand."

He hung up.

But I didn't understand.

Soon Jay was flying to Miami frequently as he worked on starting a new business. Meanwhile, I grew even more worried about our marriage. Though I was desperately trying to make our marriage work, I feared Jay was not. He was twelve years older. I was his second wife. Marriage was new to me, but not to him. Maybe the age gap gave us two different perspectives on what made a happy relationship.

Each time I did a family-type event without him, I felt worse. My heart was aching. I felt vulnerable and broken. I cried all the time. This was the man I loved more than life itself. How could this be happening? What did I do to be so horrible? I must be ugly, fat, and worthless. Was I losing my mind, or was he really breaking our vows and betraying me? I felt disrespected clear down to my soul. The deeper his lies got, the more it hurt.

I thought about the PI. I knew that soon I might need to make that life-changing phone call to put Jay under surveillance.

But then I thought of the good times, the beautiful way we'd begun our lives together. Our commitment. Our passion. Our love. And our sweet beginning.

PART 1

Love Begins

CHAPTER 1
CAUGHT BY SURPRISE

> **I**
>
> Julie: *"We talked all night."*
>
> Jay: *"I was riveted by her."*

Julie

"So, how spontaneous are you?" Jay asked on the phone.

Fresh from a hot bubble bath, I was in my sweats and ready for bed. Surprised by Jay's late night call, I said, "Depends. What do you have in mind?"

"I know we're scheduled for lunch tomorrow, but I want to know right now if you're real."

I chuckled. He wasn't the only one wondering if our impending blind date was a bad idea. My best friend Sherry was determined to get me away from Max, the guy I was dating. Though charming, successful, smart, and supportive of my business goals, Max was a freewheeler when I wasn't around—which was far too often, since he lived in Dallas and I was in Tulsa.

"You know the Full Moon?"

"Good place." Set high on a hill with a great view of Tulsa, the quaint café and bar was one of my favorites.

"You want to get a drink there?"

"Right now?" A quick calculation added up to no makeup, hair a mess, clothes unplanned.

"Yes."

"Sure." I might as well meet him and get Sherry off my back. Jay was her therapist, so I had visions of a stuffy, analytical, highly educated bore even though he'd sounded fun and full of life the few times we'd talked.

"An hour okay?"

"Make it a half hour." I might as well start the new year off with a bang, or more likely a fizzle. But at least I was getting out.

"Great."

"How will I recognize you?" I asked.

"Sunglasses."

"See you soon."

I knew I'd surprised Jay by not needing much time to get ready, but I already felt comfortable with him. Besides, I didn't see much point in my typical full face and body makeover. I pulled on jeans and a red top, twisted my hair up with a clippie, and dashed on a little makeup.

I was out the door by eleven.

Jay

The first moment I saw that woman sitting at the bar alone, I knew she had to be Julie. *Stunning.* Sherry had talked so much about her in sessions that I'd become intrigued, despite the twelve-year difference in our ages and my disillusionment with women and love. Now I'd find out if the real woman met my imagination.

Julie was stylish. She wore a crimson velvet sweater, Calvin Klein jeans, and a sexy, alluring smile. She'd pulled her long blond hair back, which accented the bone structure of her elegant face. She sat with her hands on her knees in a classy yet seductive way. I felt mesmerized by her big blue eyes.

We said hello, but no words were really necessary. Body language said it all—inviting yet cautious, intriguing yet reserved, captivating yet unassuming.

I thought of the baggage I'd brought with me that was hidden behind my designer sunglasses and acquired thick skin. Did I dare hope Julie could ignite me? Cure me of my melancholy and disillusionment?

When Julie stood up, I silently thanked my client who'd insisted I call her friend. Julie was model tall with an hour-glass figure. She had long legs, a muscular body, and a firm rear end. She moved like a runway diva, all loose-limbed, confident, and sexy. I'd never seen another woman as sophisticated and sensual.

As I followed her to the back of the restaurant, heads turned. Every guy in the crowded bar watched her first, and then us collectively. I felt a strange, primitive sensation of jealousy mingled with pride and arrogance.

When I seated Julie at a small table in front of the roaring fire, the light that played across her face revealed her many emotions and her riveting beauty.

Julie

Where did Jay get that body? He was a psychologist, but he looked like a football player. The moment he walked into the Full Moon, I thought he was gorgeous. He was tall with thick, dark hair, a muscular body, and sunglasses that mysteriously obscured his eyes. He wore a leather blazer, jeans, and cowboy boots. *Casual, cool, and good-looking.* When I realized he was the one I was there to meet, I immediately regretted not putting on my full face. I hoped I hadn't already blown our possibilities.

As we sat down near the fireplace, I admired his perfect skin and strong features. But when he turned to hang his jacket on the back of his chair, I felt horror and shock. He had a short ponytail. I hated that style on men. Though I tried not to panic, I wondered how quickly I could get out of the evening.

Then, once more Jay surprised me. He smiled, and his presence was so sweet and inviting that I felt intoxicated.

I again felt disgust when I noticed he wore a small stud earring in his left ear. It wasn't attractive, at least not to me. Nonetheless, I reassured myself that I could change this and any other small thing like his hair. Besides, I adored everything else about him. I was so smitten that I didn't care, at least not at the time.

Jay

In January 1997, when I met Julie, I was a first-time loser at marriage. I'd rushed into wedlock with my college sweetheart, stayed in mind-numbing jobs, balanced grueling graduate school schedules, and held on for the sake of Keaton, our five-year-old son. I'd finished my PhD in clinical psychology and was working on a dissertation when my marriage of thirteen years finally fell apart, divorce pending.

Julie gave me hope. Perhaps it was her youth—her twenty-three years compared to my thirty-five—or her adventurous spirit and openness to anything possible. Perhaps it was her infectious laugh and sparkling eyes. Perhaps it was her love of life.

We talked for hours. I came to know not the plastic, pretentious beauty queen that I'd imagined, but a straight-talking, soulful woman. I was struck by a strange familiarity between us. Finally, I stopped analyzing and began engaging with her.

To my dismay, love blossomed.

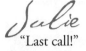

Julie

"Last call!"

When I heard those words announcing that the bar was closing at two that morning, I looked at Jay, shocked and disappointed. Where had the time flown? Jay had energized me, and we still had so many unanswered questions.

"Do you want to grab a cup of coffee at the Village Inn?" Jay asked.

"Sure." The 24/7 pancake house would give us plenty of time to finish our conversation.

"Do you want me to drive us?"

"I'll meet you there."

I had been on my own since I was eighteen. Recently, I had completed a country demo album and promoted it in Nashville. I'd met a lot of men in my careers, but none had ever deeply touched me. I'd been lonely. But as much as I liked Jay already, I still wanted the independence of driving my own car.

All evening, our conversation had been smooth and easy. I felt as if I'd known him for years and as if I should have known him all my life. I felt a deep connection with him from the first moment I saw him.

I wanted to keep him forever.

Jay

I didn't want the night to end, so I took another chance. When she agreed to continue our conversation, I felt my interest reciprocated. Could this be more than just a chance encounter? I wanted to find out.

At the diner, we talked until four in the morning. Our conversation was sometimes robust, at other times reflective and inspired. We seemed to bring out the best in each other, an unexpected but welcome surprise.

I felt as if I'd found a part of me that was missing, and I believed she felt the same.

Julie brought brilliant color into my drab, gray life.

How could I ever let her go?

> **2**
>
> Julie: *"Our courtship was short and so very sweet."*
>
> Jay: *"We rescued each other."*

Julie

We didn't have much of our own stuff. I was living with my grandmother, working part-time as a music teacher at a performance studio, and staying involved with my family and friends. He was living in an efficiency apartment, working as a counselor, finishing his doctorate, finalizing a divorce, and supporting his son. Somehow it felt only right that we were both beginning together with little more than our wits, our talents, and our love.

I admired Jay's physical and emotional strength, and his drive to succeed that matched my own. We fell in love to Toni Braxton music and the *Romeo & Juliet* movie soundtrack. I adored the lights in his apartment, blue for a soft and seductive mood.

In March, after eight weeks of dating, we moved in together. As we strengthened our relationship, Jay took me on several fantastic trips. We went first to San Francisco, that most romantic of cities. He gave a workshop at a conference. I met several people from his doctoral program. At night we went sightseeing to celebrate our life and love.

After we were engaged, we flew to Daytona Beach, Florida. I met Jay's birth father, a handsome, gregarious man whom Jay hadn't known until college. We stayed at his father and stepmother's condo and got to know them. We enjoyed watching manatees from the deck. We also walked on the beach and playfully splashed each other in the warm surf.

Marriage was the next likely step, even though it felt premature. My family and friends were happy for me. My mother and grandmother began helping me make plans for my wedding. It quickly got complicated and expensive. Jay and I wanted a simple celebration of our love and union. We wanted to begin our lives free of debt, especially since we were already house-hunting. We also wanted a special place where we could return to renew our vows and our spiritual connection.

Thorncrown Chapel suited all our needs and desires, and it was located just two hours away near Eureka Springs, Arkansas, a romantic Victorian village nestled in the beautiful Ozark Mountains. We decided to say our vows there with close family and friends in attendance. We planned to share our happiness with others later at a large reception in Tulsa.

Jay

Julie made me laugh. She gave me hope. She inspired me. I loved her with all my heart. I wanted to give her everything she wanted in life, including me. I set about doing just that, but it wasn't the first time.

When I was a child, my mother did her best, but she turned to me to cope with my stepfather's alcoholic binges and her disappointments in life. Mom was unhappy and angry; I believed it was my fault and responsibility to somehow fix that. If I were successful, then I could be loved.

When she was just a teenager, I was her surprise baby boy. My father had abandoned us, and she expected me to make it up to her by doing my duty as a man before I knew what that meant. So I role-played as best I could. I tried to be a good boy, please everyone around me, ask for nothing for myself, and become indispensible to people so that they would need me. Then I'd be safe because I was worth something. A knight was born, always heroic, when first one stepfather and then a second turned abusive and neglectful.

I learned that my value in life was to achieve, be successful so as to not need anything from anyone, deny myself, and take care of others. But for all I did and tried to do, my mother's love remained elusive, especially after my two sisters were born.

Because my mother wanted me to remain her caretaker forever, she was furious when I decided to attend college. In her eyes, I was being disloyal; I was abandoning her and a family in need. I went despite her protests. I majored in psychology. Classes came easily for me. I was already experienced as a patient, thoughtful counselor and listener to my mother and sisters. I worked hard and felt satisfied with my progress. I could help others the way I had helped myself.

Relationships were confusing to me. Love was more about finding someone to approve of me and take care of me than it was about my contributing to that person's life. Eager to find the love I craved and the acceptance I needed, I married Cindy in college. She wanted to have a child and be a full-time mother, nothing more, nothing less. I was just starting graduate school, but I supported her desire and went into action to make it happen.

We were blessed with our son, Keaton. I was a father and would be a better one than the one I'd never had. I attended college, worked full time, and did an APA clinical and counseling psych program full time, too. Exhaustion became my constant companion. Cindy wanted more of my time and energy. I was barely hanging on, but I sacrificed my personal desires for my wife and son. I soon discovered I was unprepared and ill equipped for the life I had chosen. Our marriage spiraled downward and finally ended in divorce.

I knew it took two to make a marriage work, but it took the right two. This time Julie was the right woman. I knew it.

Julie and I had a great deal in common, despite the difference in our ages and backgrounds. Tulsa and Brooklyn were worlds apart, but still we'd found each other. We'd both survived challenging issues as children and now thrived on the strengths we'd developed during childhood. We took pleasure in unifying against our demons and ghosts of the past. We were determined to support each other, even to the point of combining our last names. Together, we knew we could conquer the world, particularly our little corner of it.

Thorncrown Chapel was the beginning. It was a place to purify, to rectify, and to sanctify. Ours would be a marriage made in heaven. A marriage to last a lifetime.

3

Julie: *"I wore my mother's wedding veil."*

Jay: *"We created special memories."*

Julie

On December 18, 1997, we piled everything we needed for our wedding, even our towering cake, into our new red Isuzu Trooper, bought especially for our life together. We drove into the mountains, the trees stark and stately and a refreshing chill in the air. Arriving a day early, we registered for our marriage license and then went to the cabin Jay had rented for the weekend.

The place looked like a dump. It was dreary, old and hadn't been painted in a very long time. Despite my wanting to keep things simple the Green Tree Lodge was not what I expected. We'd reserved extra rooms for friends and family to change, too. After Jay got the keys, we drove around the corner and I knew I should have trusted him. A quaint Victorian cabin nestled in the woods. Inside, it had a living room with a pellet stove, a charming kitchen, and a bath with a huge Jacuzzi tub. Holiday decorations and a Christmas tree created a warm seasonal atmosphere. It was perfect.

We hugged and kissed. We felt as if everything would be all right now.

December 19 dawned bright and sunny, unusually warm at seventy degrees. Jay and I met family and friends at Thorncrown Chapel. This magnificent chapel, designed by Architect E. Fay Jones and set deep in the woods, towers 48 feet high and has 425 windows and over 6,000 square feet of glass (www. Thorncrown.com). That day, white poinsettias graced the interior.

Jay and Keaton looked handsome in dark tuxedos. My father and brother also arrived in tuxedos. I wore a white satin bridal gown with seed pearls and silver beading. I also proudly wore my mother's white veil from her marriage to my father. My maid of honor wore a forest green velvet and taffeta dress. My grandmother wore purple, and my mother looked beautiful in rose silk.

For me, Jay had removed his earring and promised never to wear it again. He also now had his hair fashioned without the pony tail. He couldn't have looked more perfect to me, and I marveled that he'd come to love me so deeply.

My close family and friends were there for me, but only Jay's son and a doctor friend came for him. I felt sad about that, but Jay didn't seem to mind.

When my close friend sang "The Lord's Prayer," tears gathered in my eyes. I meant it with all my heart when I said, "I do."

Jay

Winter tended to be my favorite time of year, a slower pace with happier people. I felt like a kid going on spring break—giddy, excited, playful, and full of potential. A renewed life had unexpectedly come to me.

I carried our matching wedding bands. They felt cold to the touch. I wondered if we'd turn the metal hot with our love and desire when we placed the rings on our fingers. In keeping with our wedding simplicity, we'd picked them out together at a local mall, but I secretly wished I could afford to give Julie a diamond as big as her loving heart.

At Thorncrown Chapel, I desperately wanted our wedding to be perfect. Fortunately, the weather cooperated since we held part of the ceremony outdoors. As Julie and I stood together at the altar, we basked in the sparkling rays of sunlight that penetrated the beautiful glass cathedral in the mountains. I squeezed her hand in sympathy when the stranger who was marrying us had trouble pronouncing our names.

I believed that Julie deserved a big, fancy wedding. Yet she appeared completely happy surrounded by several generations of women who had groomed her for this special occasion. One of Julie's best friends, a reigning Miss America at the time, stood by her side. I honored and respected Julie for her pleasure in our simple ceremony. Seeing her love and commitment to me, I was surprised by love.

I knew she worried that I stood so alone with my family's side of the aisle empty, but I was accustomed to it. I'd grown up strong, resilient, and independent because I had no other choice. She needed and wanted her family, just as I didn't need or want mine now. But I needed her, wanted her. I felt uneasy that I was turning my life upside down on the strength of love—even as I rejoiced in joining with her to create the loving family I'd never known.

On that day, my family lost a lot. As a therapist I watched many families benefit from meaningful involvement with each other; celebrating life's rituals and really being there for one another when it mattered. I thought my marriage to Julie would be one of those days. It was really I who lost by being alone and not having anyone there for me when I wanted it most. I'd invited them to my wedding, but because my youngest sister had recently gotten married in a lavish ceremony in New York with all the bells and whistles, my family declined to attend. They explained the timing was bad after my sister's expensive event. My birth father and his wife also decided not to share the special day with us. I wasn't too surprised that none of them came, since my family had ignored my graduation for a bachelor's degree and later a master's degree, too.

I felt a vicarious sense of belonging with Julie's big family from Oklahoma and Texas, and I chose to adopt them as my own. My son Keaton joined us, and I felt content. He completed my new family.

When I made my commitment to Julie, I meant it with my total heart. The past was past. I sealed painful memories of my birth family and my first marriage and divorce behind a locked door. The future beckoned with the strength of our convictions.

I slipped the wedding ring on Julie's finger, saw the tears of joy in her eyes, and vowed to give her everything her heart could possibly desire.

4

Julie: "We enjoyed a magical honeymoon."

Jay: "I felt like a kid again."

Julie

We spent our honeymoon in Eureka Springs. That weekend, we held hands, hugged each other, and laughed at events from the wedding as we dined in our favorite restaurants and walked the quaint streets of the Victorian village. We snuggled by the fireplace in our cabin, made amazing love, took champagne bubble baths, and sat on the balcony while we enjoyed the cold days and nights together.

Magic filled the air and our lives.

I'd felt as though I'd been suspended in time until Jay slipped the wedding ring on my finger that wonderful winter weekend. Only then did I take a deep breath and begin to live life to the fullest.

Jay

I awoke to the sound of birds flying around our cabin door the morning after our wedding. As I leaned over to kiss Julie, I marveled at her inner and outer beauty. I still felt surprised by her love, but invigorated by it as well.

Jumping out of bed, I threw on a tee and jeans. I felt ready to start my new life. After slipping into a robe, Julie followed.

We stepped outside. Sunlight warmed the cool air. A line of railroad ties separated the driveway from the large lawn that sloped into the woods. Barefoot, I leaped onto the ties and walked down them like a tightrope walker with my hands extended outward from my sides. Feeling like a kid again, I laughed as I walked back and forth and Julie cheered me on. I felt a lightness in my step that I hadn't felt in years. I was free, in love, and totally happy. It was the best time in all my thirty-five years of life.

When I turned to Julie, she rushed to me. We held hands. Our matching wedding bands glinted in the sunlight and the metal felt warmed by our love.

Together, two lonely people made each other whole.

CHAPTER 2
LIFE IN THE FAST LANE

> ### I
>
> Julie: *"We created two beautiful babies together."*
>
> Jay: *"I worked fifteen-hour days to provide the best for my new family."*

Julie

We began 1998 with a wonderful reception at the Mezzanine, a restaurant in Tulsa's trendy Brookside area. My father, mother, and grandmother happily planned the event. Tiny white lights reflected on glass brick windows and ficus trees scented the room. My mother lovingly displayed my wedding gown on a mannequin in one corner. We danced to the music of Midlife Crisis, a popular local band led by my friend's father. We laughed, talked, drank beer and wine, and enjoyed great food and my favorite cheesecake.

Two hundred guests helped us celebrate our new union. My extended family came, but Jay's family declined because they said it was too cold to travel. By then, I had begun to wonder about my new in-laws, yet I was too happy to dwell on their absence. After all, Jay's college friends and business colleagues were there, and he seemed content. We were so much in love that we had a great time with those who were able to attend.

Though the hope we shared at our reception was genuine, my faith in Jay was quickly tarnished. Over the next few weeks, I found erotic magazines and movies around our apartment, and I was awakened by middle-of-the-night phone calls from "old friends." Concerned that I'd married a man I didn't know or understand, I discussed the situation with a dear friend. I wondered how I would ever go about getting my marriage annulled if the situation didn't change. Still, I wanted our love to be enough for Jay.

When Jay realized how upset and disappointed I was, he reassured me everything was fine and that the calls were nothing. Fortunately, my anxiety subsided. I would've been humiliated to have had to tell my friends and family that I'd married someone I really didn't know.

With that settled, we turned our attention toward finding a wonderful new house. At the same time, we decided to have a baby. Though Jay had initially resisted the idea because he already had a son, I was adamant, and he eventually agreed. Doctors soon discovered that I had endometriosis. So when I had trouble getting pregnant, I began taking fertility drugs.

We spent long weekends looking for the perfect house as we tried to get pregnant. Both became big jobs. We got tired of taking temperatures, charting ovulation, and swallowing medication, but we were eager to share the experience. I was very excited. We finally conceived on Father's Day, and on the Fourth of July we learned that we were expecting.

Later that month, we closed on a darling three-bedroom house in Broken Arrow. We were finally moving forward with our new life. We spent our spare time decorating, shopping for furniture, and turning our small home into a show house. We were thrilled, not just to relocate to a better part of town but also to move out of Jay's tiny apartment to a home where we could eliminate all the things from Jay's first marriage. It was such an exciting time.

Even as we built our new life, we worried about Keaton. We did our best to integrate Jay's son into our family. He stayed with us one night a week and every other weekend, and we always supported him emotionally and encouraged his academic achievement.

During the time when we were decorating our darling nursery, we learned our baby would be a girl. I was thrilled for two reasons: first, I had always wanted a daughter, and second, I knew Keaton would feel less competitive and Jay less guilty, if we had a girl. I felt her move for the first time on October 31, a magical time not only because it was Halloween night, but also because we were together at a movie that evening.

Valentine's Day was very sweet. Jay bought presents for his coming baby daughter as well as for me. At that point he was so much the tender man that I had married, and I loved him very much. I felt lucky to have the life I lived.

Jayde Victoria was born on March 12, 1999. Jay stayed with me every moment during labor. My friends and family all came to the hospital to celebrate. Jay drove me home on a sunny day with snow on the ground. We were thrilled with our daughter.

Again, Jay's family made excuses not to be there. I was getting used to their absence from our lives, but I never understood why.

After ten days, I went back to work. Even though I didn't make a lot of money compared to Jay, I enjoyed teaching voice at a private performing school. I liked contributing to our family income, and I wanted to be a full-time mother, too. So I was fortunate to be able to take Jayde to work during the first weeks and months of her life. When she was four months old, we left her with her adoring grandmother while we went on a cruise together. We enjoyed a wonderful, magical trip.

Jay

Life got serious fast.

I made it my personal mission to be responsible for changing our lives from scarcity to abundance. Always the knight, I climbed back up on my white horse to play the hero again. With no thought to personal costs, I prepared for the mission of competing in the business world as I developed my practice, established a brand, and provided for my new family.

Even though I was still reeling from my divorce and barely recovered from six grueling years of pursuing my doctorate in psychology, I embarked on my life with Julie, fueled by the passion of our newly formed ideals. We believed that, as a team, we were ready to take on the world, a world that hadn't been friendly to either of us.

During my teenage years, my step-dad had often been unemployed, and there was constant chaos in my home because of his drinking. I worked part-time jobs to try to make up the difference, and I'd go food shopping for my mother to make sure our family had enough to eat. When I paid with food stamps, I often noticed the people around me conferring judgment that I didn't deserve. What they didn't know was that those food stamps were keeping us alive. I remember vowing, "It will be different when I have a family."

In my new life with Julie, I was still determined to prove my worth. As a result, the magic of love and marriage quickly morphed into responsibility— something I'd felt overwhelmed by during my marriage to Cindy, yet something comfortable and familiar at the same time. Julie's desire for me quickly transitioned into a drive to create life. Doctors explained that pregnancy would cure her endometriosis. It was all I needed to go into action. I loved Julie and wanted to make her happy by fulfilling her needs while healing her body.

I had a lot to prove, both to myself and to those who had witnessed my first failure in marriage. My divorce had been one of the loneliest times of my life.

During that time, I'd felt abandoned by many friends and family who were critical and judgmental. Shame, guilt, and humiliation drove me to achieve at all costs. Now, with Julie, I felt as though I'd been given a second chance at life. This time I was not going to fail.

Success and my new family became my obsession. I worked in a children's hospital full time and also began seeing private clients in the evenings and on weekends. Surprisingly, Julie and I had trouble conceiving a baby. When her endometriosis worsened and she was in pain, we started fertility treatments. Soon sex became mechanical. I felt like an automaton running back and forth to the hospital and my private practice office as I desperately tried to get us ahead and be able to pay for it all. Finally, after four months, Julie became pregnant. We were delighted. I'd achieved success through performance and felt like a man again.

We quickly closed on a new home. When I carried Julie over the threshold, I felt euphoric. Through this cultural symbol of marriage and family, I was once again legitimized. I opened a bottle of champagne, and we drank to our success and happiness. Later, we talked about our future over dinner at the Warren Duck Club, our favorite Tulsa restaurant. But my mind kept slipping away as I tried to figure out how to provide for us so that my growing family had everything they needed regardless of what it would take to make it happen.

Julie and I continued to enjoy date nights during her pregnancy. We would walk the aisles of stores in search of the ideal nursery furnishings for our coming daughter. We wanted to make sure we had everything possible for this new addition to our lives and that Julie had all the gadgets she needed to be successful in her new role as mother.

As time passed, I tried harder to be a better husband by not complaining about my growing dissatisfaction and unhappiness. I learned to numb my feelings through my pursuit of continued financial and professional success and through excursions into a private fantasy life of porn and erotica. As I increased my workload in private practice, I took on as many patients as I could. Life meant balancing priorities. I reasoned that relationships should sustain themselves on commitment and good intentions. No one was going to give me success. Seasons of sacrifice were a necessary part of getting ahead and this was our season. I simply needed to suck it up if we wanted some modicum of security and an enjoyable life.

Our growing lifestyle helped to make up for my exhausting schedule. We were in love and were enjoying creating our world, making a home together, and taking quick weekend retreats to Eureka Springs and our honeymoon cabin.

Unfortunately, those times grew further apart, as did the distance between us when we began to focus on so many other priorities besides our relationship.

With my combined East Coast, no-nonsense approach and the excellent training I'd received as a doctoral student and in post-doctoral training, my private practice grew fast. For the first time ever, I had a positive cash flow. To be in control of my own business destiny was overwhelmingly gratifying. I found a new type of adrenaline in the thrill of entrepreneurialism. I realized that the only limitations on my income and ego were the amount of hours in a day.

Everyone seemed happy and pleased with me when I was successful and our lifestyle improved. With that in mind, I defaulted to the self-discipline I had acquired during my early life: sacrifice, defer meeting my own needs, live for "someday," and provide well for others. In exchange, my life would be significant and I would receive the love and approval I craved.

Within twelve months, I was seeing forty to fifty people a week at top-rate compensation. My reputation for getting results in difficult cases grew, and soon I had a waiting list for new patients. Although success was swift, I grew restless with the limitations of my twelve-hour days and the thought of having to maintain this routine for the next few decades.

When Jayde was born, a beautiful bundle of love with jet black hair and a cherub face, I felt a strange combination of immense joy and riveting panic. From that moment on, the mounting sense of responsibility that accompanied the magical moment of her birth further fueled my obsession for success.

Now I had two women in my life to love and care for: Julie and Jayde.

2

Julie: *"I fell in love with being a mother."*

Jay: *"I found new ways to provide for my growing family."*

Julie

In the fall of 1998, I had just lost all of my baby weight and gotten back in shape when we found out that we were expecting another child. Our doctor had failed to tell us how fertile we would remain well into the first year following

Jayde's delivery. Needless to say, we were shocked and stressed at the prospect of having children so close together. But we forged ahead in our true fashion.

After deciding we needed a larger place, we began house hunting again. We found a great deal on a house in Hunter's Point, a gated community in the suburbs. In January 2000, we moved there, bought furniture, and called in a decorator to choose window coverings, rugs, and accessories. Because I'd always had a flair for decorating, it wasn't long before we had created another showplace.

Jay opened an office in our home, but it created stress since I had to keep Jayde quiet and the house immaculate. At the same time, he became more obsessed with success. I begged for time with him, we fought about it, and our relationship grew tense. As a wife, I felt emotionally neglected and abandoned by my husband even as I felt our second child stirring in my body.

Becoming a stepmother to a small child overnight was more challenging than I expected. Despite my many efforts to reach out to Keaton and be generous with time and energy, he remained critical and disrespectful of my efforts. Jay and I had many long arguments about his parenting of Keaton but seldom came to any resolution. Our "agree to disagree" approach to the problems brewing between us left me feeling misunderstood and Jay angry all the time.

Zoe Janae was born on May 19, 2000. We named her Zoe, the Greek word for life, and Janae, a French form of Jan, my mother's name. Zoe was tiny, a mere five pounds ten ounces, and absolutely gorgeous. For her "coming home" outfit, she wore a white cotton-and-Battenburg-lace dress. Jayde wore a matching one. My mother planned a special party for Jayde to celebrate her new sister's arrival.

On Sunday, Jay brought us home. On Monday, he had scheduled a school violence training several hours away. I begged him to cancel, postpone, or change it somehow, but he insisted on going. I knew he believed he was being responsible for our family, but I felt broken-hearted. Only twelve hours after arriving home from the hospital, I was left alone with my three-day- and fourteen-month-old daughters. I cried. I felt so alone and unimportant to Jay. I worried that our daughters would not feel their father's love.

I knew Jay was capable of great love, but he seemed to be pouring it all into his work and leaving little for his family. Our conflicts revolved around how he spent his time. I began to believe that he simply wanted to be rich and famous. I'd learned enough of his psychology jargon to wonder if he was a benevolent narcissist who was filling his own insatiable black hole for validation. In simple terms, I wondered if he was a jerk.

I realized that we had different values as far as family life was concerned, and it worried me more all the time. I kept teaching, and I took Zoe to work with me while my mother watched Jayde. No matter how I felt, I tried to show Jay that I loved him.

He always said that he grew up poor and never had a real birthday party. For his thirty-eighth birthday, I threw a huge party at home for him. I invited one hundred people. I had the food catered, and we enjoyed wine, shrimp, pâté, tenderloin sandwiches, and chocolate-covered strawberries. I even had the plates and glasses brought in and hired a florist to decorate the tables. Our daughters wore matching little dresses. I took lots of pictures to record the event. Jay enjoyed himself, but he didn't seem too impressed or pleased by my efforts.

A story began to reverberate in my mind and grow stronger over time: *Jay isn't available for me. Success is more important than I am. He values fame and fortune more than family. I need to withdraw and put my energies where they are needed and wanted.*

Jay

When I ended up sitting naked in a hot tub with a stranger in Santa Barbara, California, while being interviewed for seminar work, I was willing to play Brian's game. The craggy self-help guru had built an empire on self-help seminars. I wanted an association with someone very successful so that I could learn how to achieve abundant provision, be the kind of man Julie wanted and others expected, and pursue the American dream of a great lifestyle and the freedom to enjoy it. Brian offered me a peek into that world, and it changed what I knew to be possible in life.

While Julie enjoyed wine in the house with Brian's wife, I endured his interview. I knew he was trying to discover my vulnerabilities so that he could use them to figure out who I was and then control me. I was being tested and wasn't going to let a little transparency stop me, but also I was testing Brian to see if he was genuine. I quickly assessed him as an accomplished exhibitionist and decided I could learn valuable things from a successful narcissist like him.

I had grown up in poverty, always on the outside, looking in with anger and envy at the extravagant lifestyle of my uncle who was Calvin Klein's business partner in the fashion industry. Now, presumably, the same life was accessible if I was willing to do what it took to get it. Because I wanted that level of success and Brian helped me believe that I might have the right stuff to achieve it, I decided to work with him. I knew the climb to success would be steep and likely difficult, but I wanted it for my family.

Though I enjoyed helping people as a licensed clinician and seemed quite effective at it, I'd grown restless with the inherent limitations of the process.

I soon discovered that seminars, speaking, consulting, and executive coaching were a more satisfying fit for me. In October, I left the hospital to begin entrepreneurial pursuits.

Sometimes the unhealthiest people can be our greatest teachers, and Brian was the most effective unhealthy person I'd ever met. He was consumed with his own significance, and although quite talented, was as insecure as he was in need of constantly having his ego stroked. He taught me a lot about the seminar business through his mistakes as well as his effectiveness. He also taught me how to work with people in ways that were new to me.

Though Brian and I worked well together presenting nationwide personal growth seminars, our basic personalities were too different to sustain a long-term relationship. By February 1999, I'd learned the seminar business and was ready to move forward on my own, even though I knew it would create more stress in my life. That stress level increased sooner than I anticipated. I learned the hard way that no one can challenge a guru, and before I was able to chart an exit strategy, Brian fired me.

The expectation to succeed and provide for my growing family became overwhelming. In fact, it became my sole focus.

At home I felt trapped. When Julie and I had married, we'd had an explicit understanding about children. I had compromised by agreeing to one child. I was happy with one daughter and one son. In October when we learned that Julie was pregnant again, I felt a strange combination of joy, coupled with a crippling sense of anxiety over having lost control.

I grew angry at Julie, the doctor, and mostly myself for letting it happen. I wondered if Julie had gotten pregnant on purpose to fast-track to the life I knew she wanted as a stay-at-home-mom. I hated to doubt the woman I loved, but I felt unprepared for the additional responsibility so early in our new lives together.

Despite all the doubts and questions swirling around us, we took a leap of faith and bought a big, beautiful new home in an upscale community of South Tulsa. Feeling a sense of importance and validation for a job well done, I believed I was finally being rewarded for all the years of sacrifice in graduate school and all the long hours of building a successful private practice. I began working out of our new home and from a midtown office.

My success was bittersweet. I hungered for acknowledgement from Julie and my aloof parents, but I didn't get it. So I satisfied my hunger by indulging in the upscale lifestyle that I'd single-handedly created with my own hard work and determination.

I often felt criticized and attacked by Julie. What more could she possibly want from me? After all, I had given her life on a silver platter! Wasn't it the lifestyle she'd always wanted?

Soon I was nurturing a growing resentment. It felt similar to what I'd experienced as an adolescent when I was trying to please my mother and escape the inner-city gang culture by working part-time jobs between football practices. Nothing I ever did was enough—and it wasn't enough now either. No matter what I did for Julie, it didn't please. She wanted children; I gave them to her. She wanted to be a full-time mother; I made it possible. She wanted a fine home and an upscale lifestyle; I worked fifteen hour days to get it. Still, she didn't seem happy.

Underneath it all, the perceived injustice and my disillusionment with marriage were silently building into an angry, emotional storm. I felt grossly misunderstood and unappreciated. Julie expected me to do the impossible—to be there whenever she needed to lean on me for emotional support but never to meet her deeper, underlying needs. I also resented that she did little to support me as a father to Keaton and that she felt I allowed him to disrespect and manipulate her. I believed she did not welcome Keaton as part of our new family, and it upset me. Worst of all, I felt unable to voice my fears, needs, and frustrations without the situation turning toxic and fueling unending arguments. Eventually exhausted from all of it, I retreated to the certainty of success and achievement, and into the superficial comfort of pornographic images. Under the cover of being a good provider, I was slowly dying inside.

Though I'd found a larger white horse to ride, I wasn't sure how long I could stay in the saddle. So I tamped down my inner voice, the part of me that desperately wanted to be seen, heard, understood, and connected to people. I'd always hidden that part of me because I feared that if I made it known, I would be judged, criticized, and ultimately rejected and shamed—a common ritual I had endured as a child. Intimacy had become a game in which figuring out what people needed and the most strategic way of meeting those needs was the key to winning respect and self-acceptance. I convinced myself, or so I thought, not to have any needs and to "just survive" by becoming important to others. If I pleased them and they approved of me, I was needed. And if I was needed, then I was lovable and safe.

Despite the toxicity of the underlying emotional terrain in our lives, Julie and I both rejoiced when Zoe was born. I cut the umbilical cord wrapped tightly around her neck and held her close to me as oxygen filled her small body. When she looked up at me with her big dark eyes, I fell in love with her.

Julie seemed overly needy and demanding after Zoe's birth, and I grew impatient with her. I was trying to balance the pressure of caring for my new, larger family with the pressure of caring for Keaton's emotional needs, while simultaneously providing for everyone. In so doing, I felt I was steadily losing myself.

A story formed in my mind: *This isn't what I signed up for. Life is about giving others what they need to be happy. I'm alone in that effort and unappreciated for the sacrifices I make for it. My needs cannot be satisfied here.*

Within a relatively short period of time, I wrote a book to gain visibility and differentiate myself in the corporate coaching market. I also invested in a dot com start-up, launched a seminar company, began conducting executive retreats, and designed a series of leadership development courses that sold well and required me to travel around the country to deliver them.

I did my best to fulfill everyone's needs but my own, and I kept expecting things to change for the better. After all, Julie and I had started out as eager lovers and best friends, and I knew she was overburdened in taking care of virtual twins.

Quickly and innocently, we became managing partners in a new business called life. As we suffocated on chores, responsibilities, and mundane tasks, our days of love turned to seasons of sacrifice. Yet in spite of everything, we reasoned that, after the sacrifice, we would resume our love affair.

CHAPTER 3

DOWNHILL SLIDE

> ## I
>
> Julie: *"He was gone, just absent from our lives."*
>
> Jay: *"I wanted payback for all my sacrifice."*

Julie

In 2001 everything seemed to descend on us at once. Our constant fighting over Jay's workload, our time together, and how best to parent our children and Keaton sent us into separate armed camps. I hated it. For all practical purposes, I was a single parent putting up with a manipulative and disrespectful stepson. To make matters worse, Jay catered to Keaton by spoiling him and letting him get away with things because Jay felt guilty over the divorce with Cindy.

My love for Jay never wavered, but our life together didn't meet any of our emotional needs. I couldn't stand the thought of losing him or our life as a family, so I decided to focus on what I could control: our children and our beautiful home. I took satisfaction in these even if I couldn't take satisfaction in my relationship with Jay. I knew he was finding fulfillment in achievement and success, not within our relationship. I felt helpless to change our stalemate.

Our upscale lifestyle was fast catching up with us. Jay was working harder to maintain it, which caused the divide between us to grow. Then, on top of it all, we were audited by the IRS, and we discovered we owed forty thousand dollars from Jay's first marriage.

In desperation, I walked the floors of my beautiful home. I'd poured so much love and time into making it the perfect environment for our family to grow that I couldn't imagine being anyplace else. But I had to be practical, so I went into my "fix it" mode. We'd bought the house at a great price and could sell it and make money. Then we could pay off Jay and Cindy's IRS debt. It made me sick to give up my home for their debt, but I knew it was necessary. Let somebody else who could afford the home enjoy it. I called a family meeting with Jay, and we agreed to reduce our overhead to lower our stress level.

On March 1, I listed our home for sale. When it sold on the Fourth of July, we scrambled to find a new place. We decided on an older house that needed some fixing up, something I'd always enjoyed doing. This house had fewer amenities and was located in a less upscale part of town, but it had a beautiful lawn and garden. We traded Jay's sports car and my expensive SUV for a practical minivan.

We rallied around our mission of simplicity equals freedom equals more time, love, and attention at home.

Jay

As my relationship with Julie devolved, I built an epic story in my mind to explain our problems.

I screwed up and now I'm stuck. Another divorce with two more children to pay child support for is not my idea of a great life. The traditional marriage is basically another form of indentured servitude where men are objectified as success objects and women get to live free from the burden of competing in the rat race of success. The kids get all the attention and the resources. The wife gets "hair, nail, and girlfriend-lunch" days. Simply put, the family gets the benefits of my sacrifices while I get to make it all happen by working fifteen-hour days and squeezing in a few hours of sleep at night so that I can do it all over again the next day.

I got tired, angry, and depressed just thinking about enduring the grind of work for decades more. While I appreciated Julie's willingness to sell the big house, it came with a price attached to it. She was not happy and told me so with her crescendo of judgments and demands for more of whatever she felt she deserved. I thought longingly to the days when I felt free to wear an earring and a ponytail. I wanted to dye my hair orange just to shock Julie and the kids. But I pushed down the rebellion.

Every relationship has an implicit contract, a type of social exchange rate of capital expended and returned. In other words, we expect something in return for the investment we believe we contribute. Julie and I were no different. I expected, at minimum, an ounce of respect and some degree of support for what this new life was taking out of me. What I experienced in return was less support than I felt deserving of, mounting complaints from Julie that made me feel like a failure and I could not seem to quell, and a growing intolerance for the trap I felt I could not escape. Despite these growing feelings, I was unable to voice my needs and insecure about Julie's love, so I remained mute.

I judged her as a drama queen. Given all that I'd done to make her happy, I felt she was demanding and emotionally immature. The more discontented she became with my new life, the more contempt I felt for her. As a wall slowly built between us, we developed into intimate strangers. Our unresolved conflicts gradually gave way to resigned complacency. After all, we had more important things demanding our attention than our relationship.

Inside my head, questions mounted even as I went about my daily life. Had I made a mistake in marrying Julie? Was she just another impulsive solution to my failed first marriage? Had she fooled me as to who she really was, someone only wanting a meal ticket and a lifestyle, not a relationship where she would love me as deeply as she did our children? Was it possible for me to get what I needed in this relationship? Was this the best it got in modern marriage: tasks, nonstop chores, and endless responsibilities?

To make life more interesting, the IRS hit me with a forty-thousand-dollar tax bill from an audit they'd done during my first marriage. Cindy refused to help with the bill. Instead, she quickly married a man she'd only known for a few months and moved with Keaton to Florida. My conflicts with Julie over Keaton ended after he left, but the resentments remained. With all the new expenses, I didn't have the finances for a custody battle with Cindy. As a result, I experienced a deepening sense of failure and helplessness as a father to Keaton, especially since I believed Julie disrespected him and was critical of my parenting abilities.

To help us feel good about ourselves, Julie and I reverted to our prescriptive roles and responsibilities. She was the mother and I was the provider. She became a supermom; I became a workaholic on speed. We seemed to be at our best when we had a project to attack together, and it gave us a feeling of being connected even though love was nowhere to be found. Long story short, we acquired more stuff...and more debt along with it.

Then we decided the upscale lifestyle we had created was part of our problem. So we joined forces to reduce our overhead. I had mixed feelings about it because it felt like a retreat and a loss, but I went along with the choice from pure exhaustion. I desperately wanted to save our fledgling relationship and hoped this would do it. We paid off the IRS debt with the equity from the sale of our big house.

I was no longer surprised by love. I was disillusioned by it.

2

Julie: "We were like ships passing in the night."

Jay: "I was exhausted and weary. Something had to change."

Julie

Except for my adorable babies, 2002 dawned bleak and scary. Jay was becoming a stranger. He exhibited behavior patterns that I wouldn't have thought possible. Yet I remembered those early weeks in our marriage when I'd felt threatened by the erotic magazines, movies, and late-night phone calls. Had that been the real Jay and not the sweet man I thought I'd married? When had I become a suspicious, distrustful wife? Where had our love and tenderness for each other gone?

I became increasingly concerned about Jay's outside activities. When I questioned him about his pursuit of erotica, massage parlors, and strippers, he denied it all. I didn't believe him. I started watching him, looking for telltale signs. At the same time, I felt rejected and undesirable. I coped by putting up a wall of anger.

Still, we made efforts to come together. In hopes of rekindling our love, we went out on date nights and lunched together at intimate little places I'd discovered. We even spent our anniversary in Eureka Springs at our honeymoon cabin. I sincerely believed we would make it through this difficult phase of our marriage brought on by heavy child-rearing years and intense workloads. We just needed time and space.

When Jay continued to turn away from me for sexual gratification through the porn I would find on his computer, I experienced shame, disgust, and rage. I tried not to pass moral judgment on him since I believed he must have sexual addiction issues, but he simply wasn't acting like the sweet, adorable man I'd married. I wanted the old Jay back. I trusted, respected, and felt safe with that Jay, but I withdrew from this one to protect myself and my daughters.

To top it all off, Jay had the nerve to want to take even more time, energy, and focus away from our family to continue his education. I knew he'd never be happy until he had more degrees, greater fame and fortune, and a bestseller. Not only did I feel unimportant, disrespected, and neglected, I also felt alone in raising our two children.

I resolved to get out of his way and focus even harder on my daughters.

Jay

Once I'd wanted love and the intense desire that came with it. Now all I wanted was a quick, satisfying release of my tension and frustration. I also wanted to be desirable. When Julie turned away from me in disgust, I felt a deep shame and a burning anger. What right did she have to judge me? What right did she have to violate my privacy? What right did she have to disrespect me? I was providing everything she wanted in life, but she wasn't providing for my needs.

Our lunches and date nights were tawdry affairs in comparison to what we'd once shared. I was growing more disillusioned with marriage and family life by the day. I was also feeling pressured to generate more income. Though I was working long hours and doing everything needed to grow a consulting and executive coaching practice, we were simply getting by and not progressing. I needed to make more money. I decided the best way to achieve that end was to get an MBA degree, which would position me to transition from outpatient therapist (where I was burning out) to corporate coach.

Julie hated the idea. I tried to explain that I couldn't keep up the pace of my private practice, but she didn't want to understand. Again, I felt attacked and criticized instead of supported and encouraged. So I struggled on alone and did what I knew I had to do for my family. I also did what I had to do for myself as I continued to deceive Julie about my erotic desires and secret fantasy life.

At one time, we'd have been able to talk out our problems, but no more. We'd built too high a wall between us. Trust was gone.

3

Julie: *"Our marriage was on life support."*

Jay: *"Sex was a power struggle."*

Julie

Pregnancy was not how I'd planned to begin 2003, especially since I was in a marriage that I might have to pull the plug on at any moment. In raising two children, keeping up a house, and worrying about my husband, I was already stretched to my limit. Yet I felt a keen excitement and deep conviction when I learned I was expecting. I knew that this child would be loved and adored by our family.

In March, I intercepted a seductive voice-mail message for Jay from a woman promising erotic delights. Not only was I furious and hurt, but from the intimate tone of her voice and the message she left, I believed he was having an affair with this woman.

I confronted Jay. He denied a relationship with her and insisted he'd simply left a message for a massage therapist who was returning his call. Intuitively, I knew there was much more going on with his sexual addiction than I'd previously believed possible.

I threatened to leave and take the children with me. I didn't want my daughters corrupted by Jay's lack of morals, and I wasn't going to be a spurned wife. We talked—*really* talked. It was the first time we'd genuinely communicated in ages. In the end, we concluded that his behavior was a problem that threatened our relationship. He agreed to go to an intensified outpatient addiction program for a week in Arizona.

It was one of the hardest weeks of my life. I knew if Jay didn't successfully complete the program, I'd have to file for divorce. I didn't want to do that. I loved Jay. I wanted him to be with me to raise our children. I felt vulnerable, but I had to protect us all. I had finally accepted that Jay had an unhealthy relationship with sexual intimacy. It made me feel afraid, ashamed, and insignificant. I was also concerned that Jay was making the effort only because he was afraid of losing his children, not me. I fought those feelings by believing in Jay and literally willing him to finish the program and come back to his family.

Jay did all he was asked to do and then returned home. Although I felt like our relationship had a chance, tension still zinged between us. One moment he was excited about our coming son and rushed me out to buy nursery items. The next moment, he treated me with anger and contempt for getting pregnant again. I did my best to maintain a positive outlook.

On September 19, 2003, Chandler was born. Jay's ambivalence about another child disappeared, and we all rallied around this important and joyous time in our family. Now Jay had another chance to be a full-time father to a son. Jayde and Zoe thoroughly enjoyed babying Chandler. We all celebrated the event.

I turned my focus toward creating the perfect life for my three children.

Jay

I thought things couldn't get worse or harder for me, but Julie pulled out all the stops when she announced another pregnancy. Overwhelmed by the additional responsibility, I believed Julie was manipulating me so that she'd get to be a mother again at my expense. We had discussed having another child, and I'd been adamant about not wanting one. But she'd desperately wanted a son. I felt disrespected and as though I'd been taken advantage of and lied to.

Nevertheless, I kept trying to please Julie. I completed the outpatient addiction program, and though I doubted whether the model fit my particular situation, I found the program interesting from a psychologist's point of view. If I were getting what I needed in my marriage, I wouldn't be looking elsewhere. That wasn't addiction; that was a relationship problem. Still, I knew Julie felt comforted that I was in treatment and recovery, so I continued with my twelve-step group meetings back home.

I had a growing sense that Julie simply wanted to control every aspect of my life, including my sexuality, although she was mostly disinterested in me. I figured she had her children (and me to pay for them), so she was content. I was still desperately trying to please everyone, but I wasn't able to voice my own needs and desires. Thus I moved back and forth between excitement about my pending fatherhood and my fear of failure.

When Chandler was born, I felt a deep connection to my second son. I vowed to work harder to give him the best in life, everything that I hadn't had in my life. I wanted to connect with Julie again, but sex became a power struggle instead of a way of connecting to deeper intimacy. I felt I wasn't welcome to bring my erotic desires to her, and I interpreted her withdrawal as rejection and her criticism as judgment.

Finally, all we had left between us were bills, responsibilities, and our children. Passion had fled in the night. At this point, my goal was to survive my marriage, not invest in it any longer.

Julie

I still believed I could hold my family together. I felt a sense of comfort and security that Jay attended twelve-step meetings and remained committed to recovery as a solution for how he was coping with his sexuality.

Maybe I was naïve or in denial, but when Jay made a unilateral decision to quit the groups, I felt as if he never once considered my feelings. I feared his decision would lead to escalated sexual problems. I felt completely rejected and extremely angry because I believed he would not be able to control his impulses and that it would bring devastation to our family.

I tried to discuss my feelings and concerns with him, but we both ended up being defensive and blaming each other. We got nowhere except to become more distant and to increase the depth of anger and rejection we both felt. At that point, I honestly believed I had married someone without a thread of morality, a man obsessed first and foremost with meeting his own needs. I concluded that Jay's version of erotic passion was only about other women who could satisfy him, not about us as a couple. I felt deeply hurt, and I didn't want any part of his dark, deceptive world.

Jay began spending more time away from home as his business ventures thrived. Although he was making more money than ever before, I felt even more abandoned and neglected. When he presented me with a real diamond ring in celebration of our anniversary, I would have traded it in an instant for more of his time and love.

But I accepted the diamond as a bridge to strengthen our marriage.

Jay

Many people find help in twelve-step group meetings, but I wasn't one of them. I felt increasingly uncomfortable with the recovery movement. The meetings made me feel as though I had to truncate and shame my sexuality by neutering my desires in order to please Julie. Besides that, people in the groups had significantly more issues than I did, including legal problems associated with their sexual behavior. Soon they sought me out for personal counseling, and I received no support. I felt all the more diminished, lonely, and shamed—feelings that paralleled my humiliating experience in marriage. I decided to stop attending and opted for self-help.

This was about me, not Julie. I made the decision on my own and wouldn't let her change my mind. She was upset, but that was her choice. I wasn't going to sacrifice my life for her dream of life. I refused to let her regulate my sexual impulses while she remained unavailable except to judge and shame me. I wouldn't let her neuter me anymore.

As I moved on with life, Julie dragged on me like a dead weight. I decided to complete my MBA and grow my consulting practice in corporate America. I got larger projects with bigger price tags and made more money than ever before. Meanwhile, Julie criticized every choice I made. But it was the only way to sustain our lifestyle.

On our anniversary, in hopes of mending some of the holes in our relationship, I reached out to her. She liked the diamond, but I wasn't sure she liked me.

4

Julie: "Where did we go wrong?"

Jay: "I was intoxicated with success."

Julie

Nothing I did rekindled Jay's love. Many a night I cried alone in bed while he sat at the computer in his office, attended classes, worked out, or traveled. I felt like a single mom. He was rarely available to attend school or extra-curricular events. Parents at our children's school wondered if I was even married. It was deeply embarrassing. Not only that, but because he was easily bothered and agitated, our children felt as if they had to walk on eggshells around him.

Jay and I approached our date nights and lunches as if we were intimate strangers. We made shallow attempts to connect but never expressed our deeper emotions. I felt suspicious, so I watched him closely when symptoms of his addiction returned. I realized I was living with a liar and a cheat. Though I clung to the idea of our early love, my respect for Jay grew weaker with each passing day.

I was so distressed and depressed that I gained weight, and then I felt even worse about myself. When Jay was home, I went to bed in beautiful lingerie, but he refused to notice. I needed him to touch my face, hold my hand, kiss me, and make love to me. We only came together when I initiated contact, but that quickly felt worse than no contact at all. For me, sex and love went together. Without one, I couldn't enjoy the other.

Jay was so difficult to engage and be close to that I called him "my little porcupine." He lied to me even when it would've been easier to tell the truth, and it soon became a way of life for him. Early in our relationship, I'd always been able to tell by his eyes and his body language when he was lying, but the more he practiced his art of deception, the more he improved. He was putting on weight, too. I could see the toll stress was taking on him. I worried about his health and wished I could do or say something to turn back the clock.

Above all, I still loved Jay more than anything. I desperately wanted our marriage to work, but I didn't know how to reach him anymore. I kept thinking that once he achieved enough success to satisfy himself, he would be happy. He'd have time for me then and would love me again.

While I patiently waited for Jay's attention and love, I continued to focus on our children as the center of my life. I involved Jayde and Zoe in the arts at an early age. As a child, I had participated in theatre and dance events in which I learned important life skills, acquired poise, and gained friendships. I wanted our daughters to benefit from similar opportunities.

Our daughters thrived as they gained self-confidence and new friends through participating in many artistic expressions. At first, Jay and I attended their events together. We enjoyed the children's activities and agreed that they were a positive experience for us all. We were pleased and proud. Jay was very supportive, and I especially enjoyed teaching and sharing music, dance, and pageants with Jayde and Zoe.

As time went by, Jay became less supportive and questioned these activities. Our girls felt hurt. I supported them, and we continued on alone.

I still hoped Jay would come to his senses and make his family a priority.

Jay

I made up for my failure in marriage by being successful in business. Success was intoxicating and certainly more satisfying than what marriage had become; in fact, the business world was one of the few places I felt alive and good about myself. Money helped me feel powerful.

Some days it was enough. Other days I felt increasingly trapped in a life I didn't completely choose. Nothing felt fair or right. I had to put in twelve- and fourteen-hour days, seven days a week, to chase success so that we could drive new cars, the children could go to private schools, Julie wouldn't have to work, and her mother could be paid as a nanny and personal assistant. I also had to clothe and feed everyone, pay for private dance and voice lessons, and support the girls' pageant entries, which required thousands of dollars more in clothes and travel expenses. I had to deal with all this while my few needs became obliterated and nobody else cared about me.

Friendship with Julie seemed like a distant dream. I lied more and more to her because I didn't feel safe to share my deep emotions and desires. I adopted a foxhole mentality, and I wasn't about to let her lure me out of it. Her judgment and withdrawal had left me feeling abandoned and betrayed. Despite my efforts to please her, nothing had worked. I felt exploited, emasculated, and shamed.

I'd become tainted and cynical, the occupational hazards of saving numerous marriages while failing in my own. In my opinion, modern marriage was nothing more than a sham people endured for selfish reasons. I believed that survival, not fulfillment, was the mantra of marriage and that every spouse had a unique method of escape. Whether excessive golf outings; shopping sprees at Saks or Neiman Marcus; consumption of boats, cars, and lake houses; exotic trips and vacations; or addictions like gambling, booze, drugs, or sex—it all came down to the same drudgery to survive.

One morning Julie and I lay on either end of our big king bed, our three children stretched out between us. Julie was wearing a large sweat set, and I realized she looked big enough to be pregnant. I'd put on weight, too. We were a family living a great lifestyle, trapped inside a miserable life. We were in such a mess that I didn't see how we could ever get out of it.

I said to myself, "Is this what marriage is all about? Yes it is, and it sucks. I get to give everyone their life while I suffer in silence."

Now, as a successful businessman, I could have and do what I wanted. I didn't need to suffer. And I wasn't going to anymore.

PART II

Infidelity
Challenges Love

CHAPTER 4
DIZZY DAYS

I

Julie: *"I tried to bring back love."*

Jay: *"My new life caught me by surprise."*

Julie

Jay remained the love of my life, but I felt him slipping away. The love of my children, parents, and friends couldn't fill the empty place in my heart.

As he was leaving for work one day, I called him into the kitchen.

"Jay, we need to talk. Something is wrong in our marriage." I looked up from cleaning the table.

"I'm busy. You're busy," he said as he checked his watch. "We don't have time to play anymore."

"Why don't we try date nights again?" I smiled. "Remember how much fun we used to have together?"

"Yes. We could do that. I'll check my schedule and let you know what days look good."

"Thanks." I stepped close to him and straightened his tie. "I want you to know how much I appreciate your hard work. Maybe I don't tell you enough."

"Julie, let's talk later. I've got a plane to catch."

"But there's never a later. We're too busy."

"Kiss the kids bye for me."

"Jay, I love you."

"I love you, too."

After a quick hug and kiss, he was gone.

I sighed as I finished up in the kitchen. Jay and I were growing further apart all the time. I wasn't sure if our goals were still the same. Maybe I would never be able to love him the way he needed me to. I'd tried, but at times I'd turned away in frustration. He carried a big, empty place inside that he kept trying to fill. He always needed more. I hurt from not being enough for him.

But I was angry, too. How could he not give his children more love, attention, and time? For myself, I'd ask for nothing if he'd only give time to our sweet babies. But our family seemed a burden to him now.

I hoped to find a way that would turn his thoughts and his love toward us.

Jay

I was done feeling trapped. No one was going to control me anymore. The days of being suffocated by life and of watching my soul slowly euthanized by the empty structure of marriage would soon come to an end. I wanted my life back, and this time, nothing was going to stop me from taking it.

The death of a relationship happens long before the paperwork is filed. I resolved to live duplicitously. I planted my feet in two worlds and called it "complexity"—something I relished as a dysfunctional badge of courage. Here I erected walls minus any windows. Deception and presumed privacy became my MO. Girded by my uncanny ability to compartmentalize my life and look good in the process, I rationalized the unfolding situation and took a pleasantly aloof stance toward the toxicity growing in my midst.

I loved Julie and my family, but I was living life on the run. I barely had time for me, much less her. Plus, she hardly fit into my world anymore. With the growth of my consulting and executive coaching business, my business trips to Miami had become routine. It felt good being the go-to person for the corporate elite who worked in boardrooms across the country. I enjoyed helping big-name, powerful people in billion-dollar companies.

After long, arduous days, I liked to kick back in VIP clubs. I'd grown accustomed to rubbing shoulders with professional athletes, celebrities, politicians, and businessmen in places where erotica is legitimized by respectable men who had the money to gain frequent access to whatever they wanted. Booze and babes soothed our fragile egos and bolstered our fledgling self-confidence—weaknesses we'd never admit to having in the real world.

My excursions into the fantasy world of strip clubs and porn reminded me I wasn't dead yet. I thought I might still have a soul somewhere embedded deep in the armor I'd constructed to keep me safe. But I believed if people found out who I really was, they'd think I was just a fraud. So I became a master of personas—whoever people needed me to be, that's who I became. The only problem was, in pretending to be someone else, I lost any connection to my true self.

After flying in to Miami late one evening, I went to my favorite gentleman's club. As I sat drinking a glass of wine, I saw a seductive young woman walk toward me. I felt a combination of lust and fascination. At five foot two, she was tiny, but she exuded the sizzling energy of ten women. Dressed in black leather and spike heels, she drew the attention of all the nearby guests. She had dark eyes, red lips, and long auburn hair.

As a shrink, I know that most young woman working VIP clubs are fractured human beings in flight from various afflictions. A few have a life plan that includes making quick money to escape to something else. I wondered into which category this young woman fit as she walked into my space with no obvious recognition of boundaries.

"I'm Dayanara," she said. *"Hold me."*

Our first embrace seemed to slow time and unleash years of repressed passion. Vulnerability met opportunity. Then a dangerous thing happened. We talked.

In the connection of that moment, my affair began.

I handed two hundred bucks to the bartender for the pleasure of her company in a private corner of the room. At a small table, we sipped drinks. We told our life stories, or at least what we chose to reveal of them. I was struck by the contrast in her sensuality, her obvious intellect, and the brokenness within her. I recognized her as a kindred wounded soul.

Dayanara explained that she had been adopted as an infant by an affluent Miami family. Her birth mother, a South American illegal immigrant and housekeeper, was a crack addict who used rich men to support her habit. Dayanara's biological father was an ex-con who had abandoned them. The only two gifts Dayanara's mother had given her were staying off drugs during the pregnancy and giving Dayanara up for adoption so that she would have a better quality of life. Yet in spite of her hopeful beginning, Dayanara had failed to connect with her adoptive family, and her upbringing had proven quite painful.

As she spoke about her hopes and broken dreams, the seedy world of the VIP lounge melted into the background. The soul has its reasons the mind doesn't understand. I didn't plan on having an affair. I especially didn't intend to fall in love. I did both, or so I thought, when I met Dayanara. She needed a knight to rescue her, a role I knew well and longed to play, one that vitalized me and made me feel visible. I was the only one in my family who seemed to miss my playing that role. If I could help Dayanara, not only would she be better off, but I would again feel alive.

I admired the fact that Dayanara had no apparent hostility about her mother giving her up for adoption. I was suspicious about it somewhat, because I knew that abandonment issues and personality disorders usually go together. But I didn't want to see that aspect of it. I wanted to feel again. Besides, at twenty-six, she appeared mature and well integrated. I also admired her integrity, since she'd left an abusive husband and was working to pay off their credit card debts by working nights at the club on top of a day job in her own business.

Dayanara woke me up. I wanted everything she represented: eroticism, freedom, vitality, and possibility. But I had a full day of presentations to prepare and needed to leave.

"I've got to go," I said.

"I feel our deep connection." She smiled wistfully. "You've touched me in ways no one ever has before. We're soul mates. I know it." She reached into her black Versace bag, pulled out her business card, and held it out.

I took the card with her email and phone number. I didn't know whether to run away or reciprocate with my own card. Was she playing a game, trying to manipulate me?

I didn't run. I couldn't. I felt alive for the first time in years.

I gave Dayanara my card.

2

Julie: *"I kept busy."*

Jay: *"I lived life on the edge"*

Julie

Jay and I were like ships passing in the night. My love for him remained steady, and I hoped he saw it as a lighthouse beacon.

I focused on giving my children love enough for two parents. Each first step, first word, and first laugh made my heart swell with love and pride. Jay missed so much as our babies grew quickly into smart, loving little people. One day I knew he would regret the loss, but not now. For the present, he had chosen a different life, one that took him out into a big, wide world full of huge possibilities and larger-than-life individuals.

I feared that world and those people would lure him away from me and our little ones. They might make us look small and insignificant, and take him into a bright world filled with promises and possibilities. I knew Jay and that gaping hole inside him. He couldn't resist snatching everything to stuff inside.

I wouldn't allow myself to believe he would fall prey to a seductive woman who promised him the moon and took him away. I prayed he carried me, the woman who loved him with all her soul, in his heart to ward away the bright baubles that so easily tarnish.

Jay

We all possess free choice but don't always experience it as free. As I flew home from Miami the next day, I felt changed. My encounter with Dayanara had exposed vulnerabilities I didn't know I had. I had acknowledged to her that I'd become profoundly unhappy and had acclimated myself to it.

Since I couldn't seem to find happiness in my marriage, I wondered if I could pursue a friendship elsewhere. I called Dayanara. Picking up where we'd left off, we talked for three hours. My new friend's life was a mess, something I was comfortable with and knew plenty about. I became intrigued with inventing ingenious solutions for the smorgasbord of problems around her. My game was being solid, secure, smart, and unthreatened by anything. I liked who I was with Dayanara: sexy, sophisticated, and capable.

Not long after, I was planning to go to Orlando to see my son. Impulsively, I emailed Dayanara and invited her to meet me there. To my surprise, she agreed.

I rented a quaint condo on the beach where I liked to stay when I visited Keaton. Always before, I had walked the beach alone and longed for passion, touch, and a solution to my separateness. Now I had opened a door to new possibilities.

3

Julie: *"I was living on dreams."*

Jay: *"I lived my fantasies."*

Julie

I felt a strong foreboding, as if silenced sisters whispered warnings in my ear. Jay was going to Orlando to see his son from his first marriage, but I felt something was wrong.

At breakfast, I sat down across from him with a cup of coffee.

He looked up from his newspaper. "What's up?"

"Jay, is something going on with Keaton?"

"No. Why?"

"I just feel uneasy. Does Keaton want to live with us? Is that it? You know I wouldn't mind."

"Keaton's fine with his mom. He likes Orlando."

"Your business is going okay?"

"Yes. Everything's good." He glanced up over the top of his paper. "You okay, too?"

"Yes. I'm fine." I watched his attention slip back to his paper.

As we drifted further apart, I wished I knew how to bring him back to me.

Jay

As March brought spring to Tulsa, I was ready for change. Long before I met Dayanara, I'd decided that my marriage to Julie was an existence to endure but too painful to leave. With spring, I hoped for something in between.

At the Orlando airport, I watched Dayanara walk toward me. I'd seen her last at the VIP lounge in Miami with many men. Now she was here, for me alone.

Inches apart from me, she smiled. *"Hold me."*

She giggled a little-girl sound when I took her into my arms. I should have quickly run the other way, so deeply did she affect me, but I felt too alive to let her go.

I rented a car, and we inched our way through a torrential downpour toward the ocean. I felt intoxicated by the moment. Then Julie called my cell phone, and reality interrupted the dream. I quickly pulled into a gas station, got out, and returned Julie's call. I knew I must make excuses to ensure the rest of my night would not be disturbed by family matters, so I lied to her.

When I returned to Dayanara, I pushed guilt, responsibility, and accountability from my mind. We continued our escape into the night. When we arrived at my condo, the weather broke, the sky cleared, and a full moon shone down upon us.

We walked hand in hand along the beach. It was a night made for lovers. Later, we stepped inside the condo, walked upstairs, and onto the balcony. We made love in the light of the moon. Through the transparency of those moments, we found peace and healing in the seductive sharing of our bodies.

When I awoke the next morning, the world I knew no longer existed. I was angry at myself for violating my vows to Julie. Dayanara deserved better as well...yet now I desperately needed her in my life.

For me, the affair wasn't just about sex, something relatively easy to find; it was more about being true to myself. For far too long, I'd tried to live someone else's version of life instead of my own. Now I was desperate to reclaim the parts of me that I'd abandoned while trying to please Julie, our children, her family, and her friends. I was tired of trying to live up to their needs, expectations, and desires. I wanted to live life on my terms.

I believed I'd chosen Dayanara as a source of salvation, as a jagged road back to myself. I believed she'd chosen me for that same reason.

4

Julie: *"Secrets filled the air."*

Jay: *"I lived a double life."*

Julie

Even though my heart hurt when I thought of Jay, I felt happy over the success and love of my children. At age six, Zoe won an international competition and brought home over ten thousand dollars in cash and college scholarships. She was swiftly gaining poise and an understanding of her own gifts, strengths, and potential. We were all thrilled. Jay did his best to appear pleased, but his mind, if not his body, was elsewhere.

"Jay," I said, watching him grill steaks. "Won't you go to the next event with us?"

"I can't."

I walked across the patio to stand beside him. "It'd mean so much to the girls."

"I'd like to go, but work keeps heating up."

"I know. Still, it'd be so great for you to be with us."

"As soon as I get time, I'll go."

I leaned my cheek against his shoulder and savored the scent of his aftershave. "You work too hard."

"I've got to. I want us to have the best."

"We do. I just want to know that we're still working toward the same goals."

"I'm forging ahead."

"Thanks."

Jay

I still loved Julie, but not the way I wanted to anymore. Plus, I was angry at her. I resented what I perceived as years of criticism for failing to be the man she wanted me to be. I believed she took advantage of my hard work and generosity at supporting her, the kids, and her family. The situation reminded me of how I'd felt as a kid growing up in New York. I'd felt exploited then for what I could do for others, and now I felt that way again.

As the summer progressed, I stayed in touch with Dayanara, and we made a "friends with benefits" agreement. To my surprise, she had a good business head. I decided that it might be possible to blend friendship with business, make money, and have a legitimate alibi to travel the country with her. I would continue to provide well for Julie and my children. No one would get hurt. No one had to know. Everyone would benefit.

My business ventures flourished that year. I traveled from coast to coast as I delivered seminar programs to top executives and their teams. I made more money than I ever dreamed possible. Business opportunities also expanded in Miami, and I frequently stopped by the VIP lounge or called up Dayanara to meet for a drink. Our friendship deepened as we returned to Orlando for more romantic getaways.

Soon Dayanara quit her escort business. She wanted only me. I'd rescued another woman and felt good about it.

Julie

Something wasn't right, but I couldn't get the truth from Jay since he had turned so secretive. I'd finally resorted to keeping track of him as much as possible. When he came home from one of his trips to Miami, I confronted him.

"Jay, who is this woman writing you all these emails?"

"Dayanara?"

"Yes!" I got in front of him so that he couldn't move away.

"My business is growing so fast in Miami that I need help."

"How old is she?"

"Mid-twenties, I guess."

"Who is she?"

"She's a professional who is experienced in seminar work. She can help me grow the business, too."

"Are you sure it's strictly business?" I put my hands on my hips. I was determined to get to the truth of the matter.

"What do you mean?"

"Are you having an affair with her?"

"Julie, I'm sick of you checking my emails, phone records, or following up to see if I went where I said I was going. What's wrong with you?"

"Me?" I shook my head in dismay. "You aren't acting yourself."

"If anything, it's your constant checking up on me."

"It's my business, too."

"I'll take care of the business. You take care of the kids and home."

"I'm doing that." I reached out to him, but he stepped back. "Just tell me the truth. Whatever it is, we can deal with it together."

"There's nothing to tell. Life is great."

As I watched him turn and walk away, I felt a deep chill of unease.

Jay

Julie had a good reason to be suspicious, but I wasn't about to tell her the truth. I was pursuing a secret life with Dayanara and nothing was going to stop me. I felt alive for the first time in years, after so long a time of simply going through the motions.

I viewed our lives as a type of social quid pro quo. Julie got to be a stay-at-home mom, spend money, take trips, live in a big house, and drive a new SUV. I got to provide it all and do whatever the hell I wanted to do.

From my point of view, it was a fair deal.

CHAPTER 5
HOLIDAZE

> ## I
> Julie: *"I love this time of year."*
>
> Jay: *"I hate this time of year."*

Julie

Halloween, October 31, starts a wonderful time of the year. I love all the family events that come one right after another. I decorate the house with special colors and decorations for each occasion. I also plan surprises to make it fun for the kids.

That year, as always, Jayde, Zoe, and Chandler were excited about putting on their costumes and getting special treats. I desperately wanted Jay to be with us for Halloween. I'd decorated the house in black and orange. Jayde and Zoe had helped me carve a big pumpkin. I'd made my special fudge and put it in little orange treat bags to give out. I wore all black with a cute little orange pumpkin flashing necklace. I'd even found a black and white skull tie for Jay.

I wished it weren't true, but only he could make the occasion perfect for our family. I hoped he would join us.

Jay

I hated the holidays. Now they were upon me at the worst possible time in my life. I felt agitated and burdened by them. They reminded me of my childhood, a time when holiday celebrations meant alcohol and drama leading to sleepless, violent nights. As a kid, I'd always felt an overwhelming pressure to perform for everyone by putting on a happy face when all I'd wanted to do was hide and be angry.

Now the typical Halloween routine was here: dress up the kids, go over to Julie's grandmother's neighborhood, and pretend to be happy for two hours while the kids eat too much sugar and stay up till midnight.

I wanted no part of it. I'd developed friendships in Miami, and I preferred to be there. To be part of family occasions was painful for me. I'd moved from furious to resentful to contemptuous. Julie's constant questioning, intermittent accusations, and incessant policing of me were driving me further away.

My despair over our dying marriage stood in sharp contrast to the appearance of orange pumpkins, cornucopia, and Christmas lights around town. Miami was drawing me. Miami—the respite from all that was wrong with my life, just as the conflicts at home began to intensify during the holiday season.

In the end, I made it through Halloween for the kids, not because I wanted to. However, I didn't know how much more of Julie's "most wonderful time of the year" I'd be able to handle. I put a deposit down on an apartment and planned to move out after the holidays were behind us.

2

Julie: *"I was too upset to eat."*

Jay: *"I warned Julie not to police me."*

Julie

As we moved toward Thanksgiving, November 23, I became highly suspicious of Jay's activities. I believed he was lying about his relationship with Dayanara. I couldn't get the truth from him, so I became the police in my own home.

Jay started keeping confidential material in a cabinet in the roll top desk in our office complex. He kept the key so that I couldn't see inside. I hired a locksmith to make an extra key without Jay's knowledge. After that, I kept tabs on everything Jay put in the cabinet.

I was shocked to discover that he'd written letters on Dayanara's behalf suggesting that she needed medication for psychiatric issues, depression, and eating disorders. He started her in her own business, a juice product. He was building a business with her, using thousands of dollars of our personal money. I even found a signed lease for an apartment in Tulsa. If he was moving out, I needed to know, no matter how much it hurt.

I feared I was headed for divorce. I started copying everything in Jay's cabinet as I built a case to get custody of our three children.

Jay suggested we go to counseling, which I was delighted to do. On Thanksgiving eve, we went to our appointment. I felt like Jay was just dropping me off there so that the therapist could help me get through our problems.

I asked Jay directly if he was having an affair, but he denied it to the point of being self-righteously indignant, critical, and demeaning. When I asked him about his apartment contract, he blew up. Finally, I became physically ill.

On Thanksgiving morning, I felt even sicker. I went to the grocery store, but I vomited in the dairy section. I was barely able to get through our family dinner without everybody knowing about my trouble with Jay. I let everyone think I had the flu.

As soon as everyone left, I went to bed and cried myself to sleep.

Jay

Julie insisted on hosting Thanksgiving at our house for her extended family. I was angry. Julie was the drama queen. We could hardly stand to be in the same room together. By this time, we were good enough actors that nobody seemed to notice, or if they did, they looked the other way. Julie was crying and throwing up. We told everyone she had the flu.

If nothing before had convinced me that family holiday events were hell, this one certainly had.

I couldn't wait to escape and get to Miami and Dayanara.

> # 3
>
> *Julie: "I confronted Jay."*
>
> *Jay: "I refused to admit to an affair."*

Julie

On Jay's birthday, November 25, I abruptly awoke to the sound of his cell phone going off just after midnight. He was asleep, so I stumbled out of bed and stopped the noise.

I checked the text from Dayanara and read, "Happy Birthday. I love you."

Shocked, horrified, and furious, I felt tears sting my eyes. "How dare you?" I screamed as I threw the phone at Jay. It hit the bed and bounced.

Jay sat up, sleepy and confused.

I turned on the light and stalked over to him. "Read the text on your phone."

He picked up his cell and read the message. "Not what you think," he said.

I put my hands on my hips. I was so mad I could hardly keep from ripping the room apart. "I want the truth. What is your relationship with that woman?"

"Why do you insist on thinking the worst?"

"You text, email, and call her all day every day. You're in Miami all the time." I paced across the room and then turned back to face him. "How can you do this to us...to our family?"

"Julie, please calm down. Let me explain." He ran a hand through his hair. "In Miami, 'I love you' is a common phrase in her generation. They all speak to each other with terms of endearment. It doesn't mean what it sounds like to you. They're all just that way."

"They talk that way. You're sure?" I stepped closer to him and searched his face for signs of deception. He'd gotten so good at lying that I couldn't read him anymore.

"Absolutely. Dayanara is still young enough to get excited about birthdays. She and her friends give gifts and party together to celebrate their special days."

"That's not unusual for anyone."

"I know. But they go overboard." He smiled. "Look, I'm here for my birthday to share it with you, not them."

"Tell me the truth. Are you or are you not having an affair with her?"

"I'm not." He looked down and then back up. "Maybe I'm more emotionally involved than I should be, but that's all."

"If it's business, then you shouldn't be emotionally involved at all." I felt chilled and wrapped my hands around my upper arms.

"You're right. Perhaps my friendship with Dayanara is inappropriate."

"Perhaps? It is inappropriate!"

"You're right. I agree. It's inappropriate."

"In that case, what are you going to do about it?"

Glancing around the room, Jay hesitated. "I'll back off."

"Good. Business, too?"

"Yes."

I sighed in relief. "I want us to sign an agreement to rebuild our marriage. Will you do that?"

"Yes."

"If you'll work with me, whatever problems we have, we can solve."

"Sure." He smiled. "Come here. Give me a birthday kiss."

"Let's write an agreement and sign it later." I willed myself to believe him for the sake of our children and because I desperately loved him.

"Whatever you want." Jay patted the bed.

I went to him with hope in my heart.

Jay

Who I was and how I got that way were catching up to me. I'd built a house of cards on looking good, being smart and right all the time, and winning at all costs. But I felt as if all the achievement in the world wasn't going to fill the black hole that was driving me to fill my legitimate needs in illicit ways. What was worse, I didn't care anymore.

Resentment, cynicism, and disillusionment had become my friends, so I opted out of giving a damn about anyone except myself under the ruse of being taken advantage of by Julie and her family. With enough anger focused on the wrong person, anything can be justified. It felt like something had finally snapped and the illusion of a successful marriage had cracked wide open to reveal it for what it really was—a lifestyle of pretense and consumption. I wanted nothing to do with it anymore.

I'd become a highly sophisticated liar who believed his own lies. I'd divided my life into separate identities that didn't get along yet enjoyed each other's duplicity. My compulsive sexual behavior played a role in what was unfolding in my life, and I embraced its freedom without the shame. The depression driving me I attributed to my situation with Julie, not to the choices I was making and then rationalizing away. I was convinced that 60 percent of marriages ended in divorce and 40 percent were existences that people endured in a variety of creative but futile ways.

I couldn't cope with my disintegrating life and split world any longer. I wanted out. I blamed Julie, along with the institution of marriage, for my trouble. My affair with Dayanara proved that I could feel alive again. I wanted to live that way all the time.

I planned to get through the holidays without more drama. I would show up at family events in person, if not in spirit.

Lying became a warped type of grace that would spare Julie unnecessary pain. I convinced myself that my deception protected people by insulating them from hurtful truths. Besides, with all my failings, at least I was responsible enough to provide well for her and the kids. What more could she want?

4
Julie: *"I confronted Jay."*
Jay: *"I was furious."*

Julie

I felt our marriage was disintegrating before my eyes, and yet I was growing as I looked within myself, not just at Jay's behavior, for the answers as to how we got here.

As we coasted into December, Jay continued to lie and deceive me, and our conflicts increased. Then on December 3, he announced another trip to Orlando. By December 6, I felt more concerned than ever, so I confronted him once more while he was packing to go.

"Jay, are you having an affair with Dayanara?"

He closed his suitcase. "No."

"Why are you communicating with her so much?"

"I told you. It's business."

"If you'll just tell me the truth, we can work this out."

"I'm going to Orlando to see my son."

"We still haven't signed an agreement to rebuild our marriage. If I draft one, will you sign it?"

"Yes. I already agreed." He picked up his suitcase. "I've got a plane to catch. We can talk about this later."

He gave me a quick kiss and was gone.

I wandered aimlessly about my house for a while, and then I gathered my energy. Jay was almost impossible to engage in direct conversation, so I decided to email him.

Sent: *Wed, 6 Dec*
Subject: *More thoughts from the heart*

Jay,

In this journey, I am going to continue to be authentic and not pretend to be someone I'm not, just as you are doing the same. I am committed to our relationship, no matter how much it hurts. I risk being made a fool and rejected, and I accept that possibility. If that happens, I will not blame you, even though the idea of losing you crushes me. If there is any chance for us to have a future, I must be honest with you. And if there isn't because of your decisions, I will know I was true to myself.

I am burdened by the fact that you have felt shamed by me and that my reactions have hurt you as badly as I have been hurt. You think it is all about me, but it is not. Please hear me and try not to be defensive. I refuse to get nasty with you anymore about anything. I will intensely feel whatever comes up for me, but I am not going to take it out on you. I am practicing that right now. I love you.

Julie

After I opened my heart to Jay in that email, I heard nothing back from him. I so needed to communicate with him, but he was closed to me. On December 7, at 2:20 a.m., I sat alone, trying to collect my thoughts about the wind that seemed to be swirling around our lives. I decided to write my thoughts in my journal so that I could clear my mind.

I believe we marry for many reasons, but underlying many of them is one simple and powerful motivation. We all seek to fill the hole in our souls through love. Everyone included. Perhaps all of our attempts at relationship come from that driving force. It's a longing that we may keep at bay for a while, but it always comes back, often larger than before. What is the longing? The best chance for filling that hole in the soul is in a committed marriage, a mature marriage free from the expectations of society and the cultural craziness surrounding marriage and love. Marriage gives us a partial fulfillment.

Jay, I want to touch your soul. I want to love you like no other. I want you to let me in and let me love you. I want zest and passion. I want to extend grace and mercy and unconditional love to you. I promise to love, honor, and cherish all of you. I ask you to forgive me for the times I haven't. We need to sit and confess to one another our mistakes. We need to open our hearts and forgive each other. We are only human. We will never be everything the other wants. There are no perfect partners even though, in an affair, it appears there could be since there is no commitment in an affair relationship. No stresses. No financial obligations. Affairs are for cowards. They are unfair and cut like a knife. I will never do that to anyone. I promise to listen and try not to react.

I long for Jay to love me with an absolute unfailing commitment like I can offer him. I long for a physical, emotional, and spiritual relationship that continues to grow, not die. Today I feel emotionally starved. I want to learn how to love Jay so that he is not smothered. I want to know he loves me and no one else. I do not want to check up on him. I want him to want me, to be near me. It hurts me to be away from him so much. I want him to show me how he needs to be loved. I want him to talk to me.

My love and desire for Jay is sacred. I believe it is permanent. I am committed to the vows we took. I want to be one flesh with him. Even if there is no happy ending, I will never regret the stand I have taken for this relationship. I will know I made the right decision and followed the only course possible for me. I will have done all I can to save my marriage.

Depression robs Jay of his joy. It is not just sadness. It is like all of life is hopeless and bleak, and nothing he can ever do will change it. All reality and ability to reason disappear. That's the serpent of depression. Sometimes I feel alienated from Jay because of it. I get tired of hearing myself ask the same ridiculous question, "What are you thinking?" God knows Jay must just cringe when he hears me say that. I can see years of pain and hurt in him. I can see the tears behind his eyes. His tears melt my heart. I wish he'd cry so that he would feel something real.

Jay is an incredible provider. He would work till his last breath to provide for our family. I find that so admirable. I regret not saying it more often. I have taken him for granted. I think he has a need to be taken care of, and I have a need to take care of him. Will he let me? Will he open his heart to me again? I have been hardened in the heart and covered with armor. I have not been the tender woman he married. Well, that is over. I refuse to walk through life protected by my own personal armor so that I go through the motions, never intensely feeling anything.

I have learned a lesson. Reassure those you love with love. Never use affection of any kind as a weapon. Don't withhold yourself because you are hurt or don't understand. When I withdrew, it got worse. No wonder Jay hates marriage. We have created a bad one. Things must change. But it requires two. Remain committed. When it is hardest to love someone is when they need it most. Even when Jay makes me angry, he still needs my love. When I am emotionally a mental case and frustrating him is when I long to be held, to bury my head in his chest, and to feel his strong arms around me as he reassures me of his never-ending love.

Can our dreams live again? Certainly not without work. Listening, understanding, discipline, compromise, and change. God has given us the gift of choice. My question is no longer "Do you want to?" but rather "Jay, will you?"

I so struggle with our separation and being apart. I want to just say no. I can't and I won't do it. Force him to make a decision. Make him have to choose to stay or divorce. I hate feeling like I am a yoyo being toyed with. My heart cannot take much. I know that a separation is not death, but it is the valley of the shadow of death. A walk very close. Could a separation actually be the labor pains of the rebirth of the marriage? Or, is it the beginning of the end? Separation feels like intensive care. The relationship is in critical condition and can go in either direction at any given moment. If the separation happens, how we handle it will determine the quality of life for five people for many years to come. My battle for the marriage will not end until the death certificate has been signed.

Chandler needs his father around. Who will play ball with him? Who will take him camping? Who will go to Boy Scouts with him? Boys need their dads. Father hunger. It is so interesting that Jay has worked so hard to not be his birth father and has been filled with regret and guilt about his divorce. Yet he is contemplating it with three children.

I have learned so much and must see some of these things as positive: I now refuse to live in a devitalized relationship, to protect myself and not take a risk in order to find love and passion. I know I must be honest and true to myself. And I am. I have so thoroughly confused Jay, poor thing. But we both know that the changes in me probably won't influence his decision about the marriage. I do know that I am better equipped to love

with every fiber of my being in an intense way. I know that I can have
an exciting, passionate, soulful connection to another.
   I know that Julie has not died.

After I cleared my head with my journaling, I desperately tried to think of
ways to bring Jay back to me. He wasn't thinking clearly. If I could get him to
go with me, we might find a way back together through therapy. I researched
possible programs, and then emailed my results to him.

Sent: *Fri, 8 Dec 12:47 a.m.*
Subject: *Therapists*

Jay,
   I have been researching therapists that do intensive work with people
nationwide. There is a husband and wife team in Colorado that do some
interesting work. They present workshops and do marathon individual
and couples work. They also have two sex therapy workshops (perhaps we
could develop a better understanding of one another's sexuality).
   Listen, I am not above anything here. I will support you in finding
your truth, but I want it to be with someone really good. This is our life
and it is very important. The repercussions of divorce will echo for years
and years to come in all of our lives.
   I know we agree that, ideally, we can figure out how to stay together,
make everybody happy, and get our needs met. So, here is an idea. Look
at the therapists' Web site. There are bios on both of them and an over-
view of their program. I will go anywhere with you to work on whatever
we need to work on to figure out what needs to happen here. Let me know
what you think. Remember, you said for me to research it!
   Julie

Jay
   I was done and should have said so, but was too afraid to admit it. As crazy
as it sounds, I didn't want to hurt Julie any more than I already had, so I lied to
justify my actions.
   As for her latest emails and questions, I didn't respond to them at all. Her
newfound determination felt like another manipulative ploy to keep me at
home. Instead, I traveled on business as much as possible. After canceling a trip
to Disney World with Julie and the kids, I took Dayanara with me to New York
to court a new client.

Years of neglect and unmet needs, fueled by chronic resentment, had left me callous and indifferent with a novel-length story to rationalize it all. I felt empowered, even justified, to reclaim my life from Julie. I was trapped in a life where my role as a husband took everything from me and gave nothing back to me. I'd had enough of it—the lack of appreciation and respect, the judgment and withdrawal. I wasn't going to take it anymore. My new mantra was simple but provocative: "I'm all I've got, and if I don't take care of me, who will?"

I just wanted to get through the holidays as quickly and peacefully as possible, and then get on with my new life.

5

Julie: *"I audio taped him."*

Jay: *"I got caught."*

Julie

During Jay's trip to New York, I heard voicemails from Dayanara to Jay that were very upsetting to me. When I confronted him, he changed his cell phone. Yet he left the existing contract since we had to continue paying for it. He also left the cell phone bills in our company's name. I was president of the company, so from then on I obtained an itemized list of his phone messages and text messages. Jay never knew. When he was on trips, his habitual pattern was to call me and then her.

I needed to know more to protect my family. I bought a noise-activated audio tape recorder and stuck it underneath the front seat of Jay's car. Every time he drove, I got his side of conversations on tape. I couldn't hear Dayanara's words, but I could hear enough to know Jay was lying to me about their relationship. I feared the worst, so I decided to have my picture made with the kids. I had it framed in a beautiful mahogany frame so that Jay could take it to his apartment.

On December 17, we had to celebrate our wedding anniversary early since Jay was leaving town. He'd be with Dayanara two days later, our real anniversary, and I'd be home alone. Jay took me out to dinner and gave me a lovely amethyst bracelet. I gave him a new wedding band, but he didn't put on the beautiful ring.

After our tense evening out, we got home and he immediately left to buy toiletries. I knew he was really going to call Dayanara. When he returned home, I secretly got the tape recorder out of his car.

In the kitchen, Jay opened a bottle of wine, poured two glasses, and carried them into the living room. I put cheese, crackers, and fruit on a tray, and then I added the recorder and covered it with party napkins. I carried the tray into the living room, set it down on the coffee table, and joined Jay on the sofa.

We sipped wine together as classical music played softly in the background. When Jay looked relaxed, I set down my glass and uncovered the recorder.

"What's that?" he asked.

"A little something extra for our wedding anniversary." I hit a button, and his voice came out loud and clear.

Jay turned pale, jerked forward, and spilled his wine. "Turn that off!" he shouted as he reached toward the tape recorder.

I grabbed the recorder, jumped up, and stepped away from him. "Don't you like the sound of your own voice? Don't you like to hear all those sweet endearments to Dayanara?"

"Stop it!" he shouted. "How dare you secretly tape my conversations! It's a violation of my privacy."

"Listen to this." I fast-forwarded the tape until we both heard him say to Dayanara, "Can you tell me what your plans for our future are? I don't know what to tell Julie, but she is on to us and I need to tell her something. What you say to me will make a difference in what I tell her."

"That's out of context." Jay leaped to his feet. "It's not what it sounds like. We're talking business."

"Jay, I need you to admit the truth. I'm the mother of your three children. Don't I at least deserve the truth?"

He grabbed the tape recorder and threw it on the floor. It broke into small pieces. "Okay! You want the truth? I've gotten emotionally entangled with Dayanara."

"It sounds like a lot more than that."

"It's not."

"I don't know if you can be honest with anybody. Me. Yourself. Her."

"You're right. I'm wrong." He paced back and forth.

"Where is your moral compass?"

"I'll end it with Dayanara."

"You're going to be with her on our wedding anniversary."

"It's business and we are going to be separated! I can't cancel." He stopped. "I'll call you."

"Call me?" I was boiling with fury, and I felt completely devastated. "Jay, I need you to leave. Right now. You're not the man I married. I don't know who you are anymore. Just get out."

"For the record, you're not the woman I married either."

"I want your house keys and garage door opener. You'll get back in this house by invitation only."

"All right. I'll go." He handed over the keys and opener. "I'm sorry if I've caused you pain. I don't want to inflict any more."

"Leave and you won't."

As he slammed the door behind him, I whispered, "Happy Anniversary."

Jay

I spent the night in a hotel near the airport since I was flying out first thing in the morning anyway. I felt numb but also relieved that my secrets were being found out. Yet I was also furious at the loss of power and control. I felt violated by Julie's obsessive intrusions into my private little world.

After our confrontation, I wished I had avoided the holidays all together. I had assumed that placating Julie with upscale restaurants and expensive jewelry would help take the bite out of the emerging truth that we were finished. At least I'd refused to take the customary trip to Eureka Springs to revisit the glass cathedral where we had married. I hated to think what might have happened there.

A strong part of me wanted to tell Julie the complete truth, but I simply lacked the courage. Besides, I was protecting her from unnecessary pain. I was doing the honorable thing by leaving the marriage and asking for a separation so that she would be relieved of me.

Now I simply hoped to transition gradually to living alone in my apartment.

6

Julie: "We took our last family trip together."

Jay: "I was packed for my apartment."

Julie

After my confrontation with Jay, I felt so sick that I couldn't take my children to Dallas to see a high school musical concert, a Christmas gift from their uncle. My mother went in my place. Jay hadn't admitted to a physical affair, but I feared that was the truth. I was disgusted at the idea of his physical intimacy with me and another woman at the same time, so I stripped our bedroom sheets and comforter from our king-size bed and threw them away.

On December 20, Chandler, my three-year-old, went to the hospital with a serious staph infection. I called Jay to let him know that we needed him at home. Later, while I was at the hospital, he accidentally dialed me and didn't realize it. I heard him telling Dayanara how he hated to go home and deal with his wife, kids, and all the trouble in Tulsa. I felt his words like a blow to my heart. Didn't he realize he was causing all the trouble?

I stayed in the hospital with Chandler who was on IV antibiotics. Meanwhile, Jay got trapped in a snowstorm in the mountains while vacationing with Dayanara. When I confronted him about their rendezvous, he denied she was there, but I could hear her in the background.

On Christmas Eve, Jay chartered a private plane to get home in time for Christmas. By the time he arrived, Chandler was home from the hospital. Jay was very aloof, very distant. I found a wine cork, massage oil, and condoms in his suitcase. I said nothing. I just wanted to make the holidays good for our children.

For Christmas, we went to Nashville with friends to take our children to see the Rockettes. I feared it would be our last trip as an intact family. Jay and I were at odds and things were tense. He texted and called Dayanara over and over, to the point of being obsessive. We argued about it, but he didn't stop.

With all the stress in my life, I'd lost weight and was glad of it. I wanted to look like I had when Jay first met me. A nurse friend of mine in Nashville became alarmed at my weight loss. She thought I looked ashy and urged me to see a doctor when I returned home.

Once we were back in Tulsa, I muddled through the remainder of the holidays. Desperate to save my family and equally desperate for Jay to contribute something to our marriage, I pushed my fear aside when I secretly got news of a bad pap smear and spent hours on the Internet looking for the best therapists in the world. Then, because I didn't feel there were any problems in our marriage that were too big for us to overcome, I tried to convince Jay to go and get counseling with me.

To my amazement, Jay decided that on New Year's Eve he would tell our children he was leaving home.

Jay

The constant drama and unending conflict was taking a toll on everyone. So during the holidays, I lived in two different worlds as I played the role of Dad and simultaneously planned my escape to reclaim my life. Convinced it was best for us all, I continued preparing for my move and setting up my apartment.

I made it through our trip to Nashville, but the tension between Julie and me was palpable. Nevertheless, we had always been able to parent well together and this time was no exception. Once again, we rose to the occasion.

7

Julie: *"I clung to hope."*

Jay: *"I was ready for change."*

Julie

In late December, Jay gave me a separation agreement.

"This is wonderful," I said as I glanced through the document. "We have four to six months to work out our differences with the intention of you coming home."

Looking pleased about it, Jay smiled. "That's right," he replied.

"This is to lead you out of your ambivalence about our marriage, keep it intact, and not let things get toxic between us."

"Yes. It's a good plan."

"Our contract states that we will not date or be involved with anyone else during this time," I said. "What about Dayanara?"

"I'll eliminate the possibility of continuing my emotional affair with her."

"Perfect." I looked into his eyes. "And we agree to spend time together each week as a family, go once a week on a date by ourselves, and each receive weekly counseling?"

"That covers all your concerns, doesn't it?"

"Yes. I'm so happy about this agreement. It really gives us a chance."

"I want you to be happy."

We signed the separation agreement and each kept a copy of it.

For me, the contract meant everything. My life hinged on this one document. I made copies to keep in my purse, in my car, and on my nightstand. With this agreement, I believed Jay and trusted him.

Jay

I complied with Julie's demand for a separation agreement much like I had with most everything else in our life—trying to make her happy while denying what was true for me. I actually used the agreement to buy myself time to get through the holidays and begin my new life. Besides, the contract seemed important to Julie, so once again, I went through the motions of playing the emasculated good-boy role I'd learned so well in our marriage. But this would be my last curtain call.

After we both signed a copy, I filed mine and went on with life.

8

Julie: *"I had to protect my children."*

Jay: *"I was ready for the new year."*

Julie

On New Year's Eve, Jay refused to let me be part of telling our children that he was leaving home. I thought he'd probably take them to a particular sandwich and ice cream shop, so I drove past it. When I saw his car there, I felt devastated that my children would have to hear such sad news, and I went back home to wait for them.

Jay brought our children back to the house, and then left. I learned that he had sugarcoated everything. They didn't even know he was moving out of the house. I told them the truth. Afterward, we all cried together.

When Jay came home later that night, I was trying to create some sense of normalcy by making beef tenderloin. On the patio, my grill ran out of propane. Frustrated, I brought the beef in on a plate and broiled it. When I took the dish out of the oven, it exploded. Shards of glass and bits of beef flew all over the kitchen. Horrified, I realized I'd forgotten to use a Pyrex plate.

It was a poignant symbol for me. I'd tried to make the evening normal for my family, but it had turned into a mess. It would be a big cleanup job, just like my family.

I looked into the living room and saw my daughters curled up on their father's lap. Both sobbing, they begged Jay not to go.

"It's best for me to leave this house and not live with you or your mom," he said.

At his words, they only cried harder.

I felt sick. I could hardly believe the coldness of his heart. I hurried into my bedroom to get away from the sight. I reread a letter I had written to my children in my journal when I was trying to comfort them and myself.

December 29

My precious babies: Jayde, Zoe, and Chandler (7, 6, and 3),
In just a few short days you will learn devastating news from your father that will break your hearts and potentially shape your lives and relationships for years to come. I need you to know first that I am truly sorry. I would give my last breath to change this for the three of you and for myself. I know that as your mother, I am responsible for protecting you physically and emotionally and for giving you the best life has to offer so that you can grow into the adults that you are capable of being. I am so aware of how a single experience in your childhood can change the entire course of your life.
I cry tears of sadness, regret, and guilt tonight because I know that I have failed each of you. You deserve to have a happy family, one that is loving and intact. Those who dare to be authentic understand that a stable family is the environment in which children thrive best. I am broken by not being able to provide you that opportunity. The irony is

that your father and his love are the things I want most in this world. I have certainly made my share of mistakes and have contributed to this tragedy. But I have realized my mistakes and am learning from them each day. Trust me, they will never be repeated again!

Unfortunately, I realized these things after it was too late. Your father has shut his heart to me, and while I know deep down he loves and adores you, our life (wife and three kids) is no longer the life he wants for himself. Despite my best efforts, he has not changed his mind. Please do not blame only him. I have not loved him the way I should have and he has not loved me. I guess one could say we co-authored this drama and foolishly wrote it in ink. And then he made some choices which have had consequences. I promise you that I will give your dad some time. I will love him patiently from a distance and keep our front door open to him, should he decide to return. I cannot wait forever, but I will be patient. I cannot make promises for him, but I give you my word and am determined that my words will be worth something.

I adore each of you and love you with everything in me. I am heavy and burdened with guilt and sadness for you. I am also enduring the pain of my own broken heart. I feel as though I am in a one-sided love affair. I pray that you will find it in your hearts to forgive me someday. If your daddy never returns home, I promise to be everything I can to each of you.

I want you to know that I love your father and do not regret spending ten years of my life with him. Despite his stories, we had some magical times together. And he gave me three precious gifts—each one of you. I love you with every fiber of my being and wouldn't trade the last ten years for anything.

I will do my best to ensure that this situation does not negatively affect your future relationships and that you will become healthy adults and know the love of your mother. I will not stand in the way of your relationship with your daddy. We may not always live near him, but I will never keep you from seeing him. I will pray that he stays as committed to you as he is to finding himself, his new life, and his career.

My biggest fantasy (fantasy because it seems so glorious yet so far-fetched) is that your father will recognize the love we have and help me make it grow into a more mature love. Today he is unaware of the magnitude of the loss for all of us. I know if he chooses not to return, there will be a day when he lives to regret his decision. He may find himself alone and without the strongest and most pure love he has ever known.

I ask God to protect all three of you and your father. I ask Him to bestow many blessings on your innocent lives. You did not ask to be born, and you did not ask to be abandoned. I pray that no weapon formed against you will prosper, including divorce. I pray that God touches your daddy's heart and shows him the full picture. I hope your daddy will come back home and give this family the chance it deserves... healing. I know that he could be happy here, just as we all can. And I desperately want you three to grow up witnessing a healthy relationship between your daddy and me each day.

Jayde, Zoe, and Chandler, forgive us and know our love. I want you to know that your smiling faces sustain me in these dark hours. You are what gets me out of bed in the morning. I am filled with sorrow over this situation, but I promise to get help and heal my heart so that I will always be the best mother I can be. I love you so much and I am so, so sorry.

With much love today and always,
Mommy

Jay

New Year's Eve was a painful reminder of what was missing and what was to come. I took the children to lunch by myself to tell them of my decision to move out. Using the same spiel I had taught hundreds of couples when they were going through their divorces, I did the best Dr. Jay routine I could muster. This time though, I barely convinced myself, which left all of us more confused and uncertain about the future of our family.

Jayde, my older daughter, shed tears and then shut down. Zoe, my soul child, cried and then begged me not to leave. Chandler, my baby boy, just looked at me with fear in his eyes, saying, "No like this, Daddy... no like this."

I didn't like all of it either, but I was determined to save myself.

I scheduled my move to happen after the holidays when the children would be out of the house involved in activities. Determined, I prepared for it by creating a corner of our large four-car garage with things I needed to set up my new life. I'd already had furniture delivered which I'd bought the month before so that I wouldn't be removing anything from the house. It would appear that nothing had moved except my presence, which I convinced myself they would be better without.

I was ready to begin my new life.

CHAPTER 6
NEW YEAR

> ## I
>
> Julie: *"I focused on medical tests."*
>
> Jay: *"I left home."*

Julie

On January 2, I started the year by scheduling a doctor's appointment. That evening, after explaining that he was going to the office to work, Jay left the house. When I checked our cell phone bill the next day and saw that he had called Dayanara, I cried. I was desperate to do something to save my marriage, but my only comfort was our separation contract.

The next day, Jay flew back to Miami on business and left me alone with the children. Then on January 4, I had a cervical procedure, blood work, and more tests. Though the procedure caused me to cramp and to suffer other physical problems, I was determined to find out about my health. I'd had a lot of strange symptoms such as terrible congestion, profuse sweating, and constant coughing. I'd also lost a significant amount of weight. I convinced myself all the symptoms were stress-related.

The day following my tests, Jay was back in town for his move. He came to get the things that he had stored in our garage for his new apartment. I wondered how his move could be temporary because he had spent thousands of dollars on new furnishings, including living room, bedroom, and office furniture, as well as lamps, artwork, and kitchenware.

To be supportive, I gave Jay a bottle of wine and a beautiful floral arrangement. I even drove over and left Starbucks coffee on the hood of the car at his apartment complex while he was moving his things inside.

Oddly enough, at eight thirty in the evening, he left me a strange voicemail that said, "I wanted to say goodnight. I'm getting ready to go to bed."

I had never known him to go to sleep so early, especially when he had to be in the middle of an unpacking mess.

Curious, I called Jay several times. He didn't answer, perhaps because he was pretending to be asleep. Next I called a girlfriend, and she came to my home. After discussing the situation for a while, we eventually decided to go over and see if Jay was really at his apartment.

When we got there, we passed him as he drove into his apartment complex. Dayanara was with him.

Jay

Once I set foot in my new apartment, my double life was over. I felt free. I caught the scent of fresh paint, saw fabric in colors I'd chosen myself, and appreciated wall décor that meant something to me. It was an entire space designed solely by me. I felt empowered, but sad, too. I missed my children, but not the life I'd just walked away from.

Julie was gracious about my move, and that surprised me. She even brought me a care package consisting of a floral arrangement, an aromatic candle, a card full of kind sentiments that supported me despite my choices, and a mahogany-framed photograph of her and our children. This gesture reminded me of the Julie I'd known long ago, a woman of grace under fire.

When Dayanara learned about my separation, she volunteered to help me with the move, since she planned to be in Dallas on business about that time. I knew it would be a bad idea to have her in town the weekend I moved, but I wanted to assert my newfound independence. Worse than that, I had stopped caring about how everyone else felt. It was my time for a change and I was tired of being controlled by Julie. Dayanara offered me a soft place to land during a time of confusion. I took it.

On Saturday night, Dayanara and I went to Brookside to get a drink and go to a club to unwind from the move. Everything felt surreal: I was in Tulsa at midnight with an exotic dancer I had met in Miami, and we were drinking and dancing with abandon at a local hot spot. The music pulsated through my body, and with each beat I experienced another degree of freedom.

Afterward, feeling mellow and happy, I drove back to my apartment before dropping her at the hotel. As I pulled into the parking lot, I recognized the headlights of Julie's car. She was still keeping tabs on me. Furious, I got out of my vehicle and sent Dayanara on ahead with keys to the apartment so that she wouldn't have to see the coming scene.

Wearing jeans and a sweatshirt, Julie leaped out of her car and headed toward me. "What are you doing with another woman?" she cried as she thrust a piece of white paper my way.

"Julie, don't get upset." I quickly tried to talk her down.

"Do you see this?"

"Yes." I could hardly miss the paper she was waving in my face.

"It's a copy of our separation agreement."

I got her point. "I haven't broken it. Dayanara was in town on business and stopped by to help me move."

"Liar! Can't you ever tell the truth?"

"That is the truth."

"You move out of my house and five minutes later she's in your new apartment. Do you call that an accident?"

"No. She's on her way to a business meeting and came by to help."

"This is Tulsa. It's not on the way from Miami to anywhere."

"She has business in Dallas and is on her way down there. She's staying at a hotel."

"Liar!"

"Julie, I'm not arguing here in the parking lot. We're drawing attention. Pretty soon, the cops will show up."

"Oh, Jay, you're breaking my heart." She turned and quickly walked away.

I watched until I was sure she was gone and then started across the parking lot. Dayanara and I had discussed the risk of her coming to town during my move, but we had ignored the potential problems and opted instead for the draw of our emotions. Now we were paying the price.

Inside my apartment, I felt the sting of humiliation. Dayanara was visibly shaken. Taking her into my arms, I apologized and suggested she move on to someone more responsible. But she calmly accepted the situation, which validated me in a way I desperately needed after my confrontation with Julie. Her poise and strength were comforting, and only added to my fantasy of who she was and what we could be together.

> ## 2
>
> Julie: *"I kept my health issues from Jay."*
>
> Jay: *"I refused to succumb to Julie's mind games."*

Julie

Things went from bad to worse. After further medical tests, I was diagnosed with lymphoma. I didn't tell Jay because I didn't know what was going to happen and I wanted to find out first about available treatments.

I learned that I'd had lymphoma symptoms for months. I'd lost forty pounds, and at five-foot-seven, now weighed a mere one hundred pounds. I was also having terrible night sweats. At first I'd thought it all was due to stress. Now I knew differently. But at least it was still in its early stages; it appeared to be contained and not all over my body.

Jay continued to deny that he was involved in an affair. I kept trying to get the truth from him. He repeatedly told me that he couldn't be what I needed. I had no idea what he meant. It was frustrating. He could offer no specifics. He kept telling me that by leaving me, he was giving me a gift. Finally, I emailed him to explain how I truly felt about him.

Sent: *Sun, 14 Jan*

Jay,

I want you to know that I have no expectations of you. You have your space, and I am not going to question it, because I have no need to. I know you have a friend and you are very involved. I cannot stop that or try to change it. I will pose this question, however. Is it really possible for you to evaluate our marriage and its future while being emotionally and/ or physically intimate with another woman? My guess is no. And that is unfair to us and to our children. I only ask that you give this process the chance you said you would.

I know that we have been bogged down in arguments. However, as I told you a few days ago, I am finished with that. If you want to talk to me about anything, you are welcome. I am not going to fight. I am still willing to go to dinner with you on Wednesday nights so that we can check in with each other and see how things are going. I do not want to take your space from you—that space which you have resented me for having—but I am concerned about the kids having false hopes. It's important for us to check in so that we both know which direction we are headed. There is a lot happening in both of our worlds.

Jay, I do love you and would love to have you back in our home to redesign our life together. But I will not be the one to clip your wings. Go where your heart leads you. In doing so, be aware of the ramifications. Be prepared to see me with another man and also for the kids to move, because those things will quickly follow, should you decide you need your space. I want you to be clear about this and to make choices you can live with.

I appreciate it when you're nice, but your indifference is tough. Today when you said, "We are still married," I almost choked. Yes, we are. And I am happy about that because it means the marriage is not completely over yet. However, I don't feel married, which is sad. I question whether the peace and solitude you're experiencing really means divorce is the right thing for us, although that is the easy interpretation. This is not death yet, only the valley of the shadow of death.

You have retreated from the scene of the battle, but retreat is not always victory. Think about what you are doing very carefully. I am prepared to wait to file for divorce, but I am preparing myself for that reality.

Have a good day and a great trip to Florida. While you're there, envision yourself in another city visiting our children, because that may be your reality.

I do love you,
Julie

Jay

Sent: *Sun, 14 Jan*

Julie,

Thank you for your tempered response and wise words. I am thinking about all of the issues you addressed. They are complicated, have evolved over many years now, and indicate that we are at a critical crossroads.

My heart is burdened. I am pulled between honoring truths I have fought about myself and wanting to do what is customary in my life, which is to comply, please, accommodate, and take care of others. It's been gut-wrenching and confusing to try to balance the need to respect myself (by being honest about my needs and desires that you have judged and criticized for years) with the need to respect the desires of those I love and am committed to.

I still believe that my potential to be a suitable partner, someone capable of meeting your needs and contributing to your happiness, is questionable. I have agonized over seeing you hurt from things I said or did, or from things I didn't say or do that you deserved and needed.

My heart breaks because of my inability to love and be intimate in ways you certainly deserve. I am finding a type of freedom in my space, not to act out, but to go inward and find places in myself that I have ignored, neglected, or long abandoned. Marriage, while respectable, is not for everyone. This is my pervasive question: can I be the man you need and deserve? Today, I seriously doubt that I can, and I'm weary from trying.

I don't want to give you mixed messages and will not string you along. I'm trying to be as honest as I can. I'm not going to tell you any longer that I'll do something when I really can't or won't do it. I've hurt you in the past when I acted like that, and I don't want to hurt you anymore. I want to contribute to your happiness even if that means we change the structure of our relationship.

Love,

Jay

Julie

Sent: *Sun, 14 Jan*

Jay,

I appreciate your honest sharing. It is the best place for us to meet. I am glad that you are finding freedom in your space although I'm saddened that you don't hate it there without us and want to come home. You know, to the same degree that you're upset about your perceived inabilities, I'm upset about my inability to get over this. If our marriage doesn't make it, I know it will be the biggest tragedy of my life.

Jay, I'd really like to know what it is that you can't do and what it is that you've decided I must have to make reconciliation impossible. You know, you do have a lot of stories, many of which are old and need to be buried. You are still hanging on to the past. Lots of things have changed in me and in you, too.

Jay, ideally, we could talk about these changes, design some ways to move forward in our relationship, and then see what happens. I am not willing to accept it when you claim you can't be what I need. Just what is it that you think I need specifically? Your talks about accountability

are correct in that you are dishonest. If we had truthfulness and understanding, everything could change for the better.

I feel like we need to spend time together and connect, to see if our
relationship is really worth the fight. We are so bogged down in conflict
that we don't have a clue. We are so busy defending our position that we
have forgotten we have ten precious years together.

Jay, please consider what I am suggesting. You don't have to agree,
but think about it. I understand that you have things you need to honor.
If you will share, perhaps I can help you honor them. Perhaps they can
be incorporated into a life together. Perhaps not. We need to choose this
jointly. If you make unilateral choices, it will create a lot of animosity. I
am doing my best to grant you what you need despite your lack of desire
to meet any of my needs. I know it is a hard time for you right now, and
I am accepting that. Please think about the big picture when you are
making choices. These are not just decisions for you, but for five.

As you would say, "tread carefully." This decision is something you
could regret once it is too late.

Love,
Julie

Sent: *Sun, 14 Jan*

One more question.

Could it be possible that you honor your truths and needs while you
respect and care for others? Because that is really what life is about.
Not just others and not just self. Keeping and honoring commitments
and doing the same for yourself. Do you really know what I want and
need? Have you asked? Do I know what you want and need? I think not.

I hope that you will find a way to respect all of us, just as I am
respecting you and your choices.

Jay

Sent: *Sun, 14 Jan*

Julie,

Much of what I need and what I struggle with has already been
communicated to you in my journaling that I have shared with you. I
really don't have more to add to that.

Love,
Jay

3

Julie: "I found comfort in emails."

Jay: "I reached out with words."

Julie

Jay and I were now apart most of the time. It was odd, frustrating, and abnormal. Yet we reached out to each other through emails, texts, and phone calls. Our communications were a lifeline that kept me going.

Jay wanted to know about my health, but I was reluctant to share many details. I didn't want his pity. I still wanted his love.

Jay

Sent: *Mon, 15 Jan*

Dear Julie,

About last night... I was lying down in bed and trying to go to sleep when you and I began texting. Somewhere around one thirty, I fell out— although I thought we were done talking, so I put my phone down. I was not ignoring you or trying to be insensitive.

I am confused and bewildered by everything and do not know what is actually happening or what to think because I am getting the information in parts rather than a whole. I appreciate your wanting to protect me but would request you don't any further. I began researching non-Hodgkin's lymphoma, and if that is what you have, we are going to have to fight it together, despite our current difficulties. I will need full disclosure about what is happening, or it will be impossible to fight it together.

Regardless of our issues and challenges, I am your husband and will always be a committed and caring friend. While I fail miserably at many of my husband roles and expectations, I can be a very good friend and that is the best part of love in that it is pure and without conditions.

I am here to support you in any way that I can and you will allow. If you want me to cancel my Miami trip, I will do so, despite whatever client consequences might occur. If you prefer to have a friend with you,

I understand, given where we are and the fact that we need to keep your stress level down.

Love you,

Jay

Julie

Sent: *Mon, 15 Jan*

Jay,

I appreciate your words. Yes, today you are my husband and I would love to have that support. However, it feels only halfway when you have left our home and are contemplating divorcing me. Jay, the reality is that our relationship changed when you decided to leave. How can I trust you as my supporter when I know that any day in the next four months you may have an epiphany and decide you can't stay married? I have tried every way possible to work out a marriage that could make us both happy, but you are unmotivated and uninterested. That alone is crushing to me. You know I want nothing more than to have you by my side forever as my husband.

The biggest struggles in my life are the illness and the loss of you. I understand that you need to take care of you, but it is so hard to see you making these moves that are only serving your interests while our children are breaking and I am, too. Add the physical threats and demands I must face, and it tops the charts for me. I am resisting making you out to be the one who is wrong. I'm also fighting anger, and I'd be lying if I said I'm not.

I feel abandoned and betrayed by you. I keep thinking about the day you married me: for better or worse, you promised to be by my side and never leave me. What about in sickness and in health? You know it doesn't matter, and I should shut up because I don't want a partner who stays because he was forced.

Jay, with all of that said, I am uncertain how you can walk this walk and support me at the same time. You have the idea that you can be my friend, but that is the most painful thought of all. I do not want to be your friend. I want to be your wife. And just as you may find you are incapable of being a husband, I feel I am incapable of being only a friend. I can't have you in my face reminding me of what I've lost, which is what being your friend would feel like to me.

So for now, I think the best thing is for you to continue on your path of self-declaration and independence. If you decide that you think it's possible for us to work on our marriage, you know I'm game. If you think losing your wife and kids is something you aren't willing to do, let me know. If you think not, then you can make the unilateral decision. I will accept it.

As for the treatment process, sure, I'd love you with me. But how? It'd be too painful for me to know that every time you picked up your phone, you might be texting her or that at any given moment, you might decide you needed to leave. I don't trust that you've been honest with me about your hopes for reconciliation. Thank you for offering to cancel Miami and come back home. I know Miami is the pilot and it is a big deal for you, but I think you would resent me more if you had fallout over it.

Jay, frankly, I would love nothing more than for Miami to dry up and go away, for you to have no reason to return, and for you to lose contact with your friend and be able to look at our relationship without skewed perception. But losing Miami won't solve anything. I have already asked those things of you and you refused, so it wouldn't matter. I do not want you to lose business over this. You have enough ill feelings toward me and you feel taken advantage of as it is. Please go on to Miami and do your work there. You will be there for almost two weeks. I will be fine. I am hoping I can get a friend to go with me.

I will see what happens in Houston, and I will let you know. I must tell you that as private and sneaky as you are being about your life, I do not feel safe giving you many details. I am not going to have a one-sided relationship anymore. I may have to go back to Houston the following week to have more tests run or the treatment done. I am praying that I will not have to face chemotherapy.

You still need to give me an answer about Vegas. I had really hoped you and I could spend time together there. You know how important that is to me. We have not taken a trip alone in years. We neglected to do that in our marriage, and it is something I feel is very important. However, if you are not in a place of wanting to spend time with me or do anything to work on our relationship, I understand and know it is best for me to make the trip alone, if go at all. Please advise me on your plans so that I'll know whether to make new plans to go by myself or to cancel. If I decide to forget it, I'll chalk it up as another loss and sell my tickets.

I am sorry I did not tell you all of this sooner. You knew about the cervical stuff, and this all came down as you were leaving. I did not ever feel that the time was right to tell you because I feared you would call me a drama queen and not believe me, get more angry and insensitive, or stay with us out of guilt. None of those are good options. I had thought about telling you that weekend, but then I learned that you were with her.

Jay, do not change your path because of this. Perhaps it shows you how frail life is and perhaps you will feel love for me that you haven't felt in a while, but I am not counting on that. I do not want anyone to stay with me out of guilt or pity. I will be just fine even if I am alone.

Julie

Jay

Sent: *Mon, 15 Jan*

Julie,

Thank you for sharing your thoughts. I so wish I could be and give all that you need right now. The timing of this could not be worse. I love you and will be by your side to whatever degree you allow me. We are in different places, and that difference seems to cause you more pain each time we bump into an expectation that I cannot meet to your satisfaction.

That is my concern about Vegas: you have expectations that I am not in a place to fulfill. Were we to go together, it would only result in conflict and stress for us both. I think it best that you take a girlfriend on the trip and enjoy some time with friends. Rather than risk being hurt by something I cannot offer at this moment, you should go and let your hair down. Let's talk more about it later.

Jay

Julie

Sent: *Mon, 15 Jan*

Forget it. It will be miserable without you. It was planned as a trip to be spent with you in celebration of my birthday. I have no girlfriend to take. I will cancel. Thank you for your honesty.

Jay

Sent: *Mon, 15 Jan*

Julie,

    There is no reason for you to not enjoy an event that means a lot to you and have fun with your friends who will be there. I simply do not want to set us up for more drama that will cause more pain for you. You cannot afford to endure more of that right now. I am trying not to give mixed messages and to meet you in places that I can deliver without continuing to disappoint you. Please consider going and doing something for yourself. It could be an enjoyable time with people you like.

Julie

Sent: *Mon, 15 Jan*

Jay,

    My friends are at a different hotel, have tickets in different places, and I can't think of another person who'd go. And it would be plagued with "Jay should be here."

    I will skip the trip. Maybe another time. It is just another loss amidst many. I will choose to respect your choice despite the commitment we made to the trip in our separation agreement. Another breech of contract.

Jay

    I wished I could be what Julie needed when she needed it. But I was set on living my new life and she knew it. She also knew that I was there for her and our children. I'd do everything I could to help her but no longer on her terms; I also had to keep the businesses rolling to pay all of our expenses.

    I felt confused and angry at the same time. These conflicting feelings left me vulnerable, more likely to act from instinct than reason. Was Julie manipulating me again to regain the control she had lost? Would she go so far as to claim cancer to get what she wanted? I couldn't answer these questions, but even the thought of her trying to control me made me want to run further from her. For years I had felt manipulated as I complied with and placated Julie in an effort to please and make her happy while denying things important to me. Now I found myself deeper inside a despised life that I no longer recognized as my own.

It was time for me to get my life back, and lying to her was all I had left to protect her from the truth. I was done. Maybe eventually she would understand.

> # 4
> Julie: *"My PI kept tabs on Jay."*
>
> Jay: *"My privacy was violated."*

Julie

I decided to make my birthday, January 27, a turning point in my relationship with Jay. After he cancelled our Vegas plans, I discovered he had made plans for a trip to Miami. With the lymphoma, I had physical limitations. But since I had to know if Jay was having a full-blown affair with Dayanara so that I could plan my life, I hired a private investigator to get the truth about them. I went online with Jay's frequent-flier number, printed out his itinerary, and gave it to the PI firm. I also spent hours collecting pictures and data for the firm. Jay suspected nothing.

I changed my mind about not going to Las Vegas to celebrate my birthday. I flew there with friends who would support me emotionally. After Jay dropped off our kids at my parents' home, my mother called me because she knew I needed information to give the PI. Later, I learned that Jay was wearing new clothes when he boarded the airplane: a black leather blazer, white shirt, jeans, and black shoes. I also learned that he looked orange from self-tanner, and I gave all of this information to Miami PI.

When Jay arrived in Miami on my thirty-third birthday, I had six PIs on the ground waiting for him. One called Jay's cell at the luggage terminal, and when Jay answered, the PI was able to make a positive identification. A female PI who sat next to Jay on the bus to the rental car terminal asked him questions to figure out where he was staying. He explained that he didn't come there often. The PIs then deduced he was going to Dayanara's home, and they already had her address.

My PIs updated me with videos and photographs over my cell phone; but I grew progressively more distraught as I saw Jay enter Dayanara's apartment, come out carrying her in his arms, and put her in his car.

I saw their entire evening out. Jay took Dayanara to a ritzy wine bar where they danced and drank. Afterward, they went for late-night coffee, and I saw them snuggling and kissing in a booth at a pancake house. Later, he ate pancakes with blueberry topping. While he gorged, I felt sick to my stomach.

My PIs said they could watch Jay all night, but I didn't want to spend more money. In order to hire the PIs for that long, I already owed ten thousand dollars to my brother. He'd given them his credit card for me so that Jay wouldn't find out. It would take me a long time to repay him from my personal funds. Anyway, I'd seen enough. Jay was in a full-blown affair. He'd repeatedly lied to me. He'd broken our separation agreement. I was furious.

I was so angry I could hardly think straight. I finally had the facts, and I was ready to confront Jay with them. But I had to wait till I was sure he was back at Dayanara's place.

When I finally called Jay that night, I paged him to indicate that I had an emergency and that he needed to return my call ASAP. He didn't call me back, so I kept rapid-fire dialing his number.

Finally, mimicking a tired voice as if he'd been asleep, he said, "Hello?"

"I know you're in bed, but you're not sleeping." I pushed through my fury to get the words out. "Your gig is up. I know exactly what you've been doing. I even know what kind of pancake topping you just had at the pancake house."

"What?"

"Blueberry!"

"Julie, I don't know what you're talking about. I'm sick to death of you intruding into my life. I've warned you to stop it."

"You're a liar. You're a cheat."

"I'm taking care of you and the kids. Every dime I pay is so that you can live the upscale lives you enjoy. That's all you want from me anyway!"

"You're in total violation of our separation agreement."

"What do you mean?"

"I've had PIs tailing you all evening. Think back. Remember that young woman on the bus to the car rental terminal? Remember that couple at the bar and the pancake house? They videotaped your entire evening."

"No!"

"Oh, yes. You wouldn't tell me the truth. Well, now I've got it. You can't lie to me anymore."

"How dare you invade my privacy!"

"You selfish bastard! Who have you become?"

"Julie, I'm sorry. Let's talk about this when I get home."

"You bet we will." I ended the call.

By that time, I was shaking so badly, I could hardly stand up. I felt violated, betrayed, and sick my soul and collapsed on the floor. My girlfriends tried to support me, but I collapsed on the floor of the Planet Hollywood Casino. I was rushed to the hospital where I was given IV fluids because I was dehydrated from the stress and lymphoma. I missed the Miss America finals that night.

As I flew home the next day, I realized I had some hard decisions to make now that I knew the truth. Jay was supposed to come back the following day, but he delayed his return and stayed with Dayanara an additional four days. Maybe he was trying to figure out what he was going to do.

With my children around me, I gathered my bearings. After giving my situation a lot of thought, I decided my marriage and my husband were worth fighting for. I knew I loved him enough to forgive him. I decided to offer him that option one last time.

Jay

In January, Julie always had the expectation of unusually special treatment during her birthday month, and despite our separation, that remained true. She wanted me to accompany her to the Miss America pageant in Las Vegas. She was friends with several of the former and current contestants, worked in the industry, and thought it would be fun for us. I had originally told her I would go to pacify her, but the more I thought about it, the more controlled I felt.

I booked a business trip to Miami with the intention of avoiding the Las Vegas trip and spending time with Dayanara. Julie got angry and hurt. I tried not to care.

After Julie left for Las Vegas, I dropped the kids off at their grandmother's house. So I rushed to the airport, caught my plane, and was off to a new world of freedom and opportunity. Feeling like I was in my twenties again, I was intoxicated with the belief that I just might be able to have it all: love, happiness, and a satisfying relationship with someone who appreciated me and might even share in my burden of work.

On the flight to Miami, I thought about the life I wanted to create with Dayanara. I would be divorced and single. I would have time for my businesses, adequate time with my children, and time for romantic getaways around the country as I worked together with Dayanara in locations that were interesting, fun, and exciting.

In Miami, a chatty young woman asked me about places to stay and go. I tried to ignore her, but she was persistent. Finally, I picked up my car and headed for Dayanara. She met me at the door and hugged me tight. She wore a revealing blouse, tight jeans, and designer heels. When we left, I picked her up and carried her over a large rain puddle. She held me close, which let me know how much she wanted me.

The night was for partying, and we went to a local hot spot that was alive with energy. We danced with the pretty people. Dayanara was a minor celebrity, and we generated a lot of interest. I reveled in the attention.

At one point we sat in a lounge area where we cuddled close and shared drinks. I noticed a stoic couple without drinks sitting directly across from us. When I stared at them, they looked away as if I'd caught them doing something illicit.

At midnight, we went to a place for breakfast. We sat in a booth like two high school kids after a prom date. We laughed and mused about our lives. I noticed the stoic couple from the club at another table. I figured they'd gotten hungry, too.

I hadn't checked into the hotel yet, so Dayanara invited me to spend the night at her place. I hesitated, but then accepted with gratitude because I believed she was letting me know she wanted the life I had to offer. At her apartment, she danced seductively for me and then led me into her bedroom. We lay down on her bed.

My pager went off. Either a client was in serious trouble, or I was going to be. Julie's message was to the point: "Call me immediately."

I didn't want the trouble. I wanted my evening to go as I'd planned. I didn't respond. Next my cell went off. Julie wasn't going to give up.

I finally answered. Julie unleashed hell on me. I found out that I'd been tracked by a team of private investigators, my every moved recorded on video. Julie's words cut deep. My lies were exposed. So was the bankruptcy of my character and soul. I channeled my self-contempt into anger at the PIs and Julie. I felt like a child being scolded by his mother. I hated the feeling. I apologized. I had no more fight left in me.

Humiliated, embarrassed, and emotionally drained, I left Dayanara's house in the early morning hours and went to my hotel to set up the mobile office where I would work over the next several days. While I felt bruised from Julie's words, I also felt relieved that I didn't have to lie anymore to protect her. My plan for a gradual transition to a divorce was over.

Tension filled the air over the next few days. I focused on delivering with my new clients. Dayanara and I saw each other a few times over dinner, and I encouraged her to move on to someone who could offer her a legitimate relationship. She said all the right things to feed the mutual rescue mission we had embarked upon.

5

Julie: *"I was putting my life together."*

Jay: *"I was building a new life."*

Julie

When Jay returned home, we met at the Bistro Restaurant in Tulsa.

As I sat down across a table from him, I wondered what he would say about the bloody bandage on my neck. I'd recently had a lymph node removed, and the wound oozed onto the bandage no matter how often I changed it. I only had a few internal stitches holding the small incision together.

"You're looking good," Jay said.

I was so shocked at his words that I dropped the file containing photos of him with Dayanara in Miami. "You think so?" I fumbled the file back together.

"Yes. You don't look sick at all."

"Thanks. You're looking tanned from your trip."

"I got outside some in between seminar sessions."

"Jay, I want to make sure we understand our situation." I set the file on the table. "Please look at these." I slid over a photo of him kissing Dayanara in a booth at the pancake restaurant and another of them with his hands all over her in the bar.

He picked up the photos, looked at them, and then ripped them apart. "How dare you do this to me? You had no right! I'm disgusted with your actions."

Knowing so much depended on getting the moment right, I sat there calmly. "Jay, I still love you. I forgive you."

"You violated my privacy."

"I'm giving you the chance to make a choice. Dayanara or me. I'd like for you to end it with her and recommit to our separation agreement. Please agree to work with me on our marriage."

"I can't. I'll never go backward."

"I'll do whatever is necessary to make our marriage a happy one, to keep our family intact, and to spare us and our children the pain of divorce."

"I know you will, but it doesn't matter. I don't want to be married to you or anyone. I've got to have my freedom."

"All right." I took a deep breath. "I realize you feel this way at this moment, but I hope you'll change your mind."

"We can still parent the kids together. And I love you—just not the way you want anymore."

"I love you, too. I'll wait for you a little longer." I wished I could get him to wake up and get out of his fantasy world. I was sure his relationship with Dayanara would never make it, and he'd ultimately regret it.

"Let's order," he said. "And get on with our lives."

Jay

Julie looked skinny and pale. She had some kind of bandage on her neck. Though one side of the bandage had pulled away from her skin, I couldn't see an incision. I remained confused and skeptical. She was as beautiful as ever, just thinner, which I attributed to stress.

I didn't want to fix our marriage. I was furious about the PIs. I'd be watching my back for a long time. I hated the feeling of being tracked like an animal. Julie deserved the truth, but getting it this way only pushed me further from her. Her tactics reminded me of the control and manipulation I'd known during our marriage—the very things I was running from. I wanted no part of that lifestyle anymore and told her so.

I didn't want to talk about anything with her except moving forward with the divorce. I just wanted to get on with my new life. I hoped I'd made it clear enough for her to accept.

6

Julie: *"I bought my own Valentine's Day gift."*

Jay: *"I escaped to the Caribbean."*

Julie

I received an NHL stage 1 diagnosis. I feared that Jay and Dayanara would parent my children if I didn't recover quickly, and I couldn't stand that thought. So, because my kids desperately needed me to be well, I chose the most aggressive treatment possible even though the doctors recommended slower treatments. Four to five months of combo therapy would leave me sick, weak, and in bed for periods of time.

On February 10, I flew to MD Anderson Cancer Center in Houston, Texas, for my first appointment. Afterward, I flew back home and took my daughters to the funeral of Jayde's nine-year-old friend who had just died of cancer. The girls were so upset, I knew I couldn't tell them about my illness. They would just believe the worst. With their father gone, they were already crying themselves to sleep at night. I wouldn't add more to their burden.

I wanted Jay to be in our children's lives as much as possible, but he was gone a lot. I also needed his help when I knew I would be down with medical treatments. I emailed him to work out a schedule.

Sent: *Mon, 12 Feb*
Subject: *Travel schedule*

Jay,

I am still unclear as to why you will be gone next week. I have a strange feeling it is not all business. Are you going to the races that are in Florida next week? If you are, fine, but admit it. If not, I'd like to understand, since I will be doing round two of my chemo/radiation that week.

I will be scheduling my appointments for the rest of February and March. I have been asking for your schedule for several weeks but have received nothing more than the response that you will be gone all next week.

The week of March 4–10, my parents will be gone on the cruise that Dad bought Mother for Christmas. I am requesting you not leave town that week. I need someone in town with me. I may have my treatment in Houston that week, so I may need you to keep the kids and take them to school.

Jay, I am not trying to be pushy. I am in an incredibly difficult situation and am doing my best. I need your cooperation. I have already lost my health and my husband, so please don't make it any harder by getting nasty. I just need to know what to expect.

Julie

Jay
Sent: *Mon, 12 Feb*

Subject: *Re: Travel schedule*

Julie,

I am outraged at your continual insistence to know my every move, despite our separation terms and my repeated requests for you to stop violating my privacy. Unbelievable! It makes me want to push you away further and tell you even less about my whereabouts. Frankly, it provokes me to want to pursue divorce.

As for my travel, I am no longer accountable to you for every detail of what I do or where I go. However, because this involves our children, I will send you my itinerary. I will be available by phone for most of my trips and by email for all, and I will be calling regularly to check on you and the kids. I don't care whether or not you believe this.

I'm tired of the constant harassment and intrusions. I request that you do not check up on me, contact my clients, or monitor my business activities (which, by the way, enable me to support you), as this will undermine me and my credibility. If you persist in these intrusive activities, you will leave me no recourse but to file for divorce and pursue a restraining order to inhibit your violations.

As for your cancer treatments, I have been in an information blackout until very recently. You have not allowed me access to anything and have rejected my efforts and offers to support you there. You can't have it both ways, Julie. Either you're a big girl who's going to do it alone and you don't get to be a victim, or you let me know exactly what's happening and accept my support when I'm able to offer it to you. I am doing my best to support this family and you.

Jay

Julie

I needed to protect my investment in our company no matter my relationship with Jay, so I had my Tulsa PI install a GPS device on Jay's laptop.

Around Valentine's Day, Jay left town. He explained that he was going to work in the Caribbean Islands.

I needed that fact confirmed because I didn't want company funds paying for a cruise with Dayanara. My PI informed me that Jay's laptop was actually in his apartment. In order to verify that fact, I came up with a plan to discover the laptop's location.

I'd seen a spare key in the coin area of our Escalade, the car Jay used. I drove over to the airport parking lot and found the car.

Quickly, I called OnStar. "This is Mrs. Ferraro," I said. "I've locked myself out. Will you please unlock the car doors?" Of course, they did. I grabbed the key, and then relocked the Escalade.

I hoped the key fit Jay's apartment door. I drove over there. The key unlocked his front door, but I was afraid to go into his apartment without authorization. So I relocked the door and went to the apartment complex office.

"I'm Mrs. Ferraro," I said to the manager. "Jay is on a business trip. He forgot his passport and needs me to pick it up for him."

"Men!" she said. "They'd forget their heads if they weren't tied on."

"Please don't mention it to him. He'll just get embarrassed."

"I wouldn't dream of it." She held out the key. "They're too sensitive for their own good."

"So true," I agreed.

I hurried to Jay's apartment, let myself in, and found his laptop in a closet on the floor under a towel. He had to be on a cruise with Dayanara. I felt angry and devastated.

To make sure I was within my legal rights, I called my attorney, actually my friend's husband, who advised me whenever I needed help. I learned that since the manager had given me a key and I was still Jay's wife, there was no danger being in his apartment.

I took time to look around. Jay's desk was a mess. He hadn't filed anything, so everything was on top. I found copies of his cruise documents. I also found a receipt for a four-thousand-dollar diamond tennis bracelet with a copy of a note telling Dayanara how much he loved her, how important she was to him, and how he looked forward to their future together. I made copies of all these papers on his copy machine and then took the key back to the manager. After leaving the apartment complex, I made a copy of Jay's key and then put the original back in his car.

When I got home, I discovered Jay had used our company account to buy the bracelet, which made it an owner bonus. We were fifty-fifty owners in the company, so I wanted a bonus, too. I went to the bank and withdrew an equal amount of cash. Then I let Jay know that I had accidentally found the receipt, and since I was co-owner, had given myself a bonus in the same amount.

Jay

I felt stalked by Julie. At every turn, she intruded. She was obsessed with knowing my every move, despite what she had already learned and my decision to move on from our marriage. Still, I was determined to pursue my new life, regardless of her efforts to control me.

When it came to Julie's physical condition, I couldn't help but wonder if she was playing games with me. No matter where I looked, I found no information to confirm her alleged cancer. When I asked to see documentation, she denied me access. Again, I felt dominated by her. Her manipulation was a familiar pattern that I attempted to push further away from in my frenzy to find myself.

Somehow Julie kept tabs on me, and I grew more cautious about what I did and where I went. I didn't want to file for divorce with Julie supposedly sick. I offered to move back home and help with the kids, but she said she didn't want me there if I couldn't comply with her criteria. I thought her cancer scare was probably another attempt to manipulate me, so I altogether abandoned the idea of moving back home.

As time went on, she still wouldn't let me see her medical records, I couldn't find any medical bills, and she looked better than ever. She had lost a lot of weight, which I attributed to the stress of our situation. Aside from that, she looked better than I had seen her look in years. Finally, I chose a wait-and-see attitude about her health.

During our separation, I changed little about my financial arrangement with my family, and they continued to live the same upscale lifestyle I had created for them. I felt I was quite generous, and I got on with my own life.

PART III

Love Suspended and Reclaimed

CHAPTER 7
SEPARATE WORLDS

I

Julie: *"I filed for divorce."*

Jay: *"I felt a sense of relief."*

Julie

It was February 20. Though Jay and my children didn't know it, with each new treatment, the chemo had made me sicker. Sometimes I hadn't known if I'd be able to endure another round, the side effects had gotten so bad. But then I would think of my little ones, and I'd rededicate myself to following through with the treatment.

Jay told me he was on a business retreat off the coast of Florida, but I believed he was on another cruise with Dayanara. By that point, I desperately wanted him to be honest with me. I called him.

"Jay, I was wondering how your meetings were going."

"Fine," he said.

"The kids miss you."

"I miss them, too." His words were short and clipped.

"What's that I hear?"

"Nothing."

"It sounds like music."

"Oh...the radio. I forgot."

"Is that someone calling you?"

"No...I mean, it's the TV."

"Radio or TV?" I pushed him, hoping that he'd be truthful since I heard Dayanara in the background. I assumed she was dancing to the music.

"Both!" he said.

"You're on a cruise, aren't you?"

"No. I told you I'm working."

"Is Dayanara with you?"

"No. I'm with clients."

"Which ones?"

"I told you not to hound me," Jay said. "You're invading my privacy."

"It's my company, too. I want to know what's going on with it."

"I told you enough. That's all I'm giving you." He abruptly disconnected.

"I love you, too," I whispered.

With a hand to my heart, I took deep breaths and tried to still my emotional pain. While I was enduring radiation treatments, he was gallivanting about with Dayanara. He was on a cruise with her and didn't even have the decency to admit it.

I refused to let my children be exposed to this kind of a man any longer. I'd finally had enough of being rejected. I decided to move on. I picked up the phone and called my friend's husband, the attorney. When he answered, my hand shook and tears filled my eyes.

"I'm ready to retain you as my attorney and file for divorce."

Jay

When we got back from our cruise, I left Dayanara in Miami and returned to my apartment in Tulsa. Walking up to my front porch, I saw a legal-size envelope lying on the mat. I hesitated. Something felt different. It was almost as if I'd lost something or I'd somehow been disconnected from my battery.

Picking up the envelope, I noticed the unusual hand delivery. I unlocked my front door, stepped inside, and locked the door behind me. I set down my luggage.

With mounting tension, I opened the envelope and pulled out several sheets of paper. After reading a few words, I felt as though I'd taken a blow to the chest. Julie had finally done it. *Divorce papers.* She had more guts than I did to make the final cut. Now I knew what I'd felt. I had lost her—this time for good.

As I thought about our pending divorce, I realized that Julie had found her own strength, and with it, a resolve I had never before sensed in her. For my part, I felt ambivalent about the proceedings, although I knew I would do nothing to stop the forward motion of our divorce. I experienced an overwhelming sense of loss and failure as a husband, father, and man. I was staring at a second failed marriage because of my inadequacies in love.

At the same time, I felt liberated from my cramped marital cage. Prepared to pay a high price for the promise of the unknown, I embraced my newfound freedom with full force.

Julie

I knew Jay had his divorce papers. It was time to communicate with him, but I couldn't bring myself to confront him directly—not just yet. However, there was much we needed to settle, and I didn't want to wait too long to discuss things now that I was set on a divorce course. I made a firm decision to negotiate our divorce without showing Jay any emotion. I was not going to let him know the pain he was causing me. With all this in mind, I wrote him a no-nonsense email to try to iron out details and avoid a nasty court battle.

Jay

After I read Julie's email, I paced the floor of my apartment. I felt a sense of relief and hope, mixed with anger and despair. As these strong, conflicting emotions began to race through me, I suddenly realized I must block them out—I couldn't afford to let myself feel so deeply. I needed to be as practical as Julie was in settling our affairs and getting on with our lives.

2

Julie: *"I hoped for the best."*

Jay: *"My daughters rejected my new life."*

Julie

On March 1, Jay brought our daughters home from a visit with him. I opened the door with a smile. I always looked my best for him, no matter how I felt. The last thing I wanted was his sympathy.

Jayde rushed inside and flung a dark glance back at her father. "I'm never going back to *his* place."

Zoe burst into tears and ran up the stairs after her sister.

"What's going on?" I asked.

Jay trudged inside and threw himself down on the sofa.

"Jay?" I sat down across from him. My heart was racing in fear for my children.

He looked up, ran his hands through his hair, and then straightened his back. "Dayanara left a pair of shoes at my place."

"Red spikes under his bed!" Jayde shouted from the staircase.

"Go to your room," Jay shouted back.

"You tell me what is going on right this minute," I said.

"I did." Jay shook his head. "They overreacted."

"We're never going back. It's disgusting!" Jayde shouted, then ran up the stairs and slammed the door to her room.

"Is that all?" I asked.

"Yes." Jay sighed. "I wish Jayde wasn't reacting so badly to my moving out of the house. She won't even talk to me on the phone."

"All the children are upset. They won't sleep in their own beds anymore. They sleep with me."

"They need time to adjust."

"I know. We all do." Putting all my love into my words, I spoke gently. I hoped he would hear, feel, and see me for myself, not the creature he had created in his mind. Maybe we were getting a divorce, but nothing stopped my love.

"I've got to go." Jay stood up abruptly, crossed to the front door, and jerked it open.

I watched him hurry down the sidewalk and vanish into his car. A deep sadness filled my heart as I stood there alone. I watched the taillights of his vehicle race down the street and then disappear from sight.

He was gone. I closed my front door.

Jay

I drove home fast. Too fast. But I wanted to get away from their disappointed faces. I refused to feel guilty when I was doing what I needed to save myself. In time, we would all adjust and reconnect in better ways.

I was sick and tired of living for everyone else and denying what I needed for myself. I had a right to be happy and to enjoy life. Nobody was going to stop me. I saw no reason why I couldn't have it all: business success, a two-city lifestyle, fulfilling love, and a strong relationship with my children. I refused to allow Julie to think she could dictate my life and how I lived it.

Julie

No matter how my heart broke every time I thought of Jay, I had to be practical and strong. My children needed their father in their lives as much as possible. Jay was flitting here and there. I was determined for him to find ways to schedule his children into his life, and I really needed his help with them when I had treatments. I was deeply frustrated with his unwillingness to commit to even a basic visitation schedule since that left me with all the responsibility. Clearly, all he cared about was spending time with Dayanara. He was neglecting his children, and they knew it. Their reaction to him was proof positive.

Most times, I could only connect to him through emails and text messages, so once more I wrote him.

Sent: *Tue, 6 Mar*

Jay,

   Any travel dates you have and could provide me would be great. You should have both girls' practice schedules for T-ball and Zoe's itinerary for her Cayman trip. Also, you discussed going to the consulting event in May during Zoe's birthday. Remember? Are you still planning on being out of town? That week is the dance recital and Zoe's birthday party. Needing to know what to expect. Trying to work with you.
   Thanks,
   Julie

Jay

Again, I felt controlled and dominated by Julie's continued efforts to intrude into my life. Despite the fact that I had moved away from her and out of our old relationship, she seemed to be in denial about it as she continued to expect me to serve her in ways I had before. I wanted no part of it anymore.

Sent: *Tue, 6 Mar*

Julie,

   Here's my best estimate of the schedule:
   March 9: I have Chandler on Friday night. I can keep him most of the day until Saturday at three. I will be unavailable that evening because of a networking meeting in OKC. I want you to know that Dayanara will be in town doing business in OKC and working with me on a seminar program. She will be staying at a hotel, not my place.

March 14: I am going to Miami to meet with a new potential client.

March 21: I will be working in Miami Wednesday to Friday morning and home Friday night. I am available all weekend to assist in any way with the children.

April 5–6: I will be in Tampa working. I am thinking about staying in Florida that weekend.

April 18–19: I am speaking in St. Louis.

April 26–27: I am scheduled to do an executive retreat in New York.

May 14–18: I am attending the consulting event in San Francisco.

May 19: I can be home for Zoe's b-day. I have May 11–13 down for the girls' dance recital. Where is it going to be?

These dates are subject to change, and I will do my best to give you advance notice. Please meet me there.

Thanks,

Jay

3

Julie: *"We talked about our divorce."*

Jay: *"We agreed to use one attorney."*

Julie

I was determined to negotiate our divorce without getting nasty or going to court. I hoped Jay would come around and wanted to preserve that possibility. He remained the love of my life despite what he was doing to me. And since he was also my best friend, the loss of our relationship had impacted me to the very core of my being.

Nevertheless, I was beginning to understand that Jay had changed. He was no longer the man I had married. While I still loved him deeply, I did not like who he had become. I didn't like who I had become either while trying to save a marriage he was no longer committed to.

Jay

Sent: *Tue, 6 Mar*

Julie,

I need to understand what your expectations are so that I can deter-mine if we have a reasonable basis for an agreement. I am considering the numbers we discussed, but only because I want to support you with a stress-free fight against cancer and make the transition easy for you.

The context of the agreement we discussed is predicated on your staying in Tulsa and living in the current house. I see no justification for the amount you mentioned if you are to move to a lesser lifestyle. If we do not have conceptual agreement on this, I will have to take a serious look at rolling the dice in court, because I want to be generous but not taken advantage of.

I remain committed to the spirit of collaboration and generosity. I am still willing to be overly generous, but please don't take advantage of me, or my generosity will dry up. Let's talk face-to-face again soon and see where we are with realistic numbers on the budget in accordance with the lifestyle you anticipate.

Jay

Julie

Hoping Jay would be jealous, I pretended to have a "date" every now and then. It did seem to bother him. However, I desperately tried to preserve any possibility that when the smoke cleared and Jay's brain cells returned, I would not have damaged things any more than necessary by my reactions to his life-style. I sent him another email.

Sent: *Wed, 7 Mar*
Subject: *Jay, I don't want to fight you*

Jay,

You sound frustrated. I understand, and I am sorry. I hope you can remember that I love you and wanted much more than this. I wanted a marriage and our relationship to continue. You, however, prefer to provide and co-parent from a distance, an approach which I am learning to accept. For you, the downside of your choice is that you are left feeling like all we want is money. Not true. We are coping the best we can with your truths and your reality, both of which have dramatically changed our own.

You keep talking about going to court. Where is this coming from? Do you want to destroy every last possibility of a civil relationship for us? Because of our children, we will have to deal with each other for many years to come. You will have to talk to me and have a co-parenting relationship with me long after Dayanara or any other new relationship is gone.

I want to work with you and agree with you. Jay, I don't want to take advantage of you. I love you despite my hurt. I feel beaten up and bullied and threatened by you. You make plenty of money and that won't stop. I see you as being successful today and always.

I find it interesting that I go out on a date and try to move on, and that is when your attitude changes. You have been more threatening and aggressive since that time. So, in order to keep things civil between us, I am not going to go out. I will put my life on hold. It appears that you want me to have to deal with you moving on, but you don't like it that I might. It feels unfair, but then, so does this whole thing. I am not interested in a long-term relationship. I just want some companionship because I am very lonely.

I am choosing to focus on my health and my children. I will meet with you to talk about things anytime, as long as it is in the spirit of love and in keeping with what is best for the kids and me. You have chosen what is best for you, and it has come at a great cost to us. I am starting to feel like you don't care about what is best for any of us but you, and it is terribly upsetting to me.

Jay, I just want my kids to not suffer anymore. That's it. All I care about. Seriously. Please understand that. I am pleading with you to not change everything about their life. They are sad and broken little creatures, and I am doing my damnedest to take care of them when I sometimes barely have enough energy to get out of bed. I am trying to work with you and let you have Chandler often, because he needs you. I went to dinner with you, even though it was painful for me, so that I could try to bridge the gap between you and Jayde. I am not sure what you are wanting from me. I have listed the house (against the attorney's advice; he said not to change our lifestyle). I am trying to be the best I can in a situation that has broken my heart and made me angry.

I do appreciate the fact that you are a good provider. I am grateful for your hard work and generosity. I am sad you had to leave the kids and me, and I feel you are possibly being influenced to fight me and be stingy. If that is your choice, go ahead. I am not looking for a battle to fight.

I hope that you are happy and that what you end up with makes all the suffering we've endured worthwhile. I know the situation can't ever be right for the kids. But we can try to make things better for them. I really don't want to hate you. I have shared most of my life with you.

So, for what it's worth to you, I still care for you deeply and am trying my best in a situation I have never faced before and never wanted to be in.

Julie

Jay

I didn't answer her email—I couldn't. How could she still love me? Some days I couldn't even love myself. Did she see something in me I had never been able to see, despite my education, my success, my generosity? Sometimes I wondered if I even knew what love was. Sex? Smarts? Fantasy? The more I searched for answers, the more they seemed to evade me. Not only that, but the more I searched for myself, the further I seemed to recede.

I drove over to Julie's house. We needed some face-to-face time. We had too much to settle to try to do it all through phone calls and emails.

When she opened the door, warm light highlighted her features and etched lines of pain across her features. For a moment I was shocked, but then she smiled her pageant smile (the one with the bright eyes and gleaming white teeth), and she was the same lovely Julie as always.

"Jay, I wasn't expecting you." She stayed in the doorway. "Kids are asleep."

"Aren't you going to invite me in?"

"Why are you here?"

"You said in your email that we could talk anytime. I figured we could hammer out the divorce details better in person."

"You're right." She stepped back. "Your favorite chair's empty if you want it. I'll get a pad and pen."

I stepped inside and shut the door behind me.

Memories, good and bad, assaulted my senses as I sat uneasily in my recliner. She'd changed nothing about our living room. I almost wished she had.

When Julie returned, she brought a tray with an opened bottle of my favorite wine and two crystal glasses. She poured wine, handed me a glass, and took one for herself.

She lifted a glass in a salute to me and smiled. "Here's to a perfect divorce."

I saluted her and then took a sip.

"Jay, as I've said, I don't want us to annihilate each other in court. We'll be parenting our children the rest of our lives. I want to make this as easy as possible on them as well as us."

"I'll drink to that." And I did.

"If we each use an attorney, they'll get at each other's throats."

"And soon we'll be doing the same thing," I said.

"Exactly. We could lose all our money over this, and it wouldn't be fair to our kids."

"No, it wouldn't. But I want it to be fair to us, too."

"It can be." She sipped her wine. "One attorney can handle us both if we agree to deal fairly with each other."

"That sounds good."

"I'm agreeable to most anything you suggest except one vitally important issue."

"What's that?" Holding my glass with both hands, I leaned forward on alert.

"If I die—"

"Julie, don't even say such a thing."

"Stop!" Julie wiped tears from her eyes. "If I die, my mother becomes physical custodian of our children. I insist my babies be with their grandmother. I refuse to accept the idea that my children could be raised by that . . . that slut."

I dropped my empty glass in shock, picked it up, and dumped it on the tray. "Dayanara is a smart, classy businesswoman."

Julie leaped up. "If you don't agree to my condition, my one and only condition, I'll make sure you walk away from this divorce with nothing. Imagine us in front of a judge when she hears about a wife fighting cancer and raising three young children on her own while her husband traipses across the country with a girl half his age!"

I wanted to dispute her words—wanted to, but couldn't. Furious at myself as much as at her, I turned, walked out, and slammed the door behind me.

> # 4
> "Julie: *"I suffered cancer treatments in silence."*
>
> "Jay: *"I built my new life."*

Julie

I had another radiation and oral chemo round. This one made me much sicker. I spent days in bed and wore sunglasses so that light wouldn't hurt my eyes. I sweated toxins and bleached out my bed sheets. I vomited until nothing but dry heaves wracked my stomach and made my throat raw.

Fortunately, my parents took my children on a two-week-long trip to help out. Jay was out of town on business or perhaps with Dayanara somewhere—I wasn't sure. My children were still my responsibility, and I wanted it that way. But if ever I needed a husband's help, now was the time.

I was so sick from the treatments that I decided to get a second opinion at Baylor Hospital to make sure I was following the correct course of treatment. Afterward I was so sick that I had to stay in bed for a week. I went back to MDA because my second opinion agreed with the first. I had to keep going to heal, no matter how much I suffered from the cure.

I didn't want any pity. I found a hairdresser who could weave hair into mine to cover my thinning spots and spare me the embarrassment of a wig. He was out of town and expensive, but it was worth it to me because it meant that no one could see a physical sign of how horrible my life had become. Even my sunken face looked fuller because I was taking so much prednisone.

Jay

On March 12, I made sure I was home for Jayde's birthday. When I got there, I saw that Julie's mother had decorated the house in bright kid colors and set out a beautiful birthday cake and presents. I piled on more presents and then went to give my birthday girl a big bear hug.

"I'm glad you could make it," Julie said as I embraced Jayde.

I sat down next to our daughter and turned to gaze at Julie. She looked great. I didn't know how she could be sick from cancer. I knew those treatments made people lose their hair and look rough. Thinking that she was trying to manipulate me and make me appear the bad guy, I grew suspicious all over again.

"How are you feeling?" I asked.

"How do you think?

"I don't know."

"I could use more help with the kids," she said as she pushed a strand of long blond hair back from her face in a way that made her seem tired.

"I thought your mom and dad helped you."

"Kids need their father."

"I'm doing what I can. I'm traveling the country to support you and our kids in a way you are accustomed to. Nothing I do is ever good enough for you."

Julie turned away.

"Let me see your records." I reached out to her and then let my hand fall to my side in frustration.

She looked back, her blue eyes filled with scorn. "I don't want your pity or your charity."

"I can help. Maybe not as much as you want, but I'll do what I can."

"Jay, I want only one thing from you, and that's the one thing you won't give me."

"It's the one thing I can't give, not now." I picked up a plate with a piece of birthday cake. "Let's put this on hold and celebrate Jayde's birthday."

Julie nodded in agreement. "I'm glad you're here for Jayde's sake."

She tossed me a brightly colored party hat. Feeling slightly foolish but mostly sentimental, I put it on. I was glad I was there, too.

CHAPTER 8
LOVE CHALLENGES INFIDELITY

I

Julie: *"I needed to heal my emotions."*

Jay: *"I was walking a tightrope."*

Julie

In early April, my relationship with Jay went from volatile and toxic one day to friendly and respectful the next. Sometimes I'd go days without hearing from him, which made me feel sick to my stomach. Then, on the days he'd come over, I'd feel as though I were walking on eggs and trying not to break any of them. When he'd take a bathroom break, I'd pace the floor and wonder whether he was calling or texting Dayanara and lying to her. I longed for but hated the warm hug and soft kiss to my forehead he'd give me each time he left—though it brought me a moment's comfort, it was so much less than what we both deserved. Needless to say, Jay left me crying each time he came to see our children or discuss our divorce.

I kept my best face on for my dear little ones. I never told them what was going on with me. I knew they would be afraid of losing me too, especially after losing their father to another woman and their young friend to cancer.

I still refused to let Jay see my medical records. If I couldn't have his love, I didn't want his pity, nor did I want him to have the privilege of my personal information. He was shutting me out of his life, so he deserved the same in return. I felt controlled by him. He was choosing my present and my future, and our children's present and future as well. I couldn't stand the idea that he controlled me in that way, and a part of me secretly hoped he'd lost sleep worrying about me. I doubted whether he had, though; by now, I felt sure ice water ran through his veins, not blood. Still, I felt in control of one thing: the information he could receive about me. I made sure my doctors knew I was divorcing and that no one had permission to give him anything. I even had an alias put on my records; I went by "Suzanne." I hoped Jay felt as helpless as I did.

My Tulsa doctor thought I was crazy to take such aggressive cancer treatments, but he didn't understand that I would brave and endure anything for my children. I refused to let my cancer grow. I had a bone marrow aspiration to make sure that I didn't have a problem with my marrow. I knew that if the cancer spread there, I'd be in serious trouble. I wanted to do the most aggressive treatment I could because Jay and his trashy girlfriend were not acceptable parents for my children.

When I felt well enough, I recorded videotapes that explained about the divorce and about me. I made the videos for my kids to have, just in case I didn't beat the cancer. Above all, I wanted them to know I loved them and had done everything I could to remain by their side.

Jay

I wished Julie wouldn't lie to me and try to manipulate me. Cancer is a terrible thing for people to endure. She didn't need to use it as a scare tactic. Her ruse wasn't working anyway; she looked better than ever after her weight loss. Independence was becoming to her, too. I began to think I was doing her a favor. Tough love.

Dayanara had crawled into my life more than I'd anticipated she would when she first approached me in the VIP club. I began to see her in a new, not always favorable light as my initial illusions of her began to fade. Nonetheless, I needed our relationship to succeed. Failure was not an option because I had too much at stake. As a result, I fell in love with love, and I used it as an antidote for the emptiness I'd allowed my life to become. I believed that if our affair succeeded by becoming a real relationship, so would I, and the loneliness and the longing I'd felt in my marriage would be satisfied by "true love."

I responded to the problems arising from our affair by strengthening my resolve to make the relationship work. I also visualized Dayanara with characteristics I wanted her to have but she really didn't possess. In my determination to legitimize my illusions, I gave more to the affair than I'd ever given to Julie. I was left with a haunting question that kept me up at night asking, "What might have happened had I given as much of myself to my marriage as I was giving to my affair partner?"

During that vulnerable time in my marriage to Julie, I descended deeper into my infatuation. I confused my emotions for Dayanara with real love—something I was willing to die chasing.

On April 4, I wrote a letter to Dayanara to explain my feelings.

> *Dayanara,*
>
> *This divorce is hard in a lot of ways for me. I was simply blowing off steam by sharing my frustrations about it, and you went on the attack. Your voice was raised and had an irritated tone that increased in volume and intensity the more we talked. You challenged me by saying that I was out of touch with reality and needed to get a grip and stop blowing things out of proportion.*
>
> *When you approach me this way, it makes me feel like a child who is being scolded for bad behavior. When I brought it to your attention that I felt misunderstood and that I believed you were being insensitive during a very difficult time in my life, you became defensive. You denied doing anything wrong and came back with a "you can perceive things however you wish" retort. When you said that, I felt invalidated and discounted. It was as though you thought I only imagined your insensitivity, and therefore you weren't going to take any responsibility for contributing to the situation.*
>
> *Actually, I was more hurt by your reaction to the impact your behavior had on me (invalidating/discounting me) than I was about the behavior itself (lecturing/scolding me). I can deal with your humanity, bitchiness, bad days, and irritation with me. However, I find it intolerable to be told that I am alone in my experience—that it's my problem to perceive things as I may and you assume no responsibility in contributing to that perception, or that what I feel is unimportant—when you are clearly a part of it. Where did the warm, sensitive, caring woman I met go?*
>
> *I do not want to be in a relationship where it feels like I am walking on eggshells and I cannot say what I feel or mention how your actions affect me without having it interpreted as demeaning, selfish, condescending, better-than-thou, or critical; or where you think I'm blaming you for something or making you out to be in the wrong, when all I'm doing is describing how your behavior is affecting me in a particular*

moment. Perhaps we should consider going to counseling together to sort through these issues before they become a serious problem.
 With love,
 Jay

2

Julie: *"I refused to let our children meet her."*

Jay: *"I deserved a working vacation."*

Julie

In late April, Jay came over, sporting a fresh tan and a lazy smile. As he sauntered into my living room, I couldn't help but notice that he was wearing a bright island shirt, orange shorts, and leather sandals. In Tulsa, he couldn't have looked more out of place.

Unable to stop myself, I asked, "Where are you going?"

Looking pleased with himself, he smiled and said, "Not going. I've been."

"Where's that?" I had a sinking feeling in my stomach.

"Hawaii." He grinned. "Beautiful place."

I felt my heart speed up. "Did you . . . take Dayanara with you?"

He nodded. "On business. We have a client that has offices there, and we did a leadership retreat."

With my hands on my hips, I took a deep breath and I tried to control my anger. "You know I always wanted us to go there together."

"Business trip." No longer smiling, he stepped back.

"It's always business with you!" I replied as tears of anger and hurt filled my eyes.

"Without it, you'd be living in a trailer park."

"I would not! I'm talented. I can work and I will!"

"I didn't come to fight about my travel schedule."

"What do you want?"

"The kids. Dayanara is at my place. I want them to meet her."

"You what?" Feeling as if he'd hit me, I staggered backward. First he'd taken her to Hawaii, and now he wanted to take my children to meet her. "You'll have to take them over my dead body before they spend one moment in the company of that...that hussy!"

"She's a smart, professional business woman."

"Why doesn't she act like one?"

"She does."

"Does she take dictation in your bed?"

"I'm not having this discussion," Jay said. "I just came to pick up my kids."

"Go!" I pointed at the front door. "You brought nothing in. You're taking nothing out."

"Julie, be reasonable. I have a right to see my children, and you are not going to dictate my relationship with them any longer. I have to consider everyone's feelings in this predicament."

"Her feelings!" I felt like I might explode. My doctors had told me to stay calm and relaxed for my health. If they could see me now, they'd probably put me in the cardiac ward.

"Yes! Other people besides you have feelings too," he said.

"Get out!" I ran over to the door and flung it open. "If you don't leave my house this minute, I'll toss you out."

"You and who else?"

"Trust me. The way I'm feeling right now, I could throw you out with one hand."

Jay strutted to the door. As he walked out, he said, "You'd better check your blood pressure."

I slammed the door and hoped I'd hit him with it.

3

Julie: *"Jay surprised me."*
Jay: *"Apologies don't come easy."*

Jay

After my confrontation with Julie, I drove around for a while. I was determined to get my feelings under control before I went back to Dayanara. I felt trapped between two volatile women. It felt as though I were being pulled apart.

I missed seeing my children that weekend. Dayanara flew home after we made plans for me to visit her soon. Work was going great for me, so I tore into it with a vengeance. It was one of the few places I felt successful, so it got most of my time.

I felt misunderstood and rejected by everyone. I acknowledged that having an affair was obviously wrong, but I felt hurt that not one person in the family that I had been a part of for over ten years had even picked up a phone to ask me what the hell I was thinking. I wanted to communicate with them, to explain what was happening and why my marriage to Julie was failing. After some thought, I decided to set the record straight so that Julie's family and our friends would understand the truth of my situation. I wrote a letter.

Sent: *Wed, 2 May*
Subject: *Letter to our families sent by email attachment*

I respectfully request your time and attention in reading the attached.
     With love,
     Jay

May 1

Dear Friends & Family,
     I can only imagine the level of disappointment, confusion, and anger that you may feel toward me as the tragedy unfolding within our family comes to light.
     My intentions in this writing are several:
     First, I feel the need to be accountable to you who have been my family for ten years and whom I have grown to love and call my own. Despite your feelings about me or your decisions in response to my choices, we will remain connected through the lives of Jayde, Zoe, and Chandler.
     Second, I do not intend to justify, rationalize, or assign blame to anyone for the choices I have made. Rather, I intend to accept responsibility for my mistakes and also to place my decisions in a context that will assist you in understanding them.
     My contributions are as follows:
     There is no adequate justification for a betrayal of trust, and that is what I am guilty of. I have failed Julie as a husband in many ways that have been extremely painful to her. She most definitely deserved more from me. I will carry regret for the choices I made and the things I did (things I would do differently now if I had the opportunity to do them

over). Many of those decisions were simply wrong, and Julie certainly had the right to be treated differently. For my failures, I apologize from the bottom of my heart.

Our situation today exists within a complicated context where things are not simple black and white. I failed at managing my own emotional needs and did not take good care of myself in our relationship, which led directly to a combination of dangerously toxic thoughts and feelings that contributed to some of the decisions I made.

I allowed hurt, anger, and resentment to fester and grow. I tolerated intolerable conditions, attitudes, and patterns of behavior toward me because I was either too afraid to confront them and was in denial that they were there at all, or I foolishly hoped that with time things would get better and change. (They did not.) In short, I failed to do what I know works: I did not ask for what I needed. Instead, I withdrew from those who care about me and threw myself into my work, one of the few areas that remained successful for me.

This was a fatal mistake with damaging implications for my marriage to Julie. Over time, the events that took place between us eroded our bond, undermined my desire to engage in improving that bond, and damaged my respect and affection for Julie—all of which are needed to sustain motivation for reconciliation and to work on longstanding problems in our relationship.

I made the terrible mistake of linking material possessions and an upscale lifestyle with happiness and contentment. I mistakenly thought that the more pleased people were with the things we had and could do, the better things would be for us and the more my standing would be enhanced. (Although I knew better, I didn't see the forest for the trees.)

The opposite proved to be true: the larger our lifestyle became, the more imprisoned and trapped I felt. The result was that I felt a strong sense of helplessness at being unable to reverse course. (If I dismantled what we'd created, we would disappoint people.) I felt betrayed, abandoned, rejected, unwelcome, and "objectified" (viewed only as a "success object"; that is, a means to gaining success by providing children and a great lifestyle). Meanwhile, I worked around-the-clock to give everyone the life they wanted and enjoyed at my expense.

Many of you now know that I became involved in a relationship with another person prior to moving out of the home I shared with Julie and our children. Understandably, there is a tendency to associate such *a provocative event with "the reason" why a divorce happens. Nothing could be further from the truth.*

Suffice it to say that longstanding patterns of behavior between Julie and me, her chronic negative attitudes toward me, and specific actions on her part left me feeling a range of dangerously toxic emotions for years. I felt emasculated, alone, isolated, profoundly unappreciated, and taken for granted for my many contributions to my family's life. I experienced a complete lack of support and inability to get my needs met on many levels.

This experience—coupled with a variety of resentments that stemmed from feeling trapped in a role and life I did not fully choose, not being able to get my needs met, having affection and approval contingent upon compliance to certain expectations, and having an exclusive focus on a child-centered marriage—turned out to be a fatal combination that left me disillusioned, disengaged, contemptuous of married life, resentful, trapped, and dangerously vulnerable.

It is true that I did not participate for any length of time in joint counseling, largely because, at that point, I did not believe it would change our core differences. And very sadly to me, something inside me had died (my views toward marriage in general and toward Julie specifically) as this drama unfolded over the years.

I met Dayanara a year ago in a business context related to my work in Miami. That contact began as (and was in many ways primarily) a business one with mutual professional interests. She has been a caring friend to me during a very difficult time in my life.

Simultaneously, the issues between Julie and me began to deteriorate. We spoke freely and acknowledged to each other our dissatisfaction and doubts as to whether we would even choose to marry one another if given the chance to do so again. I had struggled for several years about questioning our compatibility, because significant personality conflicts had evolved.

I entered into our separation with the intention of decreasing the conflict and stress between us that was negatively impacting our children and discovering truths about myself that were impossible to assess while living with Julie. I quickly realized that what I feared was true: marriage, as we had done it, was unfulfilling and did not work for me, was constraining and suffocating, and was making me unhappy to the point of depression. In all likelihood, I could never be the person Julie needed me to be.

Regrettably, after our separation, my relationship with Dayanara changed, and it became more than a business association. I am disappointed in myself for that choice, because it not only caused pain for Julie, it also hurt many other people and was wrong and selfish of me. I will live with regret for my actions in the years to come. However, where Julie and I are today and why we got to this point has little to do with our current situation. The pathway to it was years in the making and a symptom of longstanding problems, not the cause of the problem itself.

I again apologize to you for failing to meet your expectations and for hurting the person you are rightly protective of and dearly love. Julie is the most important person for us to love, protect, and rally around, for she needs the strength of this family to fight the battle of a lifetime. I am committed to doing that alongside you, despite the realities that exist and some of the limitations our predicament presents. I ask that you join me in this effort.

Respectfully and with love,
Jay

Julie

On May 2, Jay caught me by surprise with his highly personal letter. I was outraged at the lies and justification he offered about his illicit affair. I decided not to get into a conversation that had the potential to go nuclear, should I reveal that Jay had met Dayanara at a gentleman's club and not in a corporate meeting. Who did he think he was, asking my parents and my brother to rally around me during this time? They had been fully supportive. He, on the other hand, was quite another story.

I quickly sent an email to counter his, and I later found out that my family had deleted his letter and ignored him altogether.

On another note, Jay's mother had not contacted me a single time to check on me or her grandchildren, and I hoped that she would not start now.

Sent: *Wed, 2 May*
Subject: *Re: Letter to family*

Hello,

While I will respect Jay's version of what happened and his right to speak to each of you, I feel a few things need to be said since my perspective is quite different. I am sure that the truth lies somewhere in between.

I will not discuss the painful things Jay did from the beginning of this marriage (as it is not my desire to air dirty laundry in a group email, nor is it my intention to shame or embarrass anyone), things that began six weeks after the marriage and were issues he had evidentially struggled with his entire life. Those events had a deteriorating effect on my feelings toward him from that point on.

Certainly, my reaction of criticism and withdrawal had a negative impact on the marriage. I completely lost respect for Jay as a husband and a father. However, even during the last six months of the marriage while I knew Jay was having an affair, I remained committed to our marriage. I made many suggestions to try to grow and repair what was broken. Often, I accepted my own failures and desperately expressed my wishes to work on things. Even though it may not have been felt by Jay, I never stopped loving him. Yet all of my offers made no difference to him.

Unfortunately, Jay was only willing to attend two marriage counseling sessions with me. I filed for divorce only after the affair was 100-percent indisputable and Jay had shown no willingness to keep the separation agreement we'd both signed. Until that point, I'd been open to rehabilitating our marriage. However, with his change in attitude and the unimaginable pain he was causing me, I knew divorce was the route I needed to pursue.

Perhaps Jay is finally being honest with himself, but he is no longer the man I married. I hope he finds much happiness with Dayanara, because the relationship with her and his unwillingness to discontinue the affair are the reasons I ultimately quit working on the marriage. I really felt I had no choice but to divorce or abandon my own dignity.

I was heartbroken about the loss of my husband and our family. But mostly, I felt concerned about my children, a concern I still have today. Their relationship with their father has been damaged beyond belief. I pray that I can find an opening for them so that this will not cause them lifelong problems. I am focused on my health and my kids. Fighting cancer alone as a single parent has been exhausting and emotional, and it is something I wouldn't wish on anyone. I am strong and I am doing okay.

The kids are another story. They still cry all the time. Jayde wants nothing to do with her father. She is so angry. I just found a note in her backpack that she wrote. It says, "Jayde is angry. Jayde is sad. My daddy doesn't love us anymore." Time will tell how this unfolds for the kids. Despite my encouragement and Jay's attempts to connect with Jayde, she feels abandoned. This is heartbreaking and produces a sense of failure in me each day. The kids long for a sense of family that comes with being an intact nuclear family. They beg me to find a "new husband" all of the time. I know they just want to fill the void . . . not to replace their father.

I do not feel the need to discuss any of this any further with any of you. I choose to focus on the positive, not on what I have lost. Otherwise, my health and ability to be a good mother will be affected. I will choose to see the good things about Jay. I obviously saw them at one time, or I would not have married him. Despite his poor choices, I do not believe that Jay is a bad person. Making him a villain will not get my family back.

I am surprised Jay has chosen to discuss private matters with each of you since he is so into his "privacy" these days. I feel that his need for privacy grew as his relationship with Dayanara deepened. Obviously, at home, the more I suspected he was involved with another woman, the less privacy he got; hence the source of more conflict.

Truly, I never knew he was so miserable. I wish him happiness with whomever he can find it. I am moving on with my life and am ready to close this ugly chapter. Certainly you all know that this is the very last thing I wanted for any of the five of us, especially for my kids. But I accept the reality of the situation and realize that I will be better off alone than in a marriage with a man who doesn't want to be married. The damage done is beyond repair, and we all deserve to be happy.

It is my wish that this communication be the end of our group discussion about the failure of my family. Obviously, Jay and I have very different perceptions and feelings about what has happened. Those will never change. The truth is that a family has broken and failed. Now the focus must be on helping the children cope with this reality. I respect Jay's right to communicate with you, but I want you to know that I will not respond to any further emails.

With love,
Julie

CHAPTER 9
ENDINGS AND BEGINNINGS

I

Julie: *"I planned my new life."*

Jay: *"I found trouble in paradise."*

Julie

On May 7, Jay came over to continue divorce negotiations. As crazy as it seemed, I was seeing a lot of him. Between the children and the divorce, he was at my house frequently when he was in town. He even seemed to be softening toward me. But I didn't return the favor. He'd lost me for good. No matter how much I still loved him, I was getting on with my life and considering my options.

"Julie," Jay said as he smiled, "I think we can make our divorce settlement work. What's it going to cost?"

"Five hundred if I have anything to say about it." I smiled, too. It felt good to be treating each other with respect and acting like the adults we were.

"I like the sound of that."

"Good."

Jay's phone rang. He picked it up, checked the caller ID, and then shrugged. "I've got to take this call." He quickly left the room for privacy.

I could hear his half of a conversation with Dayanara. For what it was worth, I listened. Soon, I was shocked at his words. They were in a huge fight because she didn't think he was giving her enough time. If she hadn't been the other woman, I could've sympathized with her. But how dare she attack him that way? What did she expect? Didn't she know what he had sacrificed to be with her?

Expecting the conversation to end at any moment, I sat still on my sofa and listened. But the exchange went on and on, and got more vicious by the moment. Hearing their argument gave me a sick sort of satisfaction. After listening for twenty minutes to the unrelenting tirade, I knew Jay's relationship with Dayanara was in trouble. I enjoyed that fact, but their trouble had come too late for me. I didn't want him back. I was completely disgusted with his behavior and loss of integrity.

"Julie, I hope you didn't overhear any of that," Jay said as he quickly walked into the living room. "It was just business stuff."

"I didn't hear a thing," I lied. "I was too busy making notes about our divorce."

He hesitated. "How are you feeling?"

Knowing I needed to meet his overture head-on, I stood up. "How kind of you to show concern at this late date. I'm feeling better. I'm getting on with my life. I like it." I took a deep breath. "I want to make quite sure you understand that I can never forgive you for what you've done to me and our family."

"I'm sorry I've caused you pain. You know that. I just need to get my life together."

"Go right ahead and do it. I'll go ahead with our divorce negotiations."

He sighed. "Thanks for the hard work you're doing."

"I want what's best for us all."

I led him to the front door. He leaned down to hug me, but I stepped back and opened the door. I knew I had to detach emotionally or I would constantly be in pain. I had to give up the fantasy of Jay coming back home.

"I'll call."

I shut the door in his face and let the tears fall.

Jay

I left Julie's safe haven, something I was beginning to appreciate in my rollercoaster life of excess. In an instant, I'd taken Dayanara from the bedroom to the boardroom. I had more business than I could handle, so I'd integrated her into my world, an approach which allowed us to spend time together while we worked. I'd also gotten her away from the adult entertainment industry. I still provided Julie and my children with a great lifestyle in the bargain.

For a short while I'd been proud of my clever strategy, but I was beginning to see that Dayanara was the walking wounded, something I should have recognized from the first. She lived each day in desperate need of constant adoration, sacrificial attentiveness, and compliance with her wishes from any man in her life. When she didn't get her way, her rage rivaled her passion.

She'd had me on a short leash, but I was getting restless as I realized a real relationship with her wasn't possible. I'd deluded myself into thinking I could save her from herself and that we could give each other the love we'd always wanted. Soul mates. I was learning a hard lesson. People can't be saved from themselves, and soul-mate relationships require two healthy people who create intimacy, not discover it, something which neither of us was capable of doing.

Julie's grace under fire was an inspiration to behold. I was actually amazed. Here in front of me was the woman I'd fallen out of love with after years of marital neglect had taken their toll. And yet I was flooded with irresistible fondness for her and admiration for how strong she was, no matter what life (or I) threw in her face. I thought, *Who is she, really?*

2

Julie: *"Mother's Day brought a surprise."*

Jay: *"I missed my wife."*

Julie

On May 13, I stood backstage helping Jayde put on her costume for a dance competition. I felt so very proud of my beautiful and talented daughter. Finally, I believed that I would live to see her grow up. My treatments were a success. In a few days, I'd fly to Houston for my final one. I'd be back in time to celebrate Zoe's May 19 birthday. She wouldn't know it, but I'd be celebrating much more than just her special day.

As I kissed Jayde's cheek, I heard someone behind me.

"Happy Mother's Day!" Jay said. He was holding a big bouquet of yellow roses, a large card, and a small gift box.

"Jay, you made it." I was so relieved he hadn't disappointed Jayde that I hardly noticed his gifts.

"Here, these are for you." He grinned, his teeth bright white against his tanned skin.

"You didn't need to." I felt slightly embarrassed but also very pleased that he'd remembered this important day for me.

"You know I wouldn't forget my favorite girls."

"Thank you." I quickly opened the box and discovered a jeweled bird brooch. Not his usual type of gift for me.

"It's a phoenix," Jay said. "You know, the mythical bird that rises from her ashes."

Is that how he saw me? I felt proud. "It's beautiful."

"Here. Let me put it on you."

I handed him the brooch. When he stood close with his hands touching me just above my heart, I trembled. I felt a love for him so strong it almost took my breath away.

"There." He stepped back. "Looks good on you."

"Thank you."

"Now, Jayde, let's see you go out there and wow them," he said.

I touched the brooch. *Yes, wow them, Jayde,* I thought. *Like your father just wowed me.*

Jay

After seeing Julie and Jayde, I went straight to the airport and flew to a convention in San Francisco. Dayanara met me there. I hoped to avoid one of her meltdowns, as I'd come to call them. Anytime she became jealous over the time I spent with my children or if she felt the need for more control in our business, she'd fly into a rage. It could take me hours to talk her down, even when I used my best therapeutic skills.

A frequent pattern of predictable cycles emerged whenever Dayanara felt unimportant, disrespected, or not valued. Even the slightest provocation would cause her to erupt in emotional outbursts with intense conflict. Her meltdowns were most often triggered when we had a request for more business or I had to present a solo program or we received a favorable evaluation that pointed more in my direction than hers following a joint-training event. I wondered where the liberated woman who had made her own way in the world and wanted no dependency on a man had gone. That woman was nowhere to be found.

My relationship with Dayanara was exhausting. Yet despite its downside, I'd decided failure was not an option. Always the knight, I continued to climb back up on my white horse, determined to make our relationship work. I had too much invested, both personally and professionally, to fall short. Besides, my ego wouldn't let me stop trying to get it right.

3

Julie: "I needed a new place to make new memories."

Jay: "I wanted fewer surprises in my life."

Julie

In June, I thought about what life would look like post divorce. On every corner, Tulsa held happy memories turned sad. I didn't believe I could survive if I had to confront them every day. My brother lived in Dallas, and he encouraged me to move there. Our children enjoyed each other, and I'd have family nearby.

We took several weekend trips to Dallas to look at schools and houses. The kids were excited to change the scenery of their lives. I thought by taking our children to Dallas, I would actually be protecting them from their father. His bi-monthly visits really did not give the kids enough time with him and were not reason enough for me to stick around. Also, Dallas was an easy hour flight from Tulsa, so we wouldn't be too far from my parents. I even wondered if, after my mother's retirement, my parents might consider moving south to be near all their grandchildren.

I began to look ahead to my new life. In hopes that I would get some print and commercial work to supplement my income once we moved, I even went to New York to do a photo shoot.

Meanwhile, Jay was deep into rescuing Dayanara and creating a life with her. From our bank records, I knew he was buying a house in Miami. Soon he would be living in a separate city from his children. If he wasn't going to live in Tulsa, I had no reason to keep the kids there. He hadn't even asked for a steady visitation schedule, so I wondered just how big a part he would play in their lives once he had established a permanent relationship with Dayanara.

Jay

I took Dayanara to San Francisco for an elite conference of independent entrepreneurs. It was big ticket admission for a small group of professionals to spend the week with several successful consulting gurus and obtain inside tips on how to take our businesses to the next level. One of the gurus was Eddie Reynolds, a former billionaire mentor. I credited him with my success in transitioning from an office-based psychologist to an independent consultant with a national practice.

I wanted to expose Dayanara to my world and to further legitimize our business relationship. It was a good idea that quickly turned bad.

As we ate dinner in a quaint restaurant overlooking the Golden Gate Bridge, I mentioned that Julie would be having her final treatment in Houston and I needed to keep the kids. I asked Dayanara to postpone her upcoming trip to Tulsa.

She flew into a rage. She accused me of being a selfish man who only wanted to spend time with his children. Her lack of compassion for my kids was chilling. I tried to talk her down, but she only yelled louder, made threats, and tried to embarrass me. From past experience, I knew I could stop her by getting out of her sight. I got up, walked to the maître d', and gave him money to pay my bill and get Dayanara a taxi when she was ready to leave.

Outside, I hailed a cab. At my hotel, I snagged a secluded seat at the bar and ordered a drink to calm myself. After a while, I noticed Dayanara sitting close to Eddie at a table, drinking and chatting. I felt shocked and doubly betrayed. First, I'd trusted him as my mentor and coach, tens of thousands of dollars worth. Second, I'd invested just as much in her.

But I was a betrayer too, so maybe my chickens had come home to roost. I wanted to smash his face and dump her on the street. I did neither. I left the restaurant and walked around San Francisco. As I walked, all I could think about were my precious children and my brave Julie. My knightly arrogance peeling away and my honor sadly frayed, I vowed to do better.

When I returned to the hotel, Eddie's red Ferrari was gone. I figured Dayanara had gone with him, probably to enact the ritualistic scene she had performed for hundreds of rich and famous men as a high-dollar escort. I felt humiliated. Even worse, I feared her stunt could ruin my business reputation.

I went to my hotel room alone. I waited, hours. Finally, I had to know the truth. I went downstairs to wait in a secluded corner. I watched Eddie drive up in his Ferrari and help Dayanara out, and then they walked into the bar. Just as I'd suspected, they'd gone out together. I slipped upstairs to my room and waited again.

When Dayanara finally arrived, well after midnight, she acted defiant. I confronted her with what she'd just done to me. Her rage rose to new heights. I waited her out, and then I explained that we were done and I wouldn't work on any more projects with her. At one o'clock that morning, she called her attorney at home and explained that she was going to sue me for breach of contract and ruin me. She'd done this before to men and it was no idle threat.

For the first time, I realized I was in a relationship with an extremely disturbed woman. Because of her deep childhood wounds, she manipulated men to get things she wanted and then attacked them when they didn't meet her demands.

But we were in business together, and we had contracts to fill and deadlines to meet. Plus, I needed our relationship to work. I didn't want to admit I was wrong.

4

Julie: *"Life kept surprising me."*

Jay: *"I worked to get my life on track."*

Julie

On July 7, Jay arrived at my house. I led him to the living room where we'd had so many discussions about the divorce and our children. After he sat down, I gave him something to drink.

"Jay, I'm planning to move to Dallas in August and take the children with me."

He said nothing. He just sat there with a dazed look on his face.

"I can't stand the memories in Tulsa. Besides, you'll be starting your new life in Miami. Without you in Tulsa, there's no point in keeping the kids here."

"What if I'm still here?"

"But you aren't going to be." I took a sip of wine to steady my voice. I sounded much calmer than I felt. "If you want, you can have this big house and live here till you move to Miami. That will save you some expense. I'll also take the kids out of private school so that you don't have to pay for that."

"You don't need to do any of this."

"Yes, I do. After the divorce, I can only afford a smaller house. And I hope you'll visit the kids more often if you don't have the added expense of private school." I smiled. "They're excited about getting to wear their own clothes instead of school uniforms."

"When I was their age, I envied those kids wearing uniforms and getting the stellar educations. I always vowed my children would get the best."

"In the Dallas area, our kids can attend excellent public schools. They'll do well."

"I know they will." Jay set down his glass. "Julie, what if I don't move to Miami?"

"What do you mean?" I felt my heart beat fast. Not moving to Miami could mean that he was breaking up with Dayanara. Or could he be moving her to Tulsa? My mind raced with the possibilities.

"I mean it." He leaned forward. "If I stayed here, would you?"

"I...I don't know." I jumped up. When he was so close, I couldn't think straight.

"Julie, how is your health? Will you finally let me see your medical records?"

I felt tears sting my eyes. He sounded so kind, so caring. I'd been through so much alone that I hardly knew how to handle intimacy any more. "Yes, you can see them. I'm through my treatments. I've got a clean bill of health."

"I'm thankful." Jay cleared his throat. "I've come to believe that you know more about love than anybody I've ever met."

"What do you mean?"

"I don't know a damn thing about it, but I'd like to learn."

For a moment, I thought my heart stopped. Did he mean what it sounded like he meant, or was he toying with me again? I felt confused, scared, and yet hopeful. I still loved him with all my heart, but I couldn't let him hurt me or our children again.

"Will you let me take you and our kids out to dinner tomorrow night?"

I looked into his eyes, so dark, so intense, so daring. "Yes."

He smiled. "It's a place to start."

Jay

I sat quietly in my apartment for what seemed like days. I focused on my surroundings where the remnants of my imploded life mocked me: the new couch I'd bought upon exiting the family home; a few pictures of the kids on the mantle; new appliances, some still in unopened boxes; and Julie's gift of a mahogany frame with a color photograph of her and our children crouched together on the floor, their strained smiles effervescent but their eyes betraying fear.

No doubt about it, I missed my family.

I felt as though I were awakening from a bad dream. Shocking thoughts came to me: Could I have been wrong about everything? Was divorce really necessary? Had I been wrong to believe that my marriage was dead first and the affair was just an inevitable consequence? Or was it actually the affair that had motivated my recent actions, including my decision to leave my marriage?

I felt haunted by these questions—and yet reclaimed by them, too. So I settled on a plan of action that would move me toward becoming a healthy human being again, a plan that would eventually extricate me from my affair. Because I realized I was unfit for any relationship and needed to be alone, I avoided thinking that Julie and I could work together to undo the damage of my affair. I decided I would focus on being her friend.

I began to pace the floor of my small living room. As I walked, Chandler's precious toys that were arranged in tight piles across the floor captured my attention. Only hours before he had created imaginary play worlds here: Batman battled Ninja Turtles. The plastic fish I'd bought him on our father-son trip to the Aquarium swam through the air. Later, as I'd sat with him reading him the *Dinosaurs Divorce* book, I'd heard the cry of his heart when he asked, "Daddy, when are you coming home to tuck me into my bed?"

I walked to the kids' bedroom, pulled Chandler's pajamas out of a drawer, and inhaled his sweet baby boy scent. Ever Daddy's little boy, he always begged to spend the night with me anytime I was in town. Tears filled my eyes as I imagined him just a few miles away, crying himself to sleep because I wasn't there to read him a bedtime story. At least he still wanted to be with me. My daughters refused to come to my apartment and were distancing themselves from me more with each passing day.

My tears turning to deep sobs, I made my way into the bathroom. I felt a tug on my soul that I hadn't experienced in years. It was a moment of sobering clarity. As I looked into the mirror, I tried to find the man I thought I was. Instead, I saw a stranger.

I felt chilled to the bone.

"Jay," I said aloud, "who the hell are you? What have you become?"

I blinked. Those were my eyes, but the expression in them belonged to someone else.

"You disgust me," I growled as I flung my words toward the imposter in the mirror. "The affair, the deception, the absent integrity. You're a liar, a fake, and a fraud!"

I gasped for breath.

"You know the truth. Stop selling yourself a line of crap! You left your marriage because you were chasing a fantasy with Dayanara to find an illusion of happiness. You were chasing a damn feeling that you tried hard to make real. Face it, sucker, your grand plan backfired."

I tried to get a handle on reality as I glared at myself in the mirror.

"Jay, did you really think rescuing a high-dollar stripper was going to work out? Did you think she was actually going to save you from despair and become a soul mate for life? Are you insane?"

"Yes. And yes!" I nodded at my reflection and felt a bit of sanity return.

"Why'd you give up on Julie? When you did that, you didn't just give up on your marriage; you altered the legacy of three innocent children, now victim to your selfishness. And for what purpose? So you could find yourself? You can't legitimize a fantasy. It never would've worked!"

Shivering, I felt beaten up by my own words.

Then came the words that seemed to resonate through me. For some reason, I knew they were crucial; I knew I must heed them: "Jay, there's only one pathway to wholeness. You must embrace the truth and be open to what that truth tells you."

Realizing I could no longer trust my intelligence, my beliefs, or my goals, I opened myself to the truth—wanting it, willing it, reaching out for it.

But still it seemed to elude me.

Finally unable to stand any longer, I collapsed to the floor. Perhaps it was only seconds, perhaps only minutes, but it seemed like hours that I lay there huddled on the cold, hard tile, trembling and alone. It was then that I noticed Chandler's discarded baby blanket not far from where I'd fallen. In desperation, I reached for it and clutched it close to my chest as though it might somehow give me the answers I needed.

And then the most remarkable thing happened. Though there was nothing extraordinary about the blanket itself, there must have been an element of the miraculous in the act of reaching for it; for all of a sudden, it became amazingly clear to me that I needed to reach for something beyond myself if I hoped to discover truth. I needed to reach out to a higher power. I needed to reach for God.

In the ensuing moments, I took what was perhaps the most important step of my adult life. I turned my heart back toward the God of my youth.

The past came flooding back to me as I remembered how I'd given my heart to him years earlier when I was a student at Oral Roberts University. Prayer had been a natural and important part of my life then. God was a reality and my relationship with him normal. But after college, I began to consider God irrelevant to my life, and I ended up walking away from the divine in agnostic indifference.

Now, in my hour of need, I reached for him just as I'd reached for my son's blanket seconds before. In so doing, I followed the path of many before me—I prayed out loud, pleading for answers.

"Father, it is hard for me to even call your name. Yet I will rely on the simple truth revealed in your Word to me years ago in Psalms. 'O LORD, You have searched me and you know me. ...Where can I go from your Spirit? Where can I flee your presence?...How precious to me are your thoughts, O God! How vast is the sum of them!' God, I am a broken man, a failed husband, and an unsuccessful father. I don't know how to get out from where I am, but I do know I can't do it without your presence. Please take my hand as though I am your son and be my Father. Please show me one step at a time what love means and how to love those in my life who deserve more than I have given them. Let that be my truth. Amen."

I felt peace and clarity settle over me, as warm and comforting as Chandler's blanket. God had not forsaken me. Truth was waking me up.

The next day, filled with new strength of purpose, I flew to meet Julie and our children for a dance competition. Our girls did well, and we enjoyed seeing the sights.

While we were at the competition, I snagged as much alone time as I could get with Julie. I couldn't get her out of my mind. I felt as if I'd never really seen her before, but she'd changed too. She'd been through her own dark night of the soul and had come out to a bright place in the sun. She didn't need a knight on a white horse anymore. In fact, if I'd have stepped down, she'd have let me rest my weary soul in that calm place she had created for herself and our children. But I didn't know if I could give up that much control.

One night we left the girls playing with their friends and went to a quiet, restaurant. As we dined, I reveled in the simple pleasure of her company.

"Julie," I said, "do you think we might work things out between us in the future?"

"Not if I'm a third wheel to Dayanara."

"What if she weren't in the picture?"

"You know I love you. I'll always love you. But I must be the only woman in your life."

"I don't want to be married."

"That hurts, but I accept it." Julie's big blue eyes appeared luminous and mysterious in the candlelight. "I've learned to accept things I would never have believed I was strong enough to endure."

"I apologize for hurting you." I hesitated. "Even worse, I doubted you. I checked your medical records. Everything you told me was the truth, but I was lying so much, I couldn't believe you. If I'd known, I'd have dropped everything and been by your side every step of the way. The thought of nearly losing you crushes my spirit."

"Apology accepted."

I reached out and gently squeezed her hand across the table. "Give me a chance. Stay in Tulsa. Keep the kids there."

"I'll give it some thought."

"You won't regret it."

5

Julie: *"The sweet scent of summer was in the air."*

Jay: *"I was riding on hope."*

Julie

I guess Jay could sweet talk me as much as ever. Still, if there was any possibility of our getting back together, I vowed to give love a chance. I only hoped he wasn't using me to keep his children close. I decided to stay in Tulsa, but I still planned to move out of the big house and put my children in public school. I was not willing to put myself in a situation where Jay could control me with money or ever use the kid's tuition as a weapon. I did not trust him. I also knew Jay had deep resentment toward me for the lifestyle he provided for us. I figured that once the divorce was finalized, Dayanara would start trying to control his money. I found a new house and wrote a contract to buy it. Jay took us out to dinner when he was in town.

I found out he'd gone to Cancun with Dayanara during a time when he said he'd been with his brother. I felt confused because he'd called me several times each day and had spun an elaborate story about his brother taking him on vacation. I was devastated by his choice to be with Dayanara, but I didn't back down from my commitment to give our relationship a chance.

By August 7, I was packing to move and getting my children enrolled in their new school. They grew more excited about it by the day. I realized how much they would have missed their grandparents if we'd moved to Dallas.

I went out on dates with Jay. He even took me on a flying lesson for an hour. We had great fun together. We laughed like kids. But then he flew away from me again, this time to New York City. When I talked to him, I caught him in several lies. Dayanara had joined him there, and she'd met his mother. I felt so angry, I would have moved to Dallas that weekend if it hadn't been for the children. But I refused to jerk them around since they'd been through enough.

Jay

Ending my affair proved even more difficult than my gradual resolve to do so. The fantasy I'd been chasing still had a life of its own, as did my sense of entitlement to it. As I clung to my illusions, I made a desperate attempt to breathe new life into the mistake that stared me right in the face. I lived in two worlds but knew one had to give. I just didn't know which would go first.

My relationship with Dayanara had degenerated into one of two cycles: either she placed me on a pedestal, over-idealized me, and loved me; or she criticized my character, blamed me for her outbursts, and denigrated and hated me. It seemed that every step I took to distance myself from her ushered in a new scene of mounting drama. She would verbally attack me for hours at a time while I tried to reason with her, but she'd finally convince me to question my own sanity and admit to my culpability in her problems. She was practically living on drugs and alcohol, which only aggravated her instability. Always the rescuer and the responsible one, I struggled with the thought that her demise was partly my fault. She was deteriorating, and I felt compelled to save her from herself. I had to help her, no matter what else was going on in my life.

One day as Dayanara and I waited for connecting flights from the Atlanta airport following a seminar, she started drinking before noon. When her flight to Miami was delayed due to bad weather, I warned her to take it easy on the drinks. She laughed at me. So I left her there and went ahead to catch my flight to Tulsa.

Back home, I picked up my girls and took them to the mall to shop. While they gave me a fashion show, I began receiving text messages from Dayanara that said she was being attacked at the airport. When I finally reached her by phone, she sounded drunk and belligerent. In the background, I heard airport security restrain her, and then the phone went dead. I could do nothing for her at that point. Her rage had finally sealed her own fate.

Several hours later, I took my girls home and then hurried back to my place to start my investigation. I eventually discovered that Dayanara had been arrested for public intoxication and resisting arrest. She would be taken to a downtown booking facility. I wasn't shocked, but I was worried.

I found a way to pay her bail so that she could avoid spending the night in jail. Then I arranged for a limo to pick her up and take her to a hotel near the airport. I also made travel arrangements to fly to Atlanta the next morning. I planned to pick her up and help her get to Miami.

After several more hours, Dayanara called. Sounding extremely distraught, she explained that on the way from the airport to the jail, she'd been beaten up and raped in the van they were transporting her in. She wasn't making complete sense, but I was horrified, frustrated, and deeply concerned for her safety.

Over several hours and many phone calls, I got her to the limo and talked her through the trip to the hotel. Once she got in the room, she sounded as though she felt safe. I told her to rest and that I'd see her in a few hours. I contacted Call Rape and got information on the Atlanta police and attorneys in the area. By that time it was four in the morning. I packed and caught my flight at seven.

With Dayanara, I continually needed a bigger horse to mount, but this was the biggest yet and I was flat out exhausted from all the drama. My marriage and divorce had been restful by comparison. I just didn't know where I could keep pulling up the energy from.

I arrived at nine and went straight to her hotel. As I unlocked her door, I braced myself for how she'd look after such a bad experience. She was lying in bed, watching TV—still obviously upset. I scanned her face and body for signs of physical assault, but she looked fine. In fact, I looked worse than she did.

We didn't have much time. In the next few hours, we had to catch the flight I'd booked. Her bags had already been sent to Miami. She had nothing, since all her carry-on belongings had been confiscated and were being held at the airport detention center. I hurried to a mall near the hotel and bought her toiletries and a new set of clothes. I got her dressed and ready to go.

She was scared to return to the detention center, but we had to go there to get her laptop and bags. Besides, I wanted to talk with the officers involved. Using my clinical skills and showing a copy of her driver's license, I got permission to pick up her things while she waited for me. I assumed a friendly, apologetic tone with them, and I learned that Dayanara had been labeled out of control, intoxicated, belligerent, and aggressive. She had frightened other passengers in the boarding line. A female officer informed me that she alone had accompanied Dayanara to the downtown booking center.

In the long run, she refused to file charges against the Atlanta police, and neither would she speak with the attorney I'd contacted earlier on her behalf. I was becoming increasingly convinced that Dayanara was a pathological liar who played the victim anytime she needed justification or didn't want to take responsibility for her actions. It was another chilling realization about her.

Still, I wanted to give her the benefit of the doubt. When we landed in Miami, I insisted we go to a medical facility that specialized in dealing with rape victims.

She tried to refuse, but she was exhausted and I was determined that she get help if she truly needed it. A doctor examined her and took samples. I left my business card and requested the doctor call me with her findings.

I took Dayanara home and put her to bed. Several hours later, the doctor called my cell phone. She explained that there was no sign of trauma and the tests were negative, but that she had seen the patient before.

It was confirmation of what I'd already known in my heart. Dayanara had lied to me and used me. She would continue to do so as long as I continued to let her.

But I was stronger and smarter than that. It was over.

I resolved then and there to end both our affair and our business relationship, although I had no idea how I was going to accomplish that goal. I'd made the critical mistake of integrating our personal and professional lives to the point that extricating Dayanara would have to be carefully done... or risk a high level of retaliation.

6

Julie: *"Our marriage came in like a lion and went out like a lamb."*

Jay: *"I felt free for the first time in my life."*

Julie

On September 12, Jay and I agreed on all divorce items and signed off on the papers. I wanted him to go to court with me for this final separation of our lives, but because he had to fly to Chicago on business, I met him at his apartment to obtain his signature on the documents. Afterward, I went to court by myself, outraged that he had not made time in his schedule to finalize the divorce he'd insisted on getting.

The judge's stark chambers felt cold and forlorn. She didn't like the way things were structured in the decree and required that changes be made. In the end, I had to return to Jay's apartment for him to sign off on the changes before he caught his flight. Though it seemed the drama would never end, the day finally came to a close—the divorce final, the marriage over. It was the saddest and loneliest day of my life. I had lost my greatest love.

I consoled myself by rehearsing the fact that I'd done all I could to preserve my marriage. Now I would simply go forward alone.

Jay

Our divorce felt surreal. I did nothing to stop it. I didn't even go to court, because the relentless demands of our lifestyle had me traveling all over the country again. I believed our marriage was broken beyond repair and there was nothing left to salvage. If by surprise something should happen between us in the future, so be it. However, at that point I felt I was doing Julie a favor by ending her obligation to me. I was setting her free to pursue love with someone healthier, better able to love her, and available for the type of relationship she deserved. I was convinced that guy wasn't me. My life was a train wreck.

With the divorce finalized, I received closure on the painful legacy of a relationship that had worked for everyone but me. More than ready to move on with my life, I wanted to make decisions that were right for me, not for somebody else.

As an independent, divorced man, life could only get better.

Julie

On September 15, I got up early on a bright and sunny Saturday morning. I roused my children and got them ready for our big move. We were leaving the house where we had endured so much physical and mental pain, and were making a fresh start in a new house.

I was excited to leave. My bedroom had become difficult for me to sleep in, and I wanted a new bed. I was ready to be in a place that did not reek from medication. Because my room smelled like a hospital, my kids frequently complained about the odor. Yes, I was thrilled about the move.

Jay arrived with coffee, orange juice, and donuts. We sat down at the kitchen table for one last family gathering in the house that had once held so much love and promise.

"Jay, thanks for helping us move today," I said as I wiped icing from my lips.

"I'm here for you . . . for all of you. Anything you need." He grinned. "In fact, as soon as we finish here, I'm taking you out to buy new bedroom furniture, washer and dryer, refrigerator, and a big new TV."

I laughed in delight and our children joined me.

"We need our own cell phones, too," Jayde said.

Jay looked at her in surprise. "That's something we'll discuss later, young lady."

My heart swelled with happiness. I felt almost as if he hadn't been gone from our family, as if all those dark days and nights had never been. But I couldn't forget them, not now, not ever.

"Dad," Zoe said, "we're going to Disney World!"

"Yeah!" Chandler cried out, spilling his orange juice across the table.

Glad for the distraction, I jumped up, grabbed paper towels, and cleaned up the mess. I hadn't told Jay about our trip.

"Julie, what's this about?" Jay asked.

I sat down and faced him. "I promised to take them on a trip to Disney World after the divorce was finalized to celebrate new beginnings. I wanted them to see that life will continue on in a normal and happy way. I want us to create new, positive memories." For me, this meant as a family of four. I wanted the children to know I was going to do my best and that we would get our lives back on track.

"It's a good idea," Jay said as he looked around the group. "I want new, good memories too. Can I come?"

"Yeah!" Chandler cried out, knocking over Zoe's orange juice in his excitement.

My heart beating fast and my hands clammy, I jumped up for more paper towels. What was Jay thinking? We were going to celebrate a divorce, not a marriage. What if we got into huge arguments again?

"Julie, what do you say?" Jay asked.

Feeling afraid and yet excited, I quickly mopped up the juice. Could we connect as a family at Disney one more time?

"I'll even pay for the whole trip if you agree. Who says we have to do divorce like everyone else. Like it or not, we'll always be a part of one another's life. We might as well be good friends for the sake of our kids."

I dared to look at him. Hope and fear warred in him just as much as in me. I smiled. "If you're willing to take a chance, I am. It'll be fun."

"Yeah!" Chandler cried, and then intentionally tipped over Jayde's almost-empty glass of orange juice. Pleased that he'd gotten everyone's attention, he grinned.

"You're cleaning that one up yourself," I said as I tossed him a paper towel.

"Got to train boys young," Jay said, laughing.

While Chandler made an even bigger mess cleaning up, I looked around at my precious family. We'd all grown and learned and developed through our crisis. We were better people—more tolerant, more loving, more generous.

Perhaps great loss generated great love.

Jay

As my arrogance melted, I got honest with myself about who I was and who I wasn't. The truth was that I knew little about real love or the kind of relationship needed for it to exist. I had mistaken an experience of infatuation with a stripper (a professional illusionist who spun a grand fantasy) for a person I thought I was in love with who would be the answer to my longing and loneliness. In other words, I'd confused an encounter for a person—and then I had attempted to translate my experience into something real, which it could never have been, especially since it was predicated on an illusion. The result was a false positive: I imbued Dayanara with qualities I wanted her to have, not ones she actually possessed. I also incorrectly assumed that the vitality and significance I lacked could be found in her. Now I realized I needed to find those missing parts in myself and not look for them in another.

I felt haunted by truths I could no longer deny or rationalize. Clearest of all was the fact that I'd invested more time and energy in trying to repair an affair than I had in trying to repair my marriage of ten years. I felt disgusted with myself.

Questions continued to plague me. I often asked myself, "What might've happened if I'd given as much of myself to Julie as I'd given my affair partner? Where would Julie and the kids and I be now if I'd worked on strengthening my marriage instead of chasing a fantasy?"

I felt afraid. I didn't want to endanger my fragile connection with my family by pushing too much. But I desperately missed them. I spent lonely nights sitting in my apartment, looking at their photos, and wondering how I could have thrown away so much.

Would Disney World be a mistake? Would Julie and I fight? Would our kids get the wrong idea about our relationship? I could think of a dozen reasons not to go. I could think of only one reason to go—*love*.

In the end, intrigue and a growing sense of possibility trumped my fears, and I was willing to risk being made the fool. After all, what did I really have to lose? I'd already lost the respect of everyone important to me, and I'd stopped caring about the rest. I knew I had made mistakes. It was clear that I had hurt people. There was really nothing I could do about the situation except to learn from it. As long as I wasn't leading anyone on, I felt going on the trip was worth the risk of finding out how much I didn't know.

Maybe if I went on the trip, in the long run I'd become the wiser for it: What if I discovered the truth about what had gone wrong in our marriage and why? What if Julie and I started fresh from a place of total transparency where we had nothing to protect and no power struggles to separate us? We were finally in the position of having no expectations and complete choice. We could be with each other or move on. Either way, we would remain friends and co-parents. To me, it seemed there was nothing to lose and everything to gain.

If I had a chance at finding love, not the commercial variety but real love, I had to make myself vulnerable. I had to reach out. I had to offer the best love I knew how to give. Maybe then, and only then, would I deserve to get love back.

7

Julie: "I felt like a phoenix rising."

Jay: "I felt almost new."

Julie

In October, Jay went to the back-to-school program at our girls' new school, and we all had fun. In fact, everything seemed so great and normal that we simply went back to my home as a family. We put the children to bed. Jay and I sat together in the living room, drinking wine, talking about our upcoming trip to Disney, and sharing warm, intimate moments.

I'm not quite sure how it happened, but everything was so right between us that we moved closer and closer until we were hugging and kissing. Then finally we were in my new bed, making love with nine months of pent-up longing. Our closeness took my breath away. The intimacy was exciting and wonderful, perfect in every way.

I knew I'd been right all along to wait for Jay. I'd extended my love to him long enough for him to realize he should return to me and our children.

I was desperately in love with my ex-husband.

Jay

In the year we were apart, Julie had become a new woman. I was surprised to learn what an incredible human being she was, someone I had taken for granted or perhaps never even known. As we spent time together, I came to realize that the real Julie stood in sharp contrast to the Julie I had invented in my mind. I felt shocked at what I was experiencing with my newfound friend.

Originally, friendship had been at the core of our love. So Julie and I set out to discover how we had destroyed that friendship. We discussed how we had stopped being interested in who our partner actually was and focused instead on changing our spouse into the person we thought we wanted. Rather than expressing appreciation for the contributions we'd made in each other's lives, we criticized and condemned each other for what we hadn't done. We'd also grown defensive whenever we felt rejected or judged, and we'd resorted to emotional stonewalling as we gradually disconnected from each other. During the power struggles that ensued, we'd turned away from each other in anger and hurt instead of turning toward each other with fondness and admiration. Not surprisingly, the friendship we'd built our love upon soon eroded.

As our goodwill toward each other deteriorated, we began to put our children, our possessions, and other people at the center of our worlds instead of each other. In the end, contempt struck the final blow, destroying any semblance of mutual respect—and the debris of a once-robust love turned to dust before our very eyes.

When I joined Julie at the kids' back-to-school night, I felt extremely curious about this intimate stranger I now saw as irresistibly attractive. I wanted much more of her. Though she'd lost a lot of weight and didn't look quite herself following her cancer treatment, I couldn't take my eyes off her.

Julie had become a highly independent, determined, and strong person, able to move on without me as she charted her own path. Guys from around the country had begun courting her after meeting her through Facebook and friends' introductions. Her suitors included several millionaires who were ready to hand her the moon.

I admired Julie for another reason. Instead of choosing justice, she'd chosen love. She had refused to be vindictive, resolved not to punish me, and not taken me to the cleaners as some had said she had the right to. She also was consistently classy and graceful under fire. Ultimately, it was the love Julie showed each day that nullified any remaining stories I'd told myself about her being a gold digger and taking advantage of me for my success.

Many men more successful than I stood in the wings of her life, but she refused them because of the immense integrity with which she lived. She based her values on her continuing love for me, not on the justifiable feelings of anger and hurt I had caused her. I felt humbled by who she was in comparison to who I had become.

In the warm glow of Julie's love, I came to know what love really is and how much I had to learn in order to love. I was truly surprised by love—not the mushy, sentimental kind that is driven by feelings and circumstances, but the enduring kind that is refined like steel emerging from fire. The kind that is unshakable and seasoned by the failures and struggles of life. Julie inspired me. I wanted to be like her: respected, admired, and honored.

At our children's new school, Julie filled my vision. She wore a sexy miniskirt, high heels, and a classy blue blouse. I wanted to peel off her outer wrappings and get to her core. I wanted her, a feeling that had been absent for years. I longed to hold her, touch her, and get close to her. But would she respond in the same way? To test the waters, I flirted outrageously by sending her sexy text messages. I felt sixteen. Soon, she texted me back. We flirted through the announcements and were hardly aware of anything except each other.

But I wanted more. She had earned my respect. She had professed her love. Yet the real question that remained was whether I could accept her love and grow as a man to love her in the same way.

Hungry for what only the other could provide, we took our children home, put them to bed, and then turned to each other. Love makes all the difference in sex. I'd taken a painful path to learn that truth. It wasn't one I'd ever forget. Making love to Julie felt like coming home. I was exactly where I should've been and where I wanted to be.

As for Dayanara, for all practical purposes my relationship with her had ended, but we were still in business together. I hoped that we could remain friends because I was still emotionally attached to her.

But I was in love with my ex-wife.

8

Julie: "I went back for more tests."

Jay: "I vowed to make Julie happy."

Julie

On October 11, I found a lump in my left breast. I feared the lymph nodes could be infected. Jay could feel a pea-sized mass in my breast, and he became concerned, too. We didn't tell our children. I hurried to the doctor and underwent more tests and a biopsy. We were told everything looked fine. We were relieved but still worried.

Setting aside my fear, I took my kids to Orlando where we spent a fabulous day at Disney, enveloped in a wonderful fantasy world. Jay flew in from Miami the next day. I knew he'd been with Dayanara before coming to meet us, so I worked hard to bite my tongue. I desperately tried to focus on what was in front of me, not what was behind me. For a week, we simply enjoyed each other, no arguments and no disagreements. I saw some positive changes in Jay. He was a more sensitive and caring man, but I still did not completely trust that the changes were permanent.

I could tell our children loved having their family together. I did, too. Jay had a separate room booked for himself, but the kids begged him to stay with us. He would go to his room to shower and then come back to our room. I tried not to think about the fact that he might be calling Dayanara when he left. I reminded myself that he was here with us by his own request. If he had wanted to be with her, he would have been there.

We enjoyed the Magic Kingdom as a family and laughed about the newlyweds walking around in Mickey Mouse ears with top hats and veils. We rode the monorails and the ferry across Lake Buena Vista. Some of the sweetest moments of that trip were on the boat.

At one point, Jay claimed he wanted simply to be my friend and co-parent. I was willing to accept him there. However, I let him know that if I ever met someone else, that situation would change. For now, our budding relationship worked, and I had to be content.

Later, as we boarded the ferry boat, I climbed the stairs in front of Jay. I felt someone grab my butt. Startled, I jerked around. No one was there except Jay.

He had a big grin on his face.

"Did you just pinch my butt?" I asked in shock.

He nodded as he continued to smile.

"You're assuming a lot." I tried to act huffy, but secretly I felt pleased that he still wanted me. I just wished he'd make up his mind so that I wouldn't feel so confused.

"Not my fault," Jay said. "You're irresistible."

I laughed at his words. I knew he was the irresistible one.

We all had great fun on the ride. I wasn't sure what to make of what was happening with Jay, so I decided to take our relationship one day at a time. We were a complete family again. At least for the week.

When the time came to go home, none of us wanted to leave. Our children cried when we got to the airport. We promised them that this would not be our last family vacation.

At home, I discovered the lump in my breast was gone. It felt like a miracle, but I knew the truth. Love and happiness had healed me.

Jay

Julie's second cancer scare made me realize that I couldn't imagine life without her. I vowed to do everything possible to make her happy.

Once more, I prayed to God and asked that Julie be healed and her life spared from cancer. I asked nothing for myself, only for her and our children.

At Disney World, I discovered magic with my family again. What developed between Julie and me had a momentum that no amount of past pain could stop. My intent was simply to be the best friend and co-parent I could be, since that was all I felt I could deliver on. I was surprised at how good it felt to be part of my family. I could see the joy and comfort our children experienced with Mommy and Daddy together again.

On our first day, we toured the park in the steam engine train. Chandler loved the train. He sat between Julie and me, and our daughters sat directly in front of us. At one point, I put my arm around Chandler and inadvertently touched Julie's shoulder. I felt a spark and glanced at her.

She looked back at me and smiled, her blue eyes warm with love.

Encouraged, I put my arm around her and squeezed her shoulder. When she placed her hand in mine, I felt all was right with the world.

"Julie, why did we ever divorce?" I asked. Of course I knew all the reasons, but in that moment, everything we'd gone through seemed to have happened to other people.

"I never wanted it," she chuckled. "Why did you have to get a girlfriend?"

I laughed with her at the absurd contrast of the painful past we were still transitioning from and the potent moment we found ourselves in.

Disarmed and yet disturbed at how much I enjoyed being with my family, I once again questioned all that had led us to divorce. Doubts plagued me. Had I been wrong about Julie, our marriage supposedly failing, the affair, and the subsequent decision to divorce? Had I really needed to implode my family to experience the freedom and happiness I thought I deserved? Maybe yes. Maybe no.

Whatever the case, I had to acknowledge the significant changes Julie had made. She had overcome rage and judgmental attitudes. She had displaced condescending withdrawal and lack of appreciation. She had replaced insensitivity and hard-heartedness with gentleness and true concern: instead of focusing on her own needs, she took special care to listen to my feelings, ask me my opinions, and find out what was important to me.

Now I liked who Julie was and who I was with her. I wanted to be with her. I couldn't help but wonder if a close relationship with her might one day again be possible.

One of my favorite parts of our Disney vacation was our ferry boat ride on Lake Buena Vista from the hotel to the Magic Kingdom. In our fifteen-minute trek through the enchanted world, I let my imagination roam free. What ifs abounded as I leaned over the topside rail and took in the beautiful views of the Grand Floridian and the massive theme park filled with the wonders of childhood dreams. Walt Disney's magical vision of hope and possibility connected with me.

What might be possible if a new relationship resurrected from the dust of our failures and disappointments? Could the relationship really be distinct from anything we'd experienced in our bruising past? Could we build something new out of the wisdom of experience we had gained? Though I tried to dismiss the idea of a new relationship as "nostalgic grasping for a dead past during a calm interlude of family life," a part of me could not deny the potential that was there. Perhaps it was not too late to create what I'd meant to do when I first married Julie.

After a great week at Disney World, I felt healed by the warmth of my family's love. As a result, I gave even more thought to a future life with Julie. Could we actually offer each other a mature love? More importantly, could we stay grounded in that love and separate ourselves from the painful stories and armored hearts of the past?

I wanted to believe so.

CHAPTER 10
HOLIDAZE REVISITED

> ## I
>
> Julie: *"What an amazing difference one year made."*
>
> Jay: *"I counted myself lucky."*

Julie

On Halloween, October 31, Jay came to my house to celebrate with our children. He seemed to have a good time, especially compared to the previous year. I made a point of including him in all our activities since I knew he was uncomfortable during the holidays and struggled with memories of growing up in an alcoholic home. We enjoyed his company the entire afternoon and evening.

Our kids loved being a family again. They carved pumpkins, dressed up in cute costumes, decorated cookies, and shared lots of laughter. I believed I'd succeeded in making the holiday special for us all.

I continued to be free from my cancer symptoms, another happy note for the season. I wanted more than ever to watch my children grow up.

Jay

My kids looked cute in their Halloween costumes as they laughed, ate too much sugar, and cavorted with friends. I did my best to enjoy everything with them, but I couldn't get it out of my mind that a dark cloud was looming over our future.

I knew Dayanara and I were history, but ending the relationship with her had become a torturous process. I'd made the huge mistake of trying to legitimize her and our relationship by integrating her into almost every aspect of my life.

I had put my professional reputation at stake by bringing her into my network, promoting a new product with her, and successfully landing a lucrative contract that would keep us entangled another six months. Even with my new resolve to stop seeing her, I was trapped until the contract was over.

Worse than that, I was trying to remain friends with her and keep our professional relationship civil. But she was no more emotionally stable in our business friendship than she'd been when we were lovers. Besides, she wanted it all. She didn't want to lose any more than I did. As it was turning out, she didn't want to lose me.

Beneath the glow of my unexpected courtship with Julie, all was not well within me. I knew I was in no shape for a relationship with anyone, and I worried about hurting Julie more than I already had. I was torn, confused, and afraid of myself. The deep psychological wounds that had contributed to my choice to have an affair still remained, their very presence a constant reminder of the work that lay ahead. However, surprised by my newfound love with Julie, I was determined to heal and to stop the problems of my past from dictating my behavior.

2

Julie: *"I received a fateful invitation."*

Jay: *"I turned back time."*

Julie

As the year moved into November, I felt a growing contentment with life. If all wasn't perfect, at least it was better than it had been in a long time. Though I spent quality time with friends and family, I was becoming more comfortable with being alone and was building my independence. I was determined to take control of my life regardless of what the future might bring.

My children liked their new school and were thriving there. I liked my smaller home, which was easier to manage than our previous one. I especially liked my times with Jay and enjoyed our growing romance.

One afternoon while I was packing our suitcases for a weekend in Dallas, the phone rang. I answered it.

"Julie!" Jay said. "I've got a great idea for us."

"What is it?"

"I'm sitting here at Rick's Cafe, looking at Thorncrown Chapel on my laptop."

"Seriously…why are you doing that?" I almost didn't get the words out for the rapid beat of my heart. Rick's had been our favorite restaurant when we were married. Of course, Thorncrown was where we'd married and revisited every year till Jay went away. What could he be thinking?

"Will you go back to Eureka Springs with me this weekend?"

I was shocked but did not hesitate. "I'd love to."

"Good! I'll pick you up Saturday morning at eight."

"I'll be ready." As I hung up the phone, I realized I needed to change my weekend plans.

Jay

On Tuesday night at the end of a long day of seeing private clients in Tulsa, I drove aimlessly around town as I sorted through my feelings of guilt, loneliness, and loss. I realized these were what I had destroyed a family for.

I felt hungry. Rick's Café popped poignantly into my mind. Julie and I had eaten there dozens of times during our marriage. For years, I'd avoided the place like the plague. It represented painful memories of a dying relationship we were trying to resurrect by going through the motions of obligatory date nights. Still, I felt compelled to visit the shrine, almost as if something awaited me there that I knew I must discover, no matter my fears.

I noticed a chill in the air as I walked through the entrance. The restaurant flooded me with familiar images of the life I'd walked out of. But for some reason, I felt comforted by the shadows of my past as I took my seat at the same table Julie and I had shared just a year before.

An acoustic guitarist crooned Nora Jones songs, fire crackled rhythmically in the fireplace, and scents of gourmet food filled the air. Chipper as ever, Michael the waiter asked if my wife would be joining me. I shook my head no.

Filled with nostalgia, I opened my laptop, hit the search bar, and typed in Eureka Springs and Thorncrown Chapel. When I saw the images, I was transported back to our sweet wedding and honeymoon in the Ozarks ten years earlier.

All of a sudden, with piercing clarity, a conversation began in my mind. I was not even sure who was asking the questions.

"What does legacy mean to you, Jay, and what will yours be?"

"It's a done deal. I made my bed and now I get to lie in it."

"How have you changed the legacy of the innocent: Jayde, Zoe, Chandler, and Keaton?"

"I'm not sure."

"What about the hopes, the dreams, the very soul of the woman who loved you? Are you prepared to live with the impact of that, Jay?"

"I don't have answers, especially not any good ones."

"For what purpose did you leave and destroy this family?"

"Once I knew. Now I'm not sure."

As I sat there, my future passed before my eyes like a movie on fast-forward. I saw vivid images of life's seasons: awkward graduations where my children had stilted looks on their faces as they tolerated my presence and the presence of the woman I was with at the time; forced visits and divided holidays; my kids' unending resentments that stemmed from their rage over my unfaithfulness; wedding marches with divided family sections; and on and on.

I hated the future I saw for myself, and more importantly, I hated the future I had created for the family I'd abandoned. Confronted again with the ugliness of my choices, I had to question whether those choices had really been necessary.

Maybe there was still hope for me and my family. On the spur of the moment (or perhaps under divine inspiration), I felt compelled to call Julie. I knew we must return to Thorncrown Chapel if we were ever to set our lives back on the right path. I felt blessed when she agreed to go. In no time at all, I'd made reservations for the cottage where we'd spent the first night of our honeymoon.

I felt empowered, as though I'd made a good choice—for once.

Julie

We drove through the beautiful Ozark Mountains and into Eureka Springs to the exact Victorian cabin where we'd spent our honeymoon. The interior of the cabin, complete with pellet-stove fireplace, charming kitchen, and Jacuzzi tub, was as quaint as ever. In no time at all we were settled in as though we'd never left.

During that long weekend, we recreated our honeymoon. We walked the village streets, holding hands, hugging, and laughing as we reminisced about joyous events from our past. We dined in our favorite restaurants, snuggled in front of a crackling fire in our cabin fireplace, and spent intimate time together. Once again, magic filled the air.

Though everything was the same, it was actually quite different. We had both grown during our time apart. We were aware of how we had each changed, and we liked what we saw in each other. We talked about what the future could look like for us.

On Saturday night, I nestled close to Jay in front of the fire. "If we ever make it and end up remarried, do you think we could help others?"

"You want to help others through this painful journey?"

"Yes."

"Do you think we have the strength to examine it, understand it, and explain it?"

"Yes."

"It'd be hard to do. I mean, we'd have to make ourselves transparent in order to help others."

"I know. It's scary to think about. We both brought problems to our marriage."

"But I'd have to admit to an affair."

"Are you strong enough?" I asked, clasping his big, capable hand in mine.

"I honestly don't know. We aren't even through it all."

"We'll get there," I assured him as I kissed the tip of his nose.

He returned the kiss. "One thing—with my therapist experience and your big heart, we really could counsel others through their ordeals."

"That would help to make it all worthwhile."

"This makes it all worthwhile," he said.

Then Jay covered my face with kisses.

Jay

Exactly as it had happened on our honeymoon weekend, I awoke to the sound of birds flying around the front door the morning after we'd arrived at our cabin. As I leaned over to kiss Julie, I marveled again at her inner and outer beauty—and once again, I felt surprised and invigorated by her love.

After dressing, Julie and I walked outside with our steaming mugs of coffee. We took several minutes to sit together on the porch and enjoy the beauty of the morning as the sun beamed its warming rays across the sloping lawn. When I'd finished my coffee, I ran over to the familiar railroad ties to perform my traditional tightrope walk. As Julie cheered me on, I felt a lightness in my step that I hadn't felt since the first time I'd walked those very railroad ties on our honeymoon.

Julie ran to me and I wrapped her in my arms. In that moment, two lonely people made each other whole, this time from a place of chosen love, not unconscious voids. Our once-abandoned friendship was slowly rising from the ashes of our charred life. How could we have ever forgotten our amazing connection?

Returning to our love roots and reviving the magic that had first defined us confirmed to me that our relationship was more than an attempt to elude fear or to grasp a nostalgic feeling. It was something quite real that could be built upon.

But I knew things had to change. Rather, I had to change, in ways that I had run from in our marriage. Julie and I also had a lot of work to do together if we were serious about taking another shot at love. We had to be different with each other and break the destructive patterns that had allowed our marriage to deteriorate. I had to get past my story of Julie as an opportunistic, selfish woman who'd taken advantage of me. She had to heal and move beyond the pain I'd inflicted on her. How would we ever be able to do all that?

For me, authentic change began when I made myself completely vulnerable to Julie one evening while we were dining at Rogues' Manor in downtown Eureka Springs. Looking directly into her eyes, I said, "My name is Jay. I'm interested in knowing who you really are, not what I've made up about you. I'd also like to tell you about who I am now, and who I want to become."

These few words ushered in hours of conversation. We learned things, both new and forgotten, about each other. From that point on, our love maps (long-neglected, then destroyed) were rebuilt, one chapter at a time—and with them, a new mosaic containing the seeds of nascent love.

3

Julie: *"What a wonderful holiday."*

Jay: *"I proudly carved the turkey."*

Julie

On Thanksgiving, November 22, I shared the day with Jay and our children. My extended family met in Dallas for the holiday, not yet ready to accept Jay back into the fold.

It turned out to be the best Thanksgiving of my life. I felt good and was grateful not to be dealing with cancer treatments any longer. I cooked a big turkey, Jay carved it, and we all ate so much that we had to take naps in front of the TV. We shared such a typical family day that it was hard to believe the previous year had been filled with agony and anguish.

After our Eureka Springs weekend, Jay made fewer trips to Miami, and he took no more vacations with Dayanara. Still, I worried about her. Jay hadn't told her he was seeing me again. He talked to her daily and texted her too, supposedly about business. I could tell he missed her, and I knew there was more than I was being told. So I kept my radar up.

At the same time, I felt blessed. I truly had much to be thankful for in my life.

Jay

Wrapped in the festive colors and decorations of autumn, Julie's house was alive with warmth and hospitality. As I breathed in the delicious scents of pumpkin and cinnamon that permeated her cozy home, I realized how much I'd missed and what I'd taken for granted over the years. At Thanksgiving dinner, I proudly carved the turkey and served Julie and the kids their favorite pieces. We celebrated the season simply, with great joy from being in each others' presence and being connected in ways we perhaps had never been before.

As I basked in the comfort of my loving family, my other life seemed far away. I still fantasized that Dayanara and I might someday work out our differences and have a life together, and I missed her, especially our deep emotional connection. But I had to be honest with myself. We worked well together when she was stable, yet I never knew when her mood might change. I just couldn't trust her.

Julie, however, was a different matter. I trusted her constant and abiding love. Because there was much healing and recovery ahead if we were going to succeed in reconciling, I decided it might be best if we got professional help. I was willing to fly anywhere in the country to find the support we needed. The finest people I knew were at the Gottman Institute in Seattle, so I planned to make reservations there as soon as we could get them.

> **4**
>
> Julie: *"I felt blessed that Jay chose to be with me."*
>
> Jay: *"I wanted reconciliation."*

Julie

Jay has never much liked celebrating his birthday because he has too many bad memories from his youth. So on his special day, November 25, I planned a simple event. To make his birthday as positive an occasion as possible, we gave him presents at home, and then I took him out to dinner. As we sat holding hands, I continued the subject we'd been discussing for days.

"Jay, I'd like to think reconciliation between us could work, but there's so much to consider. I'm afraid of losing you again. I don't know how I can trust you, given all that has happened."

"Why don't we decide to commit to seeing if reconciliation will work?"

"What do you mean?"

"We could live together for a few months and then decide if we believe our relationship can work."

"What about our kids? I don't want to give them hope only to dash it."

"Julie, I'm willing to take the chance if you are. I bet the kids are, too."

"We could boost our finances if we only had one house to pay for."

"Let's sell the big one and get out from under the mortgage." He smiled. "I like your cozy place better anyway."

"I could put the big house on the market at a huge discount, and maybe we'd get rid of it right away."

"Let's do it."

"And take a chance on love."

He nodded, his dark eyes sparkling with excitement.

I raised my champagne glass, clinked crystal with him, and toasted our agreement.

Jay

I felt happier than I had in years. I had hope. I had love. I had commitment. I wanted to be with Julie and my children. Even so, Dayanara still lurked in my background. I hadn't told her I was getting back with Julie. I dreaded facing Dayanara's rage, especially before our jobs were complete. At the same time, I owed it to Julie to be honest with Dayanara about the reconciliation.

5

Julie: *"We laughed together."*

Jay: *"I gave Julie diamonds."*

Julie

Our wedding anniversary, December 19, was coming up fast, but I was so busy, I barely had time to think about it. On December 7, I lowered the price of our big house and re-listed it on the market. When I received two offers in one week, I was thrilled. Soon afterward, we only had one house to manage. Jay moved into my home and right back into my big bed. He seemed happier than he had in years. My kids and I were elated, and we began enjoying our little family as never before.

Jay and I started our recovery process by attending therapy and workshops together. This step was hard yet necessary, since we both needed a great deal of healing. I saw something in Jay I hadn't seen in a long time: remorse. He had softened and was less defensive than he'd been in the past, and our friendship was flourishing as a result. I could tell he was committed.

Still, I worried about Dayanara. I wanted her out of our lives.

Jay

On our anniversary, I took Julie out to dinner. As we sat drinking champagne, we laughed together about celebrating our anniversary after our divorce. We got a chuckle when our waiter asked what we were there to celebrate. I said, "Our tenth anniversary, but we actually divorced in September," to which he offered a strained but supportive smile.

It didn't matter that people couldn't understand. Our situation felt so right, we couldn't question it.

When Julie opened my gift, she smiled in delight. I'd selected an anniversary symbol of eternal love—an eternity band, encircled with baguette diamonds. She held out her hand, and I quickly slipped the ring onto the third finger of her left hand where she'd previously worn her wedding ring.

I couldn't imagine being married again, but I wanted her to understand how much I valued our relationship.

6

Julie: *"We gifted each other with love."*

Jay: *"I enjoyed my family."*

Julie

During the holiday season, as we continued shopping for gifts, decorating the house, and taking time to share love, I could have been completely happy had it not been for Dayanara. When Jay finally told her of his intention to reconcile with his family, she went ballistic. As a result, Jay felt guilty and tried to make it up to her with business plans. But everything he did backfired. Eventually, I became concerned for my relationship with Jay.

One day when our children were away with friends, I called him into the living room and brought up the touchy subject.

"I'm uncomfortable with your continued relationship with Dayanara," I said as I sat down near him on the sofa.

"I told her I'm back with you. It's only work now."

"Maybe it is with you, but she's not letting go."

"I'm doing my best."

"I can't heal from the affair as long as she's in the picture."

"It's not like that anymore." He got up, walked away, and then turned back.

Before he could say anything, I stood up and faced him. "I can never completely trust you with the situation like this," I said.

"Julie, you're trying to control me again," he answered, his words clipped in anger.

"Do you want to be with me or with her?"

"I do not ever want to *not* be in a relationship with you."

"I want to be with you, too," I replied. I was so afraid of losing him again that my voice trembled with emotion. All the same, I couldn't put up with Dayanara. Not only was she a constant reminder of Jay's infidelity, she also was a source of irritation to me.

"If you try to control me, I'll leave again." He took a ragged breath. "I can't stand it."

"I'm not trying to control you. I love you. I want us to be together," I said as I worked to keep my rising temper under control. Why couldn't he just get rid of Dayanara?

"Feels a lot like control."

"It's not. It's love."

"Come here."

When Jay took me in his arms and held me close, everything felt right. Yet nothing was right with Dayanara still in our lives.

Jay

I felt trapped and afraid. Instinctively, I knew the relationship with my former affair partner had to end, but if I provoked her wrath, all hell would break loose and my business could be ruined. Not only that, I also felt both she and Julie were trying to manipulate me, and it was tearing me apart. At times, I almost wished I were back in my lonely apartment. But I wanted to be with my family and enjoy the holidays with them. At the moment, that was all I wanted in life.

Somehow I'd find a way to deal with Dayanara, but not till after New Year's.

Julie

On December 25, we celebrated Christmas at home. My mother and brother joined us. My father refused to come because he was still upset over the way Jay had treated us. Naturally, Dad's decision put a strain on our relationship with him, but in time I knew he would see that we were doing what was best for our family.

We enjoyed a wonderful day. Santa left quite a few presents under our tree and we opened them bright and early that morning. During the day, we shared special food, holiday treats, and a huge Christmas dinner. Maybe we went a little overboard with gift giving, but we were so happy to be together that we lavished presents on everyone.

My greatest joy and gift was to have Jay home.

Jay

What an amazing day. As the designated fix-it man, I assembled enough toys to make me glad Christmas came only once a year. Fortunately, I'd stockpiled batteries to make everything work well enough to satisfy our kids. Even if I was their dad, I had to admit they were a cute bunch. I finally had to take the candy away from them, or they'd never have gotten to sleep that night.

When our guests were gone and our kids were in bed, I turned to Julie and took her in my arms. With her nestled there against my heart, I began imagining what it would be like to share moments like this with her in forty years or so. Still spry and in love, we would have our children, our grandchildren, and even our great-grandchildren all around us at the end of a long and wonderful Christmas Day.

I kissed her forehead and realized she'd fallen asleep. I yawned and snuggled into her warm body.

She was the best Christmas gift of all.

7

Julie: *"I loved the contrast to last year."*

Jay: *"I felt blessed with love."*

Julie

On New Year's Eve, December 31, I splashed water from the Atlantic Ocean onto Jay. He roared in mock anger and chased me down the white sands of a beach in the Bahamas. We wore brightly colored swimsuits and golden tans from the warm sun. While we played, our children dug in the sand as they created an elaborate sandcastle they claimed would rival the best at Disney World.

A year earlier, Jay had told us he was leaving us, and we'd cried tears of anguish. Now we had our family back, and there were no tears anywhere to be found.

Jay

Julie looked beautiful in her bikini. The water glistened on her skin and her blue eyes blazed with energy as her laughter rung in the air.

It was hard to believe that a year ago I'd left my family for a fantasy world. Today, with Julie's love and acceptance, I'd made my way back home.

CHAPTER 11
LOVE TRANSFORMED

> **I**
>
> Julie: *"My old, painful feelings resurfaced."*
>
> Jay: *"I needed to protect my family."*

Jay

I found solace and pleasure in rediscovering my family in ways I had longed to experience during my childhood. Growing up, I had never known love, so I made it up as I went. Anything I didn't know, I invented in my imagination as I conjured up ideas of what I thought love might be. In hopes of becoming normal, I had also memorized entire books about love. The ideas from those books became the sandy soil I based my notion of love on as an adult.

Interestingly, Julie had always loved me in spite of myself. I just hadn't known how to receive her love because I didn't know what love was.

Now was the time for me to wake up, get it right, and stop hiding out as "Dr. Jay" by chasing success through constant achievement. I no longer had the luxury of using my past as an excuse not to grow up. Beneath the effervescent glow of my new courtship with Julie, all was not well inside me. I was torn, even divided in my affections, and confused and broken in my spirit. I was painfully cognizant of the damage I was responsible for and acutely aware of my own wounds that had allowed it.

I felt determined to heal—not because I was supposed to heal for anyone else, but because I had to heal, first for myself and then for Julie and our children. Now was the time for me to break the pattern of using the pain from my past as a valid reason to act out and not evolve as a man. No one but me was standing in my way of reclaiming my core, which I had abandoned through having an affair. The time to step up to the task was now.

Who I was and who I had always expected myself to be were totally incongruent. I knew I was better than the decisions that now defined me. So I committed myself to changing by returning to my clinical roots—with one exception. This time I would focus on becoming a whole person, someone capable of feeling and relating on the basis of what was real and experienced, not simply on the basis of knowledge that allowed me to feel superior, and thus safe and secure.

I understood that my infidelity had nothing to do with sex and everything to do with my inability to let my intimate partner know me fully. Simply put, I couldn't get my needs met in my marriage to Julie because the real me never "showed up" for her to see. So I ended up chasing a fantasy with an affair partner to get my needs met. The fact that my affair partner was even more damaged than I was, created a genuine recipe for disaster.

The ensuing months served as a turning point for me in recapturing my true self and learning how to love Julie as she deserved. I availed myself to various types of help and support because I realized healing and growth could not happen unless I reached beyond myself and became accountable to others. With each experience, an important piece of healing occurred and I was able to reclaim another part of myself.

In speaking to God again, I rediscovered the importance of having of a moral code that *does* make distinctions between right and wrong, as well as the importance of living for something more than just to meet my own needs.

While in therapy, I saw more clearly how growing up in an alcoholic home and being surrounded by mental and emotional abuse, domestic violence, and poverty had paved the way for me to become self-protective instead of vulnerable. Living in such a volatile environment during my formative years had planted seeds within me that influenced me as an adult not only to fear true intimacy but to avoid it all together—despite the fact that I needed it so badly. Because of this underlying fear, anytime I felt a loss of control or power with Julie, I would make up a story about her not being available for me, when in fact, I was the one not available to receive her love.

To accelerate my personal development, I attended the Landmark Forum, a three-day workshop hosted by Landmark Education. During that time, I gained great clarity. I saw that the reasons I'd used for leaving my marriage were not legitimate; I'd invented stories about our problems so that I wouldn't have to hold myself accountable to change. I realized that if I would decide how to react to situations instead of letting situations tell me how to react, anything was possible. Furthermore, I learned that I didn't have to let my circumstances dictate my possibilities to me. I could create possibilities by designing them myself, if I was bold enough to do so.

In Seattle, I met Dr. John Gottman, a therapist who taught me that love is much more than mere knowledge. Love has requirements—requirements that I was both ignorant of and ill prepared to deliver on. The gift he gave me was to help me see that love is *created* when I do certain things consistently and I choose to bring myself to my partner in ways that promote love between us. In other words, I would never find the right person capable of loving me. I had to *become* the right person capable of love. Together, two people make it possible for both to be loved and to get their needs met.

And then there were my encounters with peak-performance coach Tony Robbins. Tony challenged me to see that in many ways I was playing small in life. He helped me to see that I was sacrificing a family legacy as the result of one poor choice. Through brutal compassion, he showed me that I was much more than who I had allowed myself to become—that anytime I decided to, I could break lifelong patterns if I grabbed the right tools. With his defiant, unstoppable spirit, Tony provoked me to raise my standards significantly. He inspired me to be passionate and resolute about taking my life back in the places where I'd let it deteriorate. I'll never forget the moment he looked in my eyes and said, "Jay, it's not what we've done wrong in life that matters; it's what we do with it and who we become as a result of it that determines our destiny."

I knew Tony was right. I made a staunch decision to honor his wisdom.

Now I needed to stop the duplicity of living in two worlds. Lying came way too easily for me. The truths I was discovering required something other than deception. They required a new level of transparency that had never been a part of my life before the affair. Without integrity, life simply would not work. It was time for me to reclaim my character and my core, time to protect Julie and our rediscovered love.

I wrote a letter to Dayanara to change the pattern of lies and begin the necessary process of setting boundaries that up, until now, I had rebelled against.

> *Dear Dayanara,*
>
> *Truth often evolves over time through experience. When we find truth, we must respect what it asks of us. It is time for me to do just that by taking responsibility for the web of deception I created that hurt so many. What I now clearly see is that being friends with you will not work, is wrong, and will cause damage to everyone involved, most importantly Julie.*

An affair creates strong feelings that blind its participants to reality and truth. I have torn my soul apart in an effort to find the truth and do the right thing. Yet in trying to please too many people at once, I've lost myself and the most important things in life. As a result of the requests truth now asks of me, I have come to some clarity about the next steps I must take.

As you know, Dayanara, following our decision months ago to stop pursuing a personal relationship, I've been conflicted about the role I am to play in my relationship with Julie and my children. I have always acknowledged my love for Julie because, despite the many failures in our marriage and my decision to step out of it, the bond we share and my care for her have remained constant. I find this scenario confusing, but it is a truth I cannot deny.

Along the way, I have given you many mixed messages. I have not been candid about my conflicted feelings and have tried to hold onto the illusion of a possibility for us. My actions were selfish and unfair to all involved in our triangle. My behavior perpetuated drama that I will no longer participate in. For the way I have acted, I am truly sorry and deeply regretful. You deserve candor and truth, which I am committed to giving you from my newfound place of clarity.

Triangles don't work. Neither is it possible to live in two worlds simul-taneously, because each world requires something that compromises the other. For months I have said you need to move on and find love with someone who is available and can give to you unconditionally. Despite my inability to meet your needs, I want you to find love, fulfillment, and happiness. I hope that in sharing my truth, I contribute to that journey for you.

As you now know, Dayanara, I have decided to move back home with Julie and our children. There are many reasons for this decision, including all of those I have already shared with you. Here is what else is true for me.

I quit on my marriage and then foreclosed prematurely on any possi-bility of reclaiming it. In so doing, I did not honor the commitment I'd made to work on repairing what was broken. I failed at being responsible for getting my needs met in the marriage and then blamed the marriage for my failure. Not only did I give away my integrity, I also lacked the courage to fight for what I wanted and for what Julie and my children deserved.

I made Julie out as the one responsible for many of the issues I'd actually helped create. Because I concluded that those issues were impossible to repair, I chose not to take any responsibility for them. In the end, I blamed all of our problems on the structure of marriage. I even convinced myself that I would only survive as a man if I left the marriage structure for good. What I didn't see was that the structure was only half of the story, not the entire reason for my marriage's failure. I didn't take into accountability who I was in the story and how my corrosive choices had sabotaged any possibility for the relationship to be salvaged.

I have recently discovered more about what real love means and, in doing so, have realized how little I know about it or understand it. I've come to experience a type of love from Julie that I didn't know existed— a love of unconditional acceptance, a love devoted, loyal, and fierce. No matter how much pain I've caused her through the choices I've made, Julie has met me with love. The grace she has shown me has been totally disarming. Though she has many other more appealing options that she could be pursuing right now, she has chosen to believe in me.

I have never stopped loving Julie. Because of that fact, I owe it to myself, to her, and to our children to explore every possibility of restoring our marriage. I cannot allow myself exits and escapes that will nurture my duplicity and sabotage the integrity of what we may find in a relationship that is free from my stories, illusions, fantasies, and rationalizations.

I belong to my babies and believe they deserve more than what I gave them when I decided to end their family by having an affair. They have a right to be close to me. In the future, I will make every effort to be there for them and not make excuses for myself. I refuse to leave them a legacy of pain, emotional abandonment, and perpetual conflict due to the ravages of a blended family and the void left in my absence. They have a right to emotional health, and I will no longer take that away from them through my selfishness.

I choose to stand with Julie in her fight against cancer and to contribute to her life in ways that will keep her healthy. The demon of cancer is far from dead, and my role in her life can facilitate disease and death, or life and healing. Julie deserves my support, and it is my choice to stand with her.

Legacy matters to me; what my life contributes to others means something to me. How I live this life I've been given and who I am in the living of it means something to me. I do not like who I am when I'm deceitful and disloyal. These qualities are inconsistent with the identity I am destined to live. I want my existence to have purpose and meaning. I want my life to inspire and touch others in meaningful ways. I desire to make a difference in people's lives and to contribute to the wellbeing of children and families everywhere.

As such, I cannot live a duplicitous existence any longer. I will not live in mutually exclusive worlds that require me to compromise who I am and who I am becoming as I fulfill my purpose.

Affairs do not work. They invalidate everything sacred and pure, including the marriages they betray and the new loves they attempt to cultivate. Affairs leave their participants vulnerable, wounded, and unsafe. Affairs annihilate trust, and legacies of armored lives flow forth from their illegitimacy, such that the inherent need for intimacy is indelibly compromised. What is birthed in deception is destined to fail. We can never regain the integrity we compromise when we lie "to sustain the legitimacy" of an affair.

Passion knows no boundaries and can justify all manner of self-indulgence. I have no relationship with integrity, Dayanara. I am a hypocrite masquerading as a pundit: I dispense advice I don't follow and preach a way of living that I myself don't hold to. Frankly, I am disgusted at my character. Yet it is what it is. The most tragic aspect of this saga is the pain I have caused so many precious and innocent souls. I can never repay my debts. All I can do is to throw myself full force into becoming authentic and commit myself from this moment on to being transparent.

I learned long ago that deception was my friend. It was a survival tool that allowed me not to have to rely on others or impose myself on anyone, because it enabled me to take care of myself as I saw fit. Although the use of deception is an entirely selfish and flawed formula, it is one that was ingrained into my psyche from childhood. That is how I came to depend on deception and why it has operated freely in my life without my recognizing it for the cancer it is. I have no excuse for it, only a respect for how destructive it is and an urgency to take responsibility for changing my relationship to it.

Early in my life, in the absence of love, I invented myself as a self-sufficient orb and used deception to justify any manner of self-preservation. The creature I invented was an expression of my own narcissism, which I am only now becoming acquainted with and am repulsed by. My deceptive, egotistical behavior was wrong. It hurt you and others immensely, and I am deeply sorry for the fact I am only now able to see it, own it, and remedy it.

I am truly sorry, Dayanara, for being irresponsible early in our contact by pursuing you when I had no right to. I was and still am unavailable for a legitimate relationship, and that is what you most certainly have a right to. I genuinely regret failing and hurting you. I regret allowing my feelings and confusion to drive my decisions. What I did was wrong. For the pain I have caused you, I am so sorry.

It is time for us to move on in our lives and let go of the fantasies that have kept us connected. I am choosing to reinvest in a relationship with Julie and design a marriage based on truth and integrity. Please respect this decision as we all move forward.

Jay

Julie

After our wonderful holidays, the new year settled in on us and brought reality back into our lives. Jay was with me, but Dayanara pulled at him and tried to lure him away. He knew that his continuing relationship with her could tear us apart.

I admired Jay's letter to Dayanara, for I understood the soul-searching and inner conflict he had wrestled with to gain clarity. I felt relieved that he was finally committing to me and our children, and moving Dayanara out of his life. Yet when he tried to discontinue his relationship with her, she reacted so badly that he agreed to meet her for lunch during his next business trip to Miami. After reading his letter, I felt sure he'd decided to meet with her just to smooth things over. Still, it was extremely painful for me to experience the same old emotions that had plagued me every time I'd known he was with her and not me.

I grew even more concerned about the situation with Dayanara when we began receiving hang-up calls, many of which were in the middle of the night. Naturally, I believed she was behind the harassment. I worried about my children in particular, as I wondered how far she might go with her revenge.

Finally, I sent my one and only communication to Dayanara, an email in which I was gracious but firm with this woman who so badly wanted to take my husband from his family.

January 20

Dear Dayanara,

   I have several things to say to you, and I feel it is best to put it in writing. I also want you to know Jay has read this letter and is completely aware that I am sending it.

   Your actions have hurt me more than words can possibly express. But more importantly, they have hurt my three precious and innocent children. They are the true victims here, and the burden you will have to carry is knowing that you played a significant role in the breakup of their family. Even so, I am sure that you must have some redeeming qualities, or Jay would not have invested so much time and energy in you. Who knows, under different circumstances, perhaps we could have been friends.

   I am fully aware of what an astonishing man Jay is. I knew this from the moment I met him. We had a deep connection from the start and a precious beginning. I know him better than anyone, as I have lived with him the last twelve years and created a family with him. I have been by his side in every step of his many journeys, including the divorce, and have loved him unconditionally in spite of the intense pain he has caused me. No other woman will ever be able to love him as I have, and he knows that. I have had many experiences with him that are all over the continuum—from his intense love for me to the loss of his presence in our home during his affair with you.

   There is one thing I have never doubted: our deep love for one another, which is a bond that can never be broken. God knows that both of you tried to create such a bond, yet it did not work. The fantasy you two created did not remotely withstand reality. Had you two stayed together long term, you would have never felt secure in the relationship, for you could have never been the only woman he loved. He would have always carried a part of me and his passion for me, which would have been truly unfair to you and kept him living duplicitously.

   Jay would never have completely turned his back on me. And the fact that my children despised you for your involvement in the breakdown of their family would have made peace between you and Jay impossible. Thank God that Jay saw his mistakes and became interested in changing our relationship into something new, deeper, and more mature than ever. I always knew that Jay would eventually come back to me, and I never closed the door to that possibility.

I know that during our process of reconciliation you have not always had forthcoming information from Jay and probably only learned of much of this today when he emailed you his closure letter. Understand that this is because Jay does not want to hurt you. He knows becoming involved with you was wrong on many levels, and because he feels badly about that, he has been slowly exiting. Our process began almost seven months ago and has been steady, deliberate, and balanced. It culminated with our moving in together as a couple and putting my house on the market to buy a new one together again. You knew about our vacation to Disney World as a family but probably do not know that, together, Jay and I have attended marriage enrichment workshops, celebrated many special holidays, recently vacationed in the Bahamas, and even revisited our honeymoon cabin in Arkansas.

Dayanara, Jay is moving on. I am finally healthy, strong, cancer free, and doing great. We are talking about renewing our vows and vacating our divorce so that it will be as if it never happened. We have a brilliant future ahead. And you have a bright future, too. There is a plan for you and someone very special for you—but it is not my husband. It is essential for you to know these things so that you can move on and create something better for yourself. You deserve to be happy. I do not tell you these details to hurt you; I only tell them to you to give you the clarity you may need to be able to move on and forgive yourself for being involved in such a mess.

Jay and I plan to use these experiences and our growth in this journey to help others in powerful ways in the future. What a profound story of love and triumph to inspire other marriages that have fallen victim to the same societal pressures Jay and I fell prey to. We believe that this is one way we can make positive change in the world together. For your contribution to this process, I thank you.

I know this journey is wounding for you. You have been lied to just as I was. Yes, the whole thing was cruel, and in hindsight, Jay knows it should never have happened. He was confused and was working too much, and we had "missed" each other in many ways (though nothing in our marriage was beyond repair). But Jay did not hurt anyone intentionally. I know this as the woman he has loved for twelve years. He did not hurt our babies or me on purpose, and I know he did not mean to hurt you either. Consider the opposite: that he had good intentions, saw your vulnerabilities, and wanted to help you; that he made positive contributions to your life that you would not have otherwise experienced.

I know you are in pain. Trust me, I understand it. Just imagine for a moment how it felt for my children and me when Jay left after ten years to pursue his fantasy with you. You are not the only one who has suffered; I fought cancer alone and was a single mother to three small children while Jay was finding himself. This mistake has produced many casualties. Affairs never work. Relationships based on deception and splitting the soul are always destructive.

I know Jay has told you that we are being harassed in our home by phone, email, and now US mail. I have filed police reports in several cities and have rehired my detective and will be meeting with him tonight in Miami. I will not tolerate this behavior from anyone toward me, Jay, or our children. Certainly, I am not accusing you. I have not yet been given back the subpoenas that will lead us directly to the perpetrator. I am merely asking that if you know anything about this harassment— who, where, or how—that you ask for it to cease immediately. Whoever is responsible will be held accountable.

I also want you to know that I am aware that you met Jay in a night-club, not a boardroom. I knew this when I hired a detective in Miami to follow you and Jay, independently and as a couple. My PI did a back-ground check that quickly revealed your true profession. I needed this information so that the courts would not allow Jay to bring my children near you.

There is nothing you can tell me which will surprise me. I love Jay, and we are working through these issues together.

Dayanara, I pray that you will be able to stay strong during this difficult time. I wish you only the best for your future and your health. And I want to thank you. Thank you for contributing to the single most impacting event in my life. Though it was a source of pain, it was a great teacher. I learned much about myself and about my relationship with my husband. I am aware that the lessons we learned this past year are enabling Jay and me to have the incredible relationship we desire and will help us inspire other couples.

May your life be filled with many blessings,
Julie

Jay

In an attempt to normalize a business relationship with Dayanara, I included her in a one-day workshop in Miami. But that event did little to placate her. I'd brought a lot to her life, and she didn't want to lose it. Nevertheless, I wasn't going to let her ruin what I was building with Julie and our children. I hoped I could get Dayanara to accept our new relationship with a minimum amount of drama.

As for Julie, her letter to Dayanara further revealed the amazing person she is. Her grace, dignity, strength, and forbearance in the face of all that I had put her through, were an inspiration to me. I felt humbled when I compared her loving spirit with my own frayed character. At the same time, I was full of guilt over the pain I had inflicted on her.

Despite the certainty of my love for Julie, I was still unclear as to how to end all contact with Dayanara. I justified my business relationship with her because I feared that making her angry might elicit retaliation that could spill over into the workplace and harm our connection with our clients. As I had learned, affairs have consequences, many of which cannot be controlled, only endured.

In the meantime, I continued to move forward with Julie, as the fog of infidelity slowly began to lift.

2

Julie: *"We celebrated another wonderful milestone."*

Jay: *"In Vegas, nothing shone as brightly as Julie."*

Julie

On my birthday, January 27, Jay took me to Las Vegas to make up for not being with me the year before. In the Planet Hollywood, Jay gently took my hand.

"Julie, a thousand apologies will never make up for what I did last year on your birthday. Please accept this as a small token of my love and loyalty." He held out a small gold box.

I opened the box to find a ring with three dazzling diamonds.

"I chose a three-stone ring to represent my love for you in the past, present, and future. Julie, I want you always in my life. Please forgive me."

"Oh, Jay, it's precious."

He took the box and carefully lifted the ring from its velvet nest. I held out my hand, and he slipped the ring onto the third finger of my right hand, almost reverently.

"I love you, for now and always," he said. "Do you forgive me?"

"Yes, I do. But more importantly, do you forgive yourself?"

"I'm working on it."

"Work harder."

He smiled. "You make everything easier."

"Good." I tucked my hand in the crook of his arm. "Now let's go see just how lucky we can be."

"With us working together, the sky's the limit."

Jay

I gave Julie a three-stone ring as a small token, yet enduring symbol of how much I loved her. She was my past, my present, and my future, just as the ring represented. I wanted her to have the best birthday ever, and Vegas was the perfect place to make amends for the intense pain I had caused her just one year before. Objects could not make up for what I had chosen to do, and there was a lot of healing ahead of us, but I had to start somewhere.

Together, we set out to paint the town red and create wonderful new memories.

Julie

Our week in Vegas for my birthday and the Miss America pageant was marred by only one terrible thing. We got tons of anonymous hang-up calls, all day and all night. The calls weren't just annoying; they were nerve-wracking. Because I believed Dayanara was behind them, I hoped Jay would end his friendship with her soon.

I did my best to put her out of mind during my special week. I didn't want to worry about her and neither did Jay. But the relentless calls and constant hang-ups kept her in the shadows of my thoughts all week long.

Jay

If Dayanara was behind the irritating hang-ups, the behavior was childish and beneath her. Then again, I'd experienced the brunt of her fury more than once, so I knew she was capable of almost anything. If she was mad enough at me, she might go back to her old ways just to try to hurt me. On impulse, I checked for her photograph on an escort board that was soliciting business. I was shocked to find her photo.

I thought about firing her because of the business risk, but I decided not to hurt her further. Instead, I called her and explained my concern. She said it was all a silly mistake, and her photo quickly disappeared. After I told Julie about the situation, she checked other boards and found Dayanara's photo in other places. Once more, I called Dayanara to explain my worry about the reputation of my business, but she claimed it was all old information.

Even though Dayanara intruded into our week, Julie and I still had a great time. I could tell she was happy, and that made me happy, too.

I was learning what love actually means and finding fulfillment that only true love can offer—all because of this intimate stranger named Julie whom I was coming to know in ways I never had in over ten years of marriage.

3

Julie: *"I worried for my children."*

Jay: *"I was determined to keep my family safe."*

Julie

On February 8, we attended one of many couple's workshops on what would become our long road to recovery. We both did healing work. We were drawing closer all the time, and I couldn't have been happier. It was a powerful weekend for us, one I hoped would result in Jay finally ending his relationship with Dayanara.

Unfortunately, the harassment continued. Someone named Lisa, supposedly a friend of Dayanara's, called our home to tell me intimate things about Jay and Dayanara. During the call, Lisa even threatened my children. Finally, she told me to leave Jay alone. I told her never to call me again.

As I tried to figure out where the calls were coming from, I discovered that the caller was using an untraceable international calling card. Angry and afraid, I contacted the police about the harassment. Though they said there wasn't much they could do in a case like ours, I stayed in contact with the police detective anyway.

Jay

I fought alongside Julie to get our marriage back. With each new workshop and therapy session, we continued designing our relationship. At times the pain of looking at myself and my choices was overwhelming. We'd both made mistakes in "missing" one another, taking each other for granted, and allowing our connection to die—but only one of us had chosen to have an affair. That burden was mine. Even so, I wanted Julie to recognize how I'd been hurt by certain choices she had made in our marriage that had left me vulnerable to making such a painful choice. During one of our therapy sessions, she gave me a letter.

> *My precious Jay,*
>
> *I was wrong when I withdrew from you, neglected you, judged you, held on to anger and resentment toward you, pressured you to work harder and provide more for our family, didn't take care of myself and became unattractive to you, made you feel unimportant to me and like a success object, placed the children before you, and violated you by invading your privacy.*
>
> *I know these issues must have made you feel angry, hurt, and unimportant. Will you please forgive me?*
>
> *Love,*
> *Julie*

Julie's letter touched me profoundly. Her willingness to accept responsibility for how she had contributed to hurting me inspired me to make a deeper commitment to be accountable to her for my many failings.

We were well on our way to healing as we worked hard to create a new marriage and life together. However, the drama with Dayanara never stopped. Despite my efforts with Julie to move on with our lives, at every turn I was confronted with the consequences of my affair.

After Julie received threatening calls and someone hacked into our email accounts, I called Dayanara to ask her about the harassment. She got angry and denied any involvement. She went on to explain that she was being harassed, too. Supposedly, someone had broken into her apartment and spray-painted the names Jay and Julie on her walls. She claimed that even her parents had received harassing calls having to do with Julie and me. She blamed Julie for all her trouble.

When I asked for her father's phone number so that I could call him and verify her statements, she wouldn't give it to me. Naturally, I could only assume she was lying.

During the course of our conversation, Dayanara's anger increased to the point that she was crying and screaming. I tried to calm her down but couldn't. Finally, we reached an impasse. I told her that as long as she lied, I couldn't help her and that if she continued to endanger my family, I would have to cut her entirely out of my life, including my business.

I hoped after our conversation that she would come to her senses so that we could maintain a friendship as I transitioned out of our partnership.

4

Julie: *"I received the perfect gift."*

Jay: *"I wanted to give everything."*

Julie

The day before Valentine's Day, I arrived home to find Jay, my brother, and all three children in the living room. Jay looked secretly pleased with himself.

"Julie, come here," he said.

Smiling at him because he looked so mischievous, I set my purse down and walked over to him. "What's going on?" I asked.

"Stand over there near the window in the sunlight," Jay told me.

"Okay." I followed his instructions and felt the soft light warm me.

When Jay walked over to me and bent down on one knee, all I could do was watch him in astonishment. He reached for my left hand, placed a soft kiss on the palm, and then looked up at me as he pulled a small box out of his pocket. He snapped the box open.

"Oh, Jay!" I exclaimed as I stared in amazement at the most beautiful engagement ring I'd ever seen.

"Julie, I love you more than life itself," he said. "Will you marry me and wear this ring?"

"Yes!" I cried. Tears filled my eyes. I threw my arms around his neck and hugged him as if I'd never let go. I felt him place gentle kisses on my face. Finally, I stepped back. "I'm the happiest woman in the world," I said.

He stood up. "And I'm the happiest man."

I took off the eternity ring that I'd worn since he'd given it to me on our last anniversary and put it on my right hand. As I held out my left hand, Jay slipped the engagement ring onto my third finger. The diamond sparkled in the sunlight.

"Perfect," Jay said.

"Thank you," I whispered. I felt so grateful, not just to Jay, but to my children, my family, and the whole world itself. My constant love had been rewarded.

Before I was able to say anything else, Jay continued. "Julie, some of our happiest moments have been spent at Disney World. Why don't we celebrate our wedding there with the kids?" he asked.

"Wonderful idea! Yes, let's do."

"I don't want to wait long."

"Let's start making plans."

I heard applause and looked around at my brother and children. Big smiles creased their faces. I held out my arms, they rushed to me, and I was enveloped in their love.

Jay

When Julie accepted my proposal of marriage the second time around, I felt that my life had come full circle, and I experienced a sense of fulfillment I'd never known before. I believed we were finally at a place where we could move forward together and create a new world of love and hope. I'd learned enough to appreciate her great gifts to me, so I determined I would spend the rest of my life contributing to her happiness as I grew to become a man capable of truly loving her.

Julie

As we moved through March, we planned our Disney wedding but kept the plans a secret so that nothing could get in the way of our happiness. Nevertheless, a black cloud named Dayanara continued to hover over us.

While Jay and I were in Dallas buying a wedding band for him, Dayanara called him. I listened in as she ranted about how someone had slashed her tires and was trying to kill her. After we returned home, she texted him to say that she knew about his wedding plans, including the fact that he would be married before the first of April.

I felt chilled by Dayanara's text. I'd been emailing the wedding coordinator with the information, but she was the only one who knew about our plans. Dayanara could only have found out if she or someone she knew had hacked into my email account.

I asked Jay to get her out of our lives.

Jay

I called Dayanara and confronted her about hacking into Julie's email. Of course, she denied it, but then she escalated the harassment by saying something that shocked me. I couldn't believe she'd go so far. I hung up.

I knew I needed to tell Julie what Dayanara had said, but I didn't want to reveal this new twist in Dayanara's warped mind. Still, I was committed to being truthful, so I asked Julie to join me in the living room.

"What is it?" she asked.

"I just talked with Dayanara."

"What now?"

"Brace yourself." I took a deep breath. "She says she's pregnant with my baby."

"Oh no!" Julie sat down on the sofa and buried her face in her hands.

"It's not true." I sat down beside her and stroked her back to comfort her.

"How can you know? What if it is?" She sat up. "I can't deal with that woman being involved in our lives for the next eighteen years. The thought of it makes me sick to my stomach."

"It's not true. It's not possible. I swear it."

"Just when I thought we were finally getting her out of our lives." Julie stood up and paced back and forth.

"It can't be true," I assured her.

"But, Jay, what if it is even remotely true?"

"Please trust me. It's not."

"Oh, Jay."

Willing her to believe me and trying to relieve her anxiety, I stood up and took Julie in my arms. When she put her arms around me, I knew we would be all right.

The situation with Dayanara couldn't continue. Something had to give. I emailed her, requesting that she not contact me again except for business. She ignored my request. Once more, she upped the harassment. She insisted that she was now engaged and wanted me to come to her wedding. Also, she said she was being cyber-stalked and that the FBI would soon be arresting Julie and me for identity theft.

Dayanara's threats had become too outrageous, too unbelievable to be true. They escalated in intensity each time I didn't run to her rescue. It was obvious she was bent on revenge and was constantly harassing us so that we couldn't enjoy our lives.

Julie had finally had enough, and she insisted that I break all ties with Dayanara. I'd had enough, too, so I wrote Dayanara a letter. In the letter, I asked her to cease all contact with me except as it related to finishing our existing contract. I told her that if she made further contact, we would consider it harassment and would take whatever legal steps were necessary to protect ourselves. Julie went with me to send the letter by overnight mail with a delivery signature and confirmation. Dayanara received it on March 18, at 10:29 a.m.

We believed that Dayanara was finally out of our personal lives.

CHAPTER 12
LIFE LIVED IN LOVE

I

Julie: *"We enjoyed the most wonderful wedding imaginable."*

Jay: *"I renewed my vows with love and hope."*

Julie

On March 30, Jay, Jayde, Zoe, Chandler, and I flew from Tulsa to Orlando, Florida. Entering Disney World felt like coming home. While we realized it had taken more than Cinderella's Castle to make magic happen in our lives, Jay and I had reconnected there at Disney with our children around us. So the park held special meaning for us, and it was no small thing for us to be there again on such an important day. We were more than ready to reunite our lives with second-marriage vows.

Our children's excitement had inspired us to go all out with a Disney Escape wedding package. I wore a short white dress with a beaded neckline and had on white T-strap high heels. I carried a pink rose bouquet. Our daughters wore white dresses with pink sashes and had pink rose garlands in their hair. Jay and Chandler wore black tuxedos with pink rose boutonnieres. The five of us rode in Cinderella's crystal coach drawn by six white horses. A driver and two footmen in full regalia completed the experience. (Go to **www.drjayandjulie.com** to see our wedding ceremony.)

Jay and I held hands as we traveled in style through the fantasy world of Disney. I could hardly believe I was there with my beloved family, ready to be reunited. It proved to me that dreams can come true if someone is willing to do what it takes to make them real.

We arrived at Disney's Wedding Gazebo, set on a tranquil lake in the shadow of the Magic Kingdom. Inside, my brother and Jay's brother were there to meet us. As the ceremony began, our children walked down the aisle of the beautiful chapel with white walls and green-and-rose carpet. Our daughters went first, each carrying a white basket of rose petals, and Chandler followed, holding a plump pillow bearing our wedding rings. Jay and I went last and joined them at the front of the room. The five of us stood together in diffused sunlight that streamed in through tall windows overlooking the water. A minister smiled kindly at us from his position in front of a long table with an elegant floral arrangement of pink roses.

As Jay and I spoke the words that reunited us, I felt as if the magic of Disney swirled around us, healing, bonding, and sanctifying us. The long months of recovery had paid off, and the ceremony served as a momentous symbol of the hard work we had endured together.

Afterward, our brothers and our children joined us at a table with an elegant two-tiered, white wedding cake with a Mickey & Minnie Mouse keepsake topper. We cut the cake and each had a piece of the delicious confection. Jay opened the bottle of Fairy Tale Cuvee for our toast. Our brothers wished us happiness, and then we drank from long-stemmed crystal glasses.

No other family members chose to attend. It was a sad testimony to the pain and damage the affair had caused and to the consequences that might never be undone.

Nonetheless, Jay raised his glass and smiled. "Julie, I love you, now and forever."

Happiness bubbled up in me like our fine champagne as tears of happiness filled my eyes. "I love you, too," I replied. "This is forever."

I turned to my children and pulled my darlings close. "Dad and I aren't the only ones getting married today. We're all rejoining as a family," I told them.

"That's exactly right," Jay said. "I'm making my commitment to love, honor, and protect Julie *and* Jayde, Zoe, and Chandler for the rest of my life."

"We'll always be together," I added. I wanted my children to understand that their father would never move away from them again.

"I'll be working from home," Jay said, "so I'll be there for all your events."

"Thanks, Dad," Chandler said. "Now can we go on our Disney cruise?"

We all laughed. We could trust Chandler to get to what was most important. To him, our family was a given fact. Now he wanted us all to play together.

I wanted the same thing. From that moment on, the serious occasion was over. We set out to make the most of our honeymoon, just the five of us.

For our honeymoon, we took our children on a Disney cruise to the Bahamas. What an amazing, magical trip. We admired the wonders of the aqua ocean, the sandy beaches, and the luxurious ship. We relaxed in the comfort around us as we swam, sunbathed, and played games in the soft tropical breezes. Stress and worry fell away. We enjoyed just being together and exploring new possibilities while getting to know each other as a reunited family.

By the end of the week, I had no doubt that love does conquer all.

Jay

On my wedding day, I felt proud yet humble. I was well aware that, had it not been for the grace of one loving woman and a faithful God, I would be in a very different place. I'd made mistakes, but I'd learned from them. I'd resolved to continue learning too, not only to help myself but to help others.

I began to think that perhaps a larger purpose was playing itself out, that maybe there was an important story here, one through which others who were struggling with similar challenges might find inspiration and hope.

On March 31, the day of our second wedding, I wrote a letter to explain to Julie how much she meant to me and how much her love gave to me.

My Love,

It is the day of our wedding, the second one, and what I am witness to is the magnificence of who you are, Julie—a woman so graceful, so strong, and so unstoppable, as demonstrated in your tenacious love for me. Despite my failing you so profoundly, you have embraced me and forgiven me by giving me the opportunity for a new life with you as only a true warrior can do.

Today, I thank you, my dear, for "second chances," so undeserved yet so savored. I want you to know that I will work the rest of my days to earn your trust and respect. I commit to evolving and becoming the person you need so that I may have the privilege of loving you as you deserve to be loved by a man. As we embark on this our second life, I make this commitment both for today and for our lifetime together.

Today and every day in the future that I am blessed to be by your side, I commit to being a wise steward of the gift you chose to give me by honoring me with the privilege to love you again.

I commit to being a man worthy of you, who can contribute to you as you have so generously contributed to me.

I commit to finding joy in simplicity and laughter in the paradox that real relationships are, by playing with you and extracting the marrow from the wondrous possibility that life is.

I am determined to evolve and to take the wounds that life gave me and use them to be better, bigger, and bolder in loving you more completely.

I intend to create the conditions for us to exist as soul mates as we invent ourselves to be who we must for the magic to thrive.

I commit to being your friend, your lover, your protector, your defender, your spouse, and your partner in the gift this life is, and I invite you to lean into my being and let me hold you and keep you warm at night and nurture your soul as I embrace yours.

I commit to being transparent, authentic, and present for you each moment we are together.

I intend to live from a place of integrity so that there will never be a need to deny anything. I say this in hopes of relieving you of ever having to wonder.

I am your greatest fan, and I support you in you becoming all you are intended to become. I believe that, together, we can transform our pain into hope and possibility for others.

I love you, Julie. Thank you from the bottom of my heart for second chances to love, live, and laugh together again, both today and for an eternity.

Your husband,
Jay

2

Julie: *"The past caught up with us."*
Jay: *"Fantasy crashed into reality."*

Julie
On April 8, Jay and I wore our bride and groom Mickey Mouse ears as we exited the Disney cruise ship. We held hands like the newlyweds we were. Our

children laughed at us, and we joined in their amusement. We couldn't have been happier. Humor felt so good after so much pain. Disney magic sparkled all around us.

We walked to customs and waited to reenter the United States. When our turn came, Jay walked to the counter first. He tossed a smile back at me as he handed the agent his passport. Meanwhile, I reached up to adjust my mouse ears. *I'm wearing these all the way home,* I determined as scenes from our wonderful time at Disney flashed through my mind.

Just then, I heard the customs officer ask Jay if he lived in Miami. My hand froze on the mouse ears. I felt as if they had instantly turned from magic to plastic.

What had Dayanara done now?

Jay

As we left the cruise ship, I watched my children with pride. They now reacted to life with giddy laughter and a light-heartedness that was appropriate for their ages. I knew their joy proved the comfort and security they felt after the near destruction of our family. I could tell by their bright faces that those dark days were behind us.

I handed my passport to the customs official, and then felt a jolt of adrenaline when he asked me about Miami. I glanced back at Julie. No words were necessary. Dayanara again. I felt as if my future happiness hung on the next few moments. I knew Julie must be feeling the same. Our children moved closer to her.

Government officials led my family into a questioning area. Julie and our kids watched while I was interrogated with a barrage of accusations and questions. I did my best to answer calmly and succinctly, but inwardly, I felt as bewildered as my wife and children appeared to be. Dayanara had struck again. I didn't need to hear her name to recognize her pattern.

When all was said and done, I discovered I'd been officially declared a fugitive. Accused of a crime I didn't know about and certainly didn't commit, I felt powerless—and even more so when the officials said I would need an attorney before I could learn any details about the accusation.

Despair quickly engulfed my optimism of moments before. Was there no way I could ever move beyond past demons? Were the many months I'd invested in healing my mistakes worth it? I'd been through therapy, attended workshops, made amends, and created new memories—all in an attempt to restore my frayed integrity. Was I doomed to failure despite these efforts? Dazed and disillusioned, I struggled to remain strong for my family.

When the officials said I was free to go, we caught our flight and headed home. Needless to say, my thoughts had turned from Julie to Dayanara. I marveled at the human capacity to harm not only self but others. Dayanara had finally pushed me too far. Dead was any fantasy of a civil future between us. Gone was the possibility of a strictly business partnership. Absent were my unconditional support and knight-on-a-white-horse rescue missions for her. She could forget about receiving any more high-level earnings from our businesses. I felt a sense of satisfaction in knowing that she'd never be able to replace what I'd brought to her life. But maybe the money was what she'd always cared about anyway. Not me.

This last bit of drama had finally made me wake up to who Dayanara was, what she was actually capable of, and how to end the affair.

Julie

I gathered my strength for our next battle with Dayanara. I knew without a doubt that, just as with any affair, this one would carry consequences. Once Pandora's box is opened, events and emotions can't be controlled, handled, or stuffed back inside.

I felt scared, hurt, and angry as I wondered whether the results of Jay's affair would ever end. More time, energy, and money would have to be spent on Dayanara. I could hardly stand the idea. Yet I wouldn't let my husband go through this alone.

When we got home, I called the PI in Miami that I'd hired before. He put us in touch with an attorney to help with this new problem.

We learned that the Miami police had issued a warrant for Jay's arrest for "threats against a person or property," which meant a domestic violence complaint. If Jay set foot in Miami, he'd go to jail.

The complaint didn't make sense. I'd never known Jay to be violent. He was a psychologist, a kind, caring individual. I could only conclude that Dayanara was determined to make Jay pay for rejecting her. But she was also making three innocent children pay.

Once more, I vowed to protect my family.

Jay

I quickly learned from my attorney that I had no options. If I wanted to clear my name and do business in Miami, I had to go there and turn myself in to the police. Turning myself in also meant being treated as if I were guilty, which, due to the way domestic violence laws are written, included being booked and processed, and spending time in a jail cell. Somehow, Dayanara had made sure I would suffer—and that meant Julie and my kids would suffer, too. This was my final wake up call. Not only did I recognize the mess I'd caused through my infidelity, I also realized the truth about Dayanara. She was dangerous and sick, and would stop at nothing to secure her revenge by delivering whatever final parting blows she could.

When I chose to enter my affair, I knew there would be consequences. What I didn't know was how severe those consequences would be and how little control I would have over their impact—and certainly, not once did I ever imagine they would involve my going to jail.

3

Julie: *"We had to be brave for our children."*

Jay: *"I knew I was innocent."*

Julie

On April 24, at seven in the evening, Jay and I went to a Miami police station. The moment didn't seem real. Yet we had to deal with Dayanara's latest manipulation.

Jay was full of rage over the situation, but he went to jail with his head held high. He knew he'd done nothing bad to Dayanara. He'd been good to her. He'd given her a job she wasn't qualified for that paid her much more than she ever could've earned on her own. He'd helped to rescue her and further her education. Her life was so much better since he'd been a part of it. Perhaps that was why she wouldn't let go or give up.

I wondered if we'd ever be done with her revenge.

Jay

As I stepped into the Miami police station, the moment felt surreal. I was about to surrender my freedom in order to clear my name.

Earlier in the day, Julie and I had concluded meetings in which we had led over 150 executives from around the country in a two-day leadership forum. We had spoken, coached, and trained people. We had received standing ovations. Many executives had asked me to sign my self-help book. Others had requested more speaking dates on a range of other topics. We'd been wined and dined at the best of restaurants by one CEO and her senior executive team.

Unfortunately, none of those meetings had any bearing whatsoever on my current predicament. I straightened my shoulders in my power suit and glanced over at my attorney. Of course, I had hired the best. I hoped he would make a difference.

As the law stands, a person need only file a report and claim that a crime has occurred for someone to be charged with that crime.

My attorney and I had figured out the truth about my case. Moments after Dayanara had signed for my certified letter (which had put her on notice and officially cut off all contact with me unless it related to business), she called a former police officer boyfriend. Three hours later, a police report outlining my alleged crimes against her was filed on her behalf. Due to the fact that we had been in a relationship, she could file the complaint under domestic violence. She even claimed that I had threatened to hurt her and to send other people after her to hurt her and to damage her property.

Anyone accused of a domestic violence offense must go to jail for at least one night whether he is guilty or not. That meant I was going to spend a night in jail, thanks to Dayanara.

Julie held tightly to my arm as we walked with my attorney to a thick bullet-proof window.

My attorney nodded at the officer behind the window. "I have Dr. Jay Ferraro here with me, whom I'm representing as his attorney. You have a warrant for his arrest, and he is voluntarily surrendering."

The officer appeared surprised. "What did you say?"

My attorney repeated his words.

"I'm here voluntarily to clear my name," I added. Yet it wasn't voluntary. Dayanara had taken advantage of a system designed primarily to help abused women.

The officer nodded, and then he walked around through the metal detectors. "Dr. Ferraro, please step forward."

I did as he said.

"Please remove your belt and jacket, and put your hands behind your back."

Again, I did as he said.

He snapped stiff handcuffs into place.

With the cuffs around my wrists, I felt trapped. All the same, I glanced over at Julie and mouthed the words, "Don't worry."

Tears slipped from her eyes. "I love you," she whispered.

I tried to give her a comforting smile, and then I was led away.

Julie

Jay's attorney held my arm as he led me away from the jail. I was trembling so badly, I could hardly stand up. My heart was almost broken at the idea of leaving Jay in that horrid place. What would he eat? Where would he sleep? Would he be hurt? The attorney tried to console me, but his words made me cry all the more.

Afterward, as I was checking into a nearby hotel, I grew angry when I considered my luxurious surroundings in contrast to the harsh environment Jay was experiencing in jail. The situation seemed so unfair. Nevertheless, I knew I had to be strong for my husband, so I resolved to make it through the ordeal.

I finalized plans to meet Jay's attorney the next day and go to court at noon. I hoped the judge would allow Jay out on bail. I had a wallet full of cash to rescue him with if that possibility arose. Whatever the case, once I had Jay back in my arms, we'd hurry home to our children.

Jay

Two officers escorted me to a booking area. Using my best clinical skills, I quickly developed a rapport with them. They invited me to watch the hockey game during their questioning session.

"Let me guess," one officer said after reading my report, "an old girlfriend with an axe to grind?"

"Have you seen this a time or two?" I asked.

He nodded, obviously sympathetic.

The other officer glanced at my report. "Too bad he can't be bonded out tonight. It's a domestic."

The officers allowed me extra time to sit and watch the game. I realized they were showing mercy. They even called and tried to get me a special cell, but the place was too crowded. Eventually, my hour of reprieve was over.

"Thanks for the help," I said.

"Good luck and keep your spirits up," one of the officers said as he turned me over to the jail guards.

The jail intake area was a different universe from the booking area. Everything was rougher, louder, and more aggressive. The guards were armed with mace and .45 Glocks.

"Welcome to hell, gentleman," one of the guards said to the men being held. "If you mess with us, you will be hurt and no one will listen to your complaints. I suggest you do exactly what we tell you."

The power play was on.

I was shoved into a cell and instructed to strip down. Over the course of an hour, I had to swallow my humiliation as I was ordered to stand, sit, face the wall, and spread my toes while officers used electric probes to check for contraband. The sound of jeers, threats, and abusive comments from the jailers invaded any sense of calm I had. I felt victimized and wanted to lash out in self-defense. But I held my temper, controlled my fear, and put on my game face as I went through the process of entering the felon population.

About nine thirty that evening, the intake ordeal was over. I was escorted along with about a dozen other men to the actual jail cell blocks. My clean, corporate appearance a sharp contrast to the other felons' gang regalia of tattoos and baggy clothes, I stood out like a sore thumb. Inmates hollered derogatory words at me.

I had once been a member of a New York street gang. For the first time ever, I was thankful for that childhood I'd left behind at seventeen. Now was not the time to be the intuitive shrink who had served me well in the boardroom and with the intake officers. Now was the time to draw on a different archetype, the bold Yankee jock. Old instincts kicked into gear. I manned-up and eye-balled the guys.

I arrived at my new home—dark, dingy, and filled with inmates screaming obscenities as they banged on their metal doors for attention. The guard escorting me announced my arrival through a handheld radio attached to his uniform. A huge cell door slowly slid open.

I caught the strong stench of urine and feces as I was thrust into the cell. The room was cinderblock and concrete with no windows except for the scratched Plexiglas rectangle on the steel door that shut behind me.

I felt trapped. My panic spiked. I instinctively grabbed the door to test its strength. When it didn't budge, I took stock of my surroundings and saw I'd hardly be able to take a step without bumping into my cellmate or the broken, reeking toilet. The walls seemed to close in as the other guy in my cell focused on me.

Only one language is spoken on the street: respect. Nothing else is understood or obeyed. I had spoken that dialect as my childhood language. Though I thought I'd left it far behind, I knew I needed it now. I had to face down my cellmate and do it fast. He was a muscular gangbanger who didn't fear or respect what he saw as a corporate yuppie.

He stepped forward and bumped his chest against mine, a male ritual I knew only too well. I almost wished for an original move, something to show that street gangs had improved or guys had gotten smarter since my youth. At any rate, with my past martial arts experience I knew I could gain his respect.

I gave a sharp thrust with my right hand to the guy's windpipe and then grabbed his esophagus and squeezed out his breath. When he tried a thrust to my ribs with his right hand, I got hold of his wrist and twisted hard.

Up close, I stared him down. "If you mess with me, I'll rip your throat out. Do we understand each other?"

He nodded.

I eased my grip on his throat.

"We're...cool, man. We're...cool...," he said as he gasped and choked on his words.

I let him go. No need for anything else. We'd reached an understanding. He lay down on the bottom bunk. I took the top one.

A few hours later, guards moved my cellmate elsewhere and left me alone with my blanket and my Bible. Time was hard to judge. It passed slowly. I didn't try to sleep. I tried to meditate, read psalms, and move about some in the small cell. Nothing much helped. For seventeen hours I went without food, help, or communication.

Around five in the morning, I learned that I'd be among the last to leave. The felons and serious criminals were rallied first thing that morning. The DVs would be left awhile longer.

At one in the afternoon, my cell door opened. My time had come to see the judge and get out. I was hungry enough to eat jail food, if there'd been any. Handcuffed, I was led to a waiting room and left with other DVs to wait our turn.

Finally, I entered the courtroom. I saw Julie. She sat calmly and defiantly, with the grace of an angel and the class of a queen. She smiled, and her love for me shone in her beautiful blue eyes. I hadn't committed a crime, but I had chosen to commit an affair. For me, she was enduring this sad drama. For me, she was fighting the system. For me, her love had never wavered.

I was surprised yet again by such love.

I was called first. I walked to the podium with one thought in my head: *This is the high price of infidelity.* As I stood before the judge, he informed me that, to be released, I must agree to a page of civil rights restrictions, from no alcohol and no firearms to a full protective order, among others. Then Dayanara would receive her victim status and I would gain my freedom.

Of course, I agreed to the court's terms. I wasn't released at that point, however, because the bonding process would take several more hours to complete. I was sent back to my jail cell to wait.

Hours passed as I stewed in my noisy, smelly cage. But the moment finally came when I was truly free.

Julie welcomed me with open arms and a waiting limo. We headed straight for the airport and left the jail and its horror far behind us.

4

Julie: *"I wanted to win."*

Jay: *"I wanted my day in court."*

Julie

On July 2, Jay and I went back to Miami for his court date. I wanted to confront Dayanara. I wanted to disprove her lies. I wanted to watch her face when she realized all she had lost.

In the courtroom, Jay and I stood side by side, more in love, more committed, more a family than ever before. We waited for our moment of truth.

But Dayanara didn't come to court. Maybe she felt satisfied in her revenge. Maybe she didn't want to face Jay in person. Maybe she'd moved on in her life. It didn't matter.

Jay and I had won. Our love had survived infidelity.

Jay

Dayanara didn't show. I felt disappointed. I wanted her to see that nothing she'd done had tarnished my love for Julie or broken my family. I could only assume that Dayanara knew she couldn't win, and she'd gotten her revenge by putting me in jail for a night.

What she didn't realize was that I'd learned something important during that long twenty-four hours. I now valued the strength, courage, and knowledge I'd gained from my youth. I was proud not to have ended up like so many of those other guys in jail. Any one of them could have been me, but I'd saved myself from that fate. And by saving myself, I'd met Julie, who had made it possible for me to finally understand and accept love.

Julie

We moved again. Compared to our previous homes, our new one wasn't our biggest or smallest, our most upscale or most downscale. It was just right. With Jay working from home, we spent more quality time together than ever before. Our lives were happy, our marriage a far cry from the one we'd left behind in the debris of divorce and infidelity.

Looking back, I realized Jay and I had stood together in our darkest moments and overcome every obstacle, despite the relentless adversity that should have destroyed us. Then, almost as if awakening from a revelatory dream, we had emerged from our trial with the strength and tenacity to turn tragedy into triumph, disrespect into respect, and loss into love.

In response to our pain, Jay and I had created something new, different, and lasting. Now I wondered if we were we being called to a new task. Had we gone through our difficulties for a bigger reason than to rescue our small family? Had we learned lessons we might teach? Could we help save other marriages?

I hoped so.

Jay

I felt bone-tired, weary from the inside out, more exhausted than I had ever been. With a groan, I sat down on the end of the king-size bed and cradled my face in my hands. Even though I was emotionally drained, I couldn't shut off my mind. Events kept replaying in my thoughts: Julie's tears, my remorse, Drs. John and Julie Gottman's wise counsel during the healing months there in Seattle, and my shame. *Always my shame.* Inwardly, I berated myself. What kind of man cheats on his wife? What kind of father inflicts the pain of divorce on his children? What kind of guy has an affair?

Sensing my deep despair, Julie sat down and held me while I mumbled yet another tearful apology.

When my sobs finally subsided, she drew me to the window overlooking Nantucket Bay, a picturesque scene in Seattle's rare afternoon sunlight. Watching the parade of sailboats and slow-moving ferries, I held her close and savored the fragrance of her perfume and the touch of her hair against my cheek.

"I love you, Jay," she said softly as she tilted her face up toward mine.

Unable to meet her eyes, I looked away. I couldn't accept her love. I wanted to, but I didn't think I was worthy. Yet she was my lifeline.

In the background I heard the television, and after a few minutes the sound intruded into my consciousness. I clasped Julie's hand and drew her over to look at the TV screen. We watched as New York Governor Elliot Spitzer stepped to the podium. He acknowledged assignations with a high-dollar escort, expressed regret for his poor judgment, and apologized to his family and constituents. Finally, he announced his resignation.

In the ensuing moments, I experienced the shame and guilt all over again, especially since I couldn't get the image of Spitzer's wife out of my mind. As he'd made his announcement, she had stood to one side and a little behind him, her face clearly visible and full of pain. I knew that look well. Julie's face had held the same combination of disbelief and betrayal.

As my agitation overcame my exhaustion, I stood up and paced the room. "Infidelity is pandemic, and the fallout is toxic," I said. "In real life, adultery isn't anything like the romanticized version displayed on the big screen. Sure, there are moments of illicit pleasure. But they pale in comparison to the pain and suffering that inevitably follow. The emotional trauma of divorce, of which infidelity is a significant contributor, lives on for generations in the relationships touched by it."

"You're right," Julie agreed.

"Someone must tell the truth about infidelity," I muttered as I continued to pace back and forth. "Someone who can speak from experience. Someone who will tell the absolute truth no matter the consequences. Affairs need deception to exist. The anecdote for the deception that fuels infidelity is transparent truth. Nothing less."

Turning on my heel, I caught sight of my reflection in the mirror. I froze in place. As I stared at the man who looked back at me, I had an epiphany. I realized that if someone was going to tell the truth about adultery, that person would have to be me. My life experiences, as well as my training, had uniquely prepared me.

I don't make a habit of saying, "God told me to do something," but that day, deep inside, I felt a surge of renewed energy and purpose. Maybe the terrible mistakes I'd made could be redeemed. Maybe the wisdom I had gleaned at so great a cost could be used to help others. Maybe that was my destiny, albeit not the one I'd signed up for in graduate school. But so be it, if Julie and I could make a difference in the legacy of even one family.

> ## 5
> Julie: *"True love."*
>
> Jay: *"Soul mates."*

Jay and Julie

And so began the creation of *Surprised by Love*, our way of reaching out through our story of hope, healing, and relationship transformation to others who have been affected by infidelity.

Second chances are real. A new legacy can be built on true love. If not now...then when?

CHAPTER 13

WISDOM EARNED: THE LESSONS

Jay

If you are a betrayed spouse, an important question you will ask is, *why* did this happen? If you had an affair, you will ask, *how* did this happen? Both questions require an answer if you hope to heal from an affair and, more importantly, if you want to protect your marriage and prevent an affair from ever happening again.

Before my affair, I was an adept liar. The practice of telling the truth was indeed foreign to me. In finding my way home, I had to begin by telling the truth—all of it—first to myself and then to Julie.

Every affair has a purpose and a design to it. There are no accidents in infidelity. It is rare that an affair will rear its ugly head in a "good marriage," one in which partners are consistently getting their needs met. *An affair is the failure of a relationship and the people within it to meet each other's needs adequately, despite the fact that only one partner may choose to be unfaithful.*

Many of us who engage in the destructive choice to commit infidelity do so for the same reasons. All of these reasons are rationalizations. My rationalizations had everything to do with my failings and little to do with Julie's. She was merely a victim of the choices I made in response to our problems—problems that were actually solvable. Yes, Julie contributed to the problems in our marriage, and her choice to accept responsibility for the role she played was instrumental in our healing. However, she was not to blame for the choices I made in dealing with those problems, including my choice to have an affair.

How did a marriage to a beautiful human being who was a professional model and former pageant queen with three adorable children end in an affair and divorce? I will tell you.

I created the conditions where *vulnerability* met *opportunity* in the perfect storm of self-destruction and hedonistic indulgence. I myself did this, all in the name of survival and self-preservation, which were the excuses I hid behind to justify my exit.

As I suspect is true with many affairs, the anatomy of my affair was found in those parts of me that I denied, refused to acknowledge, or ran from being honest about. In lying to myself and others about those parts, I severed them from my life. Once dissociated, they remained unknown to me, which left me in a dangerous and intolerable state in a world replete with opportunities for escape and threats to deep intimacy. My ignorance about my own brokenness rendered any smarts I'd acquired in getting a PhD in clinical psychology useless. My broken condition allowed me to fail in taking responsibility for those severed parts—something that true love requires of us all.

Perhaps in reading our story you've asked yourself, how could he do this? If that is the case with you, I'll attempt to offer you an answer here. I do so, not as an excuse to justify my actions, but rather as an explanation to provide insight into how someone who took his marriage vows seriously and intended to live by his Christian faith and value system could fail everyone he loves so profoundly.

1. *I believed that the rules didn't apply to me.* As a highly credentialed, licensed clinician, I offered thousands of patients my professional advice on retaining integrity in their relationships, the importance of good communication, and the need for honesty. Yet there was little congruence between what I sold and what I lived. I believed my own press clippings and rationalized my character defects with psychological justifications. While I was significantly involved in other people's lives as their therapist, I never showed up for and was disengaged in my own life—which is the essence of hypocrisy. In fact, my profession was an occupational hazard that allowed me to hide better than most people because I was able to concoct fancy excuses.

The casualty, of course, was truth. Truth is a key ingredient to growing up and maturely loving another. As an arrogant, successful fraud who dispensed anecdotes I barely believed in myself, I was hiding behind the cloak of "expert." Simply put, I was a hypocrite masquerading behind a socially-sanctioned mask. As long as I continued to look good in other people's eyes and I maintained the appearance of normalcy, my lies had a context I could easily hide behind. Arrogance and a dangerous form of entitlement gradually replaced honest self-reflection. The Dr. Jay narrative of "successful, smart, driven, and alpha" became my new mantra. This theme equipped me with a temporary narcissism that set the stage for the risks I was willing to take, but gave little regard to the impact those risks would have on those around me.

2. *I confused significance and self-worth with financial success.* I believed I was worthy, and therefore lovable, only if I surrounded myself with the standard trappings of wealth and prestige. Intent on achieving at any cost, I became a workaholic. I attached my value to success in the world, not to relationships with people. Achievement became my pathway to legitimacy—and legitimate I would be, regardless of the cost to others or myself.

Under the guise of "I have to do this to please Julie and to take care of our family," I built a large practice with multiple revenue streams and then expanded nationally to executive and corporate coaching, training, and consulting. I quickly became one of the most successful and financially independent consultants in the country with a large database of Fortune 500 clients. The result was that I felt imprisoned by the success I had built. However, I blamed Julie and the life we had created together—and in fact the entire institution of marriage itself—for the grueling work it took to generate and maintain my success.

The more lavish our lifestyle became, the stronger my justifications for pursuing success and lying to preserve the illusion of a "great" marriage became. A vicious cycle of self-imposed servitude fueled my rationalizations for the illicit happiness I chased with Dayanara. The need to achieve empowered me to justify *any behavior* as service to the consumption monster Julie and I had constructed. Achievement was also a convenient diversion that allowed me to ignore what was actually happening in my marriage and offered me an excuse to exit the relationship.

I assumed those around me saw me as a "success object," that I was there just to provide them with a great life at my expense. This belief allowed me to claim victim status, a dangerous banner indeed. I believed I was only valued by Julie and others for my ability to provide for them. This was fodder for the story I'd told myself, and it fueled enough anger and self-pity in me to assuage any guilt that arose from having sex with a woman other than my wife.

The truth is, I set it up that way, not to serve others, but to serve my own ego, and then I blamed everyone in sight for taking advantage of me. It was a perfect way to justify leaving my marriage.

When success to bolster insecurity becomes a mission more important than anything else in life, we become blind to how the isolation and loneliness we feel in pursuing that success happen in the first place. It's hard to think clearly on a treadmill going full speed. Instead of thinking, we're merely surviving, and humans in survival mode can justify any behavior that allows them to breathe.

3. *I believed that my spouse was the cause of my unhappiness.* In trying to maintain the illusion of normalcy and self-importance while I built my businesses,

I made some significant errors: I allowed myself to be alone often and did not have an adequate support system, and I neglected many of my personal wants and needs. As I tirelessly provided for others, I gradually euthanized my soul. I didn't effectively communicate to Julie the anger, resentment, and frustration I felt. I wrongly assumed that she should have known or cared enough to figure all this out. No one is that good, nor should anyone have to be. One's partner and marriage are not responsible for making a person happy—only that person is responsible. In my case, I told myself Julie was controlling me, and then I allowed myself to *feel* controlled. In so doing, I unconsciously demonized Julie. Using passive-aggressive behavior, I blamed her for my issues, but I never let her in on the game I was playing.

Placing responsibility on Julie and the circumstances of our life caused me to feel victimized by them; once anyone becomes a victim of something, it's possible to justify any type of behavior to change that "victim status." At that point, it's easy to rationalize an affair.

4. *I was an accomplished liar.* In order to protect the private universe I had created, I lied to Julie when she asked for and deserved the truth. The reason I could do this is that men have an uncanny and dangerous ability to compartmentalize their lives. They place the various areas of their lives into mutually exclusive rooms whose walls have no windows or doors. As a result, what happens in one compartment is completely cut off from what happens in another. In this split, dissociative state, a man can rationalize anything—even leaving a woman who was recently diagnosed with cancer, which is a painful reality I struggle to live with to this day.

I deceived myself into thinking Julie was *the reason* for my misery. I believed she had manipulated and taken advantage of me, didn't love me, and was only using me to gain the lifestyle she wanted. I told myself, "This whole thing is unfair and unjust, especially in light of all you've done for Julie to make her life wonderful. You have no choice but to leave and reclaim yourself. After all, if you don't take care of yourself, who will?"

This deception opened the door for me to justify having an affair. Under the assumption that Julie was exploiting me, I excused myself from having to care about what was going on in her life and from taking any action to put a stop to my behavior and get my life back. This limiting belief empowered my self-absorption.

The truth is, other people are never all that powerful over us and are certainly not responsible for our emotional state; we alone are responsible for our emotions because we alone can exert control over them. Our partners can't victimize us without our permission and active participation; however, when I was on the path to infidelity, that fact seemed to escape me. At the time, I was too consumed with injustice and entitlement (a toxic alchemy of dysfunctional emotion) to see my self-inflicted victimization; in turn, the perfect storm of my affair's anatomy began to form.

I made Julie out to be wrong in our relationship so that I could justify my unavailability. Since I didn't want to give my valuable energy to what I saw as a dying connection between us, I didn't show up for what I claimed to want in my relationship with her. As long as I wasn't available, we couldn't be intimate. After all, intimacy requires that a person show up for it, not demand it while running in the opposite direction!

My choice to remain unavailable positioned me to use the lie that many adulterers finalize the deal with: "We're simply incompatible. I can't get what I want from this marriage. I *must* do something to survive, so I'll just get my needs met elsewhere and lie about it. That way, no one gets hurt."

In making this choice, I sabotaged any possibility for *true intimacy*. Mature love requires *transparency*, *self-disclosure*, and bold *vulnerability*. Not only was I ill equipped to give these to Julie, I was not present to give them to her. If we don't show up for what we say we want in life, we forfeit our right to expect it. This is particularly true in authentic relationships.

5. *I confused sexual fantasy with real love.* Early in life, I learned to use sex as a drug and means of escape. Instead of coping with stress or conflict in a productive manner, I turned to fantasy to fill the existential void in my soul. I spent more time viewing porn and visiting strip clubs than I did connecting with Julie, which set the stage for unrealistic expectations of sexual fulfillment in the context of genuine love and marriage. Rather than use my psychological acumen to take responsibility for confusing sex for love, I used it to rationalize my flights into fantasy and my frantic efforts to interpret shallow sexual attraction as real love.

Love is a form of energy. Where you focus that energy determines the quality of love possible. It's absurd to think that I expected from marriage what I was unwilling to invest in it. The illicit lure of fantasy can never compete with the sobering realities of a real relationship. Where you invest your emotional energy *will determine* the degree of passion and intimacy you can experience. When you take that energy and put it anywhere except into your marriage, you've set the stage for infidelity.

Through stonewalling and disengagement, I cut off my healthy emotions from Julie. Then I invested those emotions in exits and escapes she couldn't compete with. Not only did I make myself unavailable emotionally, I also put Julie in a competition she could never win. She was up against a fantasy, and no one can win when competing with a fantasy. For me, the fantasy included the deception that if a sexual attraction was there, *it meant something* and if it was missing from my marriage, *that meant something too* (that I didn't love Julie anymore), which gave me yet another reason to commit adultery! This shallow version of immature love based on adrenaline and emotion required the opposite of what a deep relationship based on true love requires.

The anatomy of an affair is a series of choices. Each choice is a *commitment* to a way of thinking that involves three phases: assigning inaccurate meaning to an idea, drawing faulty assumptions and conclusions about the idea, and taking improper action in accordance with the idea. The territory of an affair is so replete with illusions and distortions that most, if not all, of its commitments are flawed. They are based on poor information and vain imaginations that spurn dangerous, driving emotions. Such flawed commitments set the stage for my flights into fantasy and my frantic efforts to legitimize what could never be with Dayanara—a real relationship. *An affair is predicated on deception and, therefore, can never be legitimized. True love it is not.*

6. *I didn't take responsibility for my mental health.* I've suffered from clinical depression since childhood. In marriage, this looked like being sullen and withdrawn, frequently irritable, extremely moody, chronically unhappy, and easily agitated. Sounds like a fun guy to be in a relationship with, doesn't it? The impact this behavior had on Julie and the kids was that they walked on eggshells around me in an effort not to make things worse. I'd taken antidepressants on and off at different times in my life, but never consistently. Despite going to therapy intermittently and attending hundreds of hours of professional development workshops as a psychologist, I convinced myself that I was above applying my medical know-how to my personal life and could figure things out on my own. Being a mental health professional was actually a liability that allowed me to hide behind the illusion of having my act together. After all, I was "Dr. Jay" and had helped hundreds of people save their marriages, tame their past demons, and redesign their lives.

Emotion is *energy*, and how it is managed affects the success of a marriage. Passion and connection, the stuff soul mates are made of, are by-products of the *quality of energy* people choose to bring to each other in their relationship. How much and what type of energy you bring to a relationship and what you do with your own negative energy determine the culture of that relationship; the *emotional state* of your relationship will be shaped by its culture.

If I'm consumed with misery from my past pain or disappointments, along with misery from my current stressors and any unfinished business from prior events, I can't be in relationship with anyone in the present; my past is what I'm in relationship with. This condition was true for me, and yet I didn't see it. Because of that fact, I didn't accept responsibility for doing anything about it until after the affair when the situation became clear to me. The impact my relationship with the past had on our marriage was corrosive, and there was nothing Julie could do to stop the corrosion or to help the situation.

I grew up in emotional and financial poverty. The byproduct of an unwanted teenage pregnancy, I was raised by a mother and several stepfathers consumed with their own emotional demons and addictions. I entered adulthood alone and deeply wounded. My choice to be a mental health professional was a desperate attempt to rescue myself by becoming a savior to others (and, as I often jest, to save money on therapy!), a creative compensation for my deep-seated feelings of inadequacy and illegitimacy as a person.

The plan was simple: if I could be important and relevant enough to others that needed me, my significance would be enhanced and my legitimacy as a person affirmed. This plan worked pretty well for a while, and I even helped a lot of people when I was using it. The problem was that the plan wasn't sustainable. I burned out and ended up giving away more than what I actually had, which left the well dry. As a result, I drilled deeper into fantasy relationships and other escape routes so that I could continue supplying myself with validation.

My mother was chronically depressed and emotionally unavailable; my father, whom I never met, abandoned me before birth so that he could chase women, drink alcohol, and race cars. My initiation into manhood came through competing on the football field and fighting in the back alleys of Brooklyn, New York, as a gang member in a drug-infested neighborhood. I grew up with two surrogate fathers, one who was indifferent to me and the other who was chemically dependent and violent. Fresh from the jungles of Vietnam, my second stepfather forced me to learn how to fight him because I had to protect my family from his physical abuse and other violence.

In spite of all this, my past was not the problem. How I chose to deal with my past was the issue. Despite many years of clinical training and my insight into how the past affected me, I had never dealt with who I'd become in response to it. I couldn't *transcend* my emotional wounds by trying to be someone other than myself. In hopes of having my love returned, I became someone others needed; in so doing, I overcompensated for the terror of not being loved or wanted. This is a formula that simply does not work.

We can only transform wounds by embracing the truth about them, that is, by owning what happened in all its ugliness and even its brutality and, most importantly, by owning what we made up about ourselves, others, and the world around us in order to survive. Then, and only then, can we change our wounds into something else as we *become someone* distinct from the survival methods we used in the first place to cope with life. *It is within the borders of our decision to embrace the truth that our destiny is forged, and with it, the legacy of marriages and families.*

I don't believe we "find" ourselves; I believe we "invent" ourselves. A great marriage is a product of *design* brought to life by new choices. Too many of us waste too much valuable time by searching for solutions, either in a past that is no longer relevant or among insights that do nothing to improve the patterns of our failed relationships.

The only good choice we have is to be instructed by the wisdom found in dealing with our past demons. Then we can recreate ourselves in such a way that honors what was without being defined by its limitations. Because I failed to go through that process, I remained unconsciously wounded and therefore un-evolved. As a result, I was pseudo-sophisticated—capable of helping others succeed in their relationships but uninterested in showing up for mine.

The bottom line is this: I failed to manage my depression, evolve beyond my psychological ghosts, and attend to my own mental health. By failing to do the necessary work to grow and heal, I didn't mature into someone capable of giving and receiving mature love. True love requires that we evolve beyond our wounds and not demand our partners or the relationship to heal us from those wounds.

We have to grow in order to love. Intimacy is both an art and a science that many of us are ill equipped for. Still, we expect intimacy in our relationships anyway. To love another person requires that we grow up, rise above our wounds, and take responsibility for what we need as adults. I made the mistake of trying to use relationships to validate what was missing in me. This process was a black hole of empty, cyclical dissatisfaction. When my marriage failed and I no longer felt validated, I held Julie responsible.

Of course, relationships can never validate us because people can't fulfill us. We can really only find fulfillment for ourselves and then share it with someone from the place within us that comes from being a whole person.

Jay and Julie

In life there will be pain. In relationships there will be both pain and suffering of one kind or another. Pain isn't the problem; what you do with the pain and "who you become" in response to it can be, however. If you choose to use the pain to mature and evolve and to grow your relationship up into something it might never have become in pain's absence, only then will the pain have purpose. That is what it takes to transform pain into something different.

Whereas *suffering* is pain without any meaning, *transformation* is pain with a purpose. With transformation, the meaning you create out of your place of pain takes you to a new place within yourself and your relationship. At that point, both are changing for the better because you experienced the pain, and both are evolving because you lived through the pain. Simply put, when an affair has been a part of your life and you choose to grow instead of recoiling from life because "life hurt you," your pain is transformed into something meaningful.

Emotions can use you, or you can use them. Sometimes the feelings you don't deal with can destroy you if you let them. But suffering can offer a gold mine of wisdom if you're persistent enough to dig it out. Viktor Frankl taught from behind barbed wire at Auschwitz that the greatest freedom human beings possess is the ability to choose how to respond to negative circumstances and adversity. So, although you may have no control over adverse situations, you can control the meaning you assign to them—and that's where your destiny will be determined, one choice at a time.

During times of suffering, you can *complain* or you can *create*. The former leads to further suffering, while the latter allows you to design a love and a relationship that may never have existed before. In our relationship, the affair is a poignant reminder of the deep pain we chose to learn rich lessons from. In that sense, the affair is a painful, cruel "gift" because we chose to allow ourselves and our relationship to be transformed by it.

Life never turns out the way it "should"; it always turns out the way it "does." The secret to designing an outstanding marriage is to accept this fact and get into a powerful relationship with "what is," not "what we wished for," "hoped would have happened," or "thought we deserved." Affairs are horrible life experiences, but they are a part of the risk we take in being in an intimate relationship. It is a fact that betrayals of trust occur in relationships. The gift we have is what we can learn from these disloyalties when they do occur. In other words, our gift is that we get to design our lives according to the lessons the betrayals teach us.

We have learned many wisdom lessons on our journey of transforming the ugliness and tragedy of infidelity into the triumph of a beautiful, new marriage and family, and true love. In hopes of contributing to your life and your relationships, both present and future, we now share some of these lessons.

TO LIVE IS TO LOVE—
EVERYTHING ELSE IS NOISE

Love is a force to be reckoned with. It was because of Julie's persistent refusal to quit on love and her defiant stand for a possible future (which, at the time, was nowhere in sight) that we are married today and able to tell you our story. Despite the fact that Julie needed to protect herself by moving on with the divorce, she took this stand and continued to offer me the purest form of love possible—unconditional love. Her remarkable decision birthed the seed of possibility between us that became the basis of our new relationship. And upon that new relationship we have been able to design our present life together.

There is nothing more powerful than defiant love that refuses to be defined by the circumstances it is thrust into, and instead, acts on principle, values, core beliefs, and unconventional choices. Julie *lived* love. She never withdrew it, even though she would no longer allow me to mistreat her. As a matter of fact, she modeled a lifestyle of love throughout our journey, and ultimately, when I was ready to change, her example humbled me and made her irresistibly attractive to me in a place where passion was once dead. Her choice to love unconditionally and contribute to my life when I least deserved it was *the* connection that stopped me from moving on to what I was frantically pursuing. *That connection stemming from her decision to love me, birthed a new intimacy that allowed us to create a new marriage.*

Even if you must move on and leave a relationship, never underestimate how influential the choice to love can be. It can powerfully influence the future state of the relationship, no matter what it looks like at present or how far it is from what you had first hoped for or expected. If you choose to love, sometimes magic can be the result.

HONOR THE "THIRD" PERSON IN YOUR
MARRIAGE—THE RELATIONSHIP

It's interesting what passes for a marriage today. We start off best friends, get engaged and commit a lifetime of love to each other, sanctify our commitment through marriage, become passionate lovers, have a brief celebration of all the above, and then become parents, housemates, and business partners of "Life.Inc." Before long, we discover we are intimate strangers who merely coexist and tolerate one another. Many of us invest more time and effort into purchasing a car than we do in working on the most important relationship of our life, the relationship with our partner whom we have vowed to love and cherish for a lifetime.

In an outstanding marriage, there are really three "people," not two. There are you, your partner, and "the relationship" itself—all three of which deserve energy, time, and attention if you want the marriage to grow. Clearly, it was the "third person" in our marriage that was most neglected and left us vulnerable while we raised children, built businesses, and did life in grand fashion. Through our healing and redesign process, we learned the difference between a "real relationship" and an "arrangement." The saddest marriages in the world are not the ones with problems and rancor, but those void of any passion at all—the "good enough" relationships you can take or leave, where indifference and apathy are their defining states.

In our book *The Truth about Love: How to Design a Relationship of Your Dreams* (see www.prevent-a-divorce.com), we capture the essence of what was missing in our first marriage and what defines our second one:

- **You choose to put your *relationship first*, period**. No questions about it and no excuses standing in the way. No justifications for why you don't have the time or for why other things are more important that would force the relationship to wait or take second or third place in your list of priorities. You have time for what you value, and not investing time in something means it simply isn't a priority. Good intentions don't work in this territory, because great relationships require more than that. They require consistent time, focused energy, and sustained attention through your presence and by bringing all of who you are to one another in love.

- **As an act of grace and love, you give your partner your unconditional presence, time, energy, and focus**. This means you not only respond to your partner's needs, but you also consistently contribute to your partner in a positive way regardless of how you feel physically, what mood you're in, or what your external circumstances are. You are *present* and *engaged* in the relationship. You honor your commitment and remain true to your word as an expression of who you are and because it's what you said you would do when you chose to love your partner. Stressors and circumstances have no bearing on whether you will give love, for in an outstanding relationship, you live by high standards and will not tolerate anything less than your personal best.

- **It means you take full responsibility for growing up.** Knowing *how* life has wounded you and who you became in response to the pain, you evolve beyond it so that you are actually capable of being intimate with another person. Intimacy, like success, has requirements, and one of them is to evolve by growing up. This means you no longer dominate others by using defense mechanisms on them or by acting out your hurt, pain, and disappointments to cover up the festering wounds you received from another time and place. It means you choose to be accountable by owning your life and doing whatever it takes to heal and become a healthy human capable of loving another person to the fullest.

- **In a *real relationship* you understand the games you've each played in other relationships and the ways you've learned to keep yourself safe or hidden from your partner by defending yourself from pain, rejection, or the lack of approval or acceptance.** Then, you choose to take responsibility for those games anytime you use them (as we all occasionally do to protect ourselves in the day-to-day living of a *real relationship*). It means you stop playing those games, come out from behind them, and *enter into the conversations that are missing* between you and your partner—those conversations that can create intimacy and fulfill your longings and needs.

- **A *real relationship* occurs when you create love through who you are and what you bring to your partner.** The creation of love is a by-product of the *energy* you invest in your partner and the relationship itself. You cannot hold back and wait for it to show up from some source other than your investment itself. It's NOT where you "find the right partner" to love you perfectly; rather, you actually bring something to the table, which inspires your partner to reciprocate in kind because they so value what you have with one another that they fight to keep it great.

- **In a *real relationship* you don't expect your partner or the relationship to fill or fulfill you.** Rather, you design a culture, or place, in which fulfillment can develop through the energy you and your partner invest in the relationship. In this place, your life dreams, aspirations, and shared meaning can be created, which, in turn, will lead to fulfillment in your relationship.

The issue here is not in "finding" that kind of person or relationship that will lead to fulfillment. It is in *becoming* the kind of person capable of creating the conditions inside a relationship for fulfillment to happen. We really have it backwards in our culture. *It's NOT about learning how to find the right person to love us; it has everything to do with being the right person—someone capable of giving and receiving love.*

NEVER SACRIFICE A LIFESTYLE FOR A LIFE

Success has its costs, and pursuing success comes at a price. In our marriage, we made the mistake of putting consumption and lifestyle before relationship with each other. As a result, we didn't make each other a priority, which left us both susceptible to not getting our important needs met. While I (Jay) turned my attention to building businesses and net worth, Julie invested everything she had in the kids. In the long run, we learned that even though our intentions were good, the path to accomplishing our goals was at times seductive. We also learned how easy it was to commit marital neglect when pursuing our goals.

We were best at neglecting each other when we were pursuing ambitious goals such as acquiring a bigger house, putting our kids in private schools, purchasing a new car or motor home, and taking exotic vacations. Although we planned our pursuit of these goals together, during the time we were working to achieve them, we spent less time with each other, focused our attention on things other than the relationship, and supported patterns that distracted and distanced us from each other.

The consumption bug is easy to catch and difficult to get rid of. In chasing a lifestyle, we compromised our core values, which almost cost us our lives. Today we carefully plan what we want our life to look like. We begin by mapping out the time we will invest in our marriage and family. Then we systematically build everything else that is valuable to us around that schedule. One thing that has helped us to follow this model is that, after the affair, we downsized our lifestyle by two-thirds. I got rid of my expensive midtown office and staff, and now I work just a few feet away from Julie and the children. This design allows me to be connected intricately to the flow of the family and to court Julie all week in between business meetings!

WITHOUT INTEGRITY,
LIFE DOESN'T WORK

Life simply will not work without integrity. Your actions must be congruent and consistent with who you are at your core, what you say you're about, and what you claim to stand for. The greatest challenge in our relationship, and we believe in most relationships, is that we didn't tell the truth. Deception existed at so many levels that it choked out any chance for cultivating the trust so essential to deep intimacy. In our own way, we each secretly conspired to hide important parts of ourselves due to fear of rejection. Afraid to be fully known and discovered by each other, we avoided the potential for conflict that neither of us was courageous enough to use to grow in positive ways.

I (Jay) was the greatest offender. I lied habitually even though it would have been just as easy to tell the truth much of the time. In part a remnant from my alcoholic family past (one that I accepted as normal), I failed to evolve beyond my early learning. With Julie, I became very adept at lying and covering my tracks, whether to maintain my privacy, ward off an intrusion into my secret life, or simply exert power and control by not allowing myself to be dominated in any way by her. The causality, of course, was my ability to be transparent and to risk vulnerability, two conditions required for intimacy even to exist. I substituted instead a cast of characters in the form of personas and pretenses that sucked the soul right out of our relationship.

Lying comes in many forms, and it wasn't just the "commission" ones that were a problem in our marriage. We never risked being honest about what we really wanted and needed from one another. We pretended instead that "everything was all right" and that if it wasn't, "it was a season of sacrifice" which would soon pass. This pattern was a dangerous form of deception in that it bred complacency and acclimated us to what was actually dysfunctional and needed to change.

The principle that *without integrity, life doesn't work* is especially true in the area of intimate relationships. Today we live by the commitment to tell the truth no matter what. Honoring this agreement has allowed us to share things with each other that we were afraid to before the affair and has also helped us to avoid sabotaging opportunities to grow closer in areas that are truly meaningful to us both.

WE MUST GROW UP

Personal evolution is a prerequisite for a successful relationship. You cannot be successful in a relationship if you remain unconscious as to how life wounded you. All of us have been wounded in some way by life. We all have demons from our past that we must learn to understand, take responsibility for, and ultimately tame. True love demands that we grow up and live in ways above and beyond those that wounded us in the past.

Certainly a relationship can rub our nose in the slime of life; however, nothing can be more growth-producing than letting a relationship grow us into who we were created to be. The truth is, any "problem area" we see in our partner is usually an area that we need to grow in ourselves. In other words, the relationship's challenges are opportunities for us to evolve and call forth those aspects of ourselves that are underdeveloped. The real problem is that we often miss this point. We focus on the splinter in our partner's eye and overlook the log in our own.

When we enter marriage, we bring with us a community of people and experiences from childhood and early adulthood. Many of us are clueless about the extent to which those past relationships and experiences have shaped us. People and events have touched our lives in the most vulnerable of places, in those inward parts that we must draw upon if we hope to love and be intimate with another. These hidden places involve our basic insecurities: being able to trust someone else fully, having a correct body image which allows us to be vulnerable and naked with our partner, and connecting emotionally to our partner by allowing ourselves to feel need or dependency.

Ironically, I (Jay) was highly educated and understood a fair amount about relationships and love. Yet all of my knowledge did little to help me take responsibility for my own pain and for how my childhood experience of growing up in the midst of poverty, addiction, and various types of abuse had impacted the person I became, especially in my most intimate relationship.

When we experience pain without the support we need to understand and make sense of it, we become invulnerable and self-protective in various ways. Some of us use achievement and success, some manipulation and deception, others domination and control, and still others various addictive behaviors. Regardless of the method we choose to survive the terror of not being loved or not feeling worthy enough in intimate relationships, our survival strategy makes it impossible to get from a relationship what we claim to want from it—satisfaction, closeness, intimacy, love, and care. Why? Because we never really show up for those things when we're self-protective; we can't, because we're too busy defending ourselves from what we fear.

The love I was surprised by in Julie was there all the time, and yet, because I was not able to "be present" for it, that love evaded me. You must show up for what you say you want, and if you are unavailable or unwilling to do the work necessary to understand and be responsible for your wounds, you give up the right to expect a fulfilling relationship.

I (Julie) had to learn why I was reacting to Jay, and though some of my reactions were justified, I had to take responsibility for how I too had been influenced by growing up in an alcoholic home and how many of my reactions to Jay were also influenced by my experiences of growing up in that environment. Today we both have ongoing commitments to our individual and relationship support. In addition, we continue to invest time and resources in workshops, personal and joint therapy, coaching, and professional development conferences and seminars, which help us to stay alert as we continue to design the love and the relationship of our dreams.

FRIENDSHIP IS THE CORE OF AN OUTSTANDING MARRIAGE

Have you ever asked yourself, what's the real secret of lasting love and a great marriage? We found the answer, and it's simple but not easy to do! The "secret" is friendship: a true and rich *friendship* is the foundation for lasting love and an outstanding relationship that can endure the test of time and circumstances.

But what does that actually mean to befriend your spouse? I (Jay) will describe this concept from a husband's perspective, but it could just as easily be told from a wife's. It means to invest your interest and curiosity into who your partner is and to be intimately acquainted with her map of the world so that you can defend and contribute to it; it means to give your fondness and admiration to those parts of your partner that you can adore, respect, admire, and appreciate; it means to bring your presence to your spouse by turning toward and into her, as an act of delight in those aspects of who she is; and it means to move toward your spouse as an expression of love and passion in anticipation of what is possible, not what is wrong about her that you'd like to change.

As we (Jay and Julie) felt progressively devalued and unimportant in our marriage due to our neglect of each other and to making other things our priority (e.g., work and children), a strange thing happened: we needed someone to blame, so we recruited a scapegoat for our feelings. In our relationship, that scapegoat became each other, such that we stopped giving one another the benefit of the doubt, assumed bad and negative intentions in the other, and became filled with toxic feelings toward one other. In a word, our friendship was destroyed, and instead of being each other's biggest advocate, we became each other's most avid critic. Instead of embracing and adoring the parts in us we fell in love with, we became judge and juror of each other and demanded that we each become a version of the person we had invented in our stories.

Love is an act of contribution in which you selflessly inquire as to what fulfills, moves, touches the heart and spirit, and meets the needs of your partner. You then choose to nurture those parts of your spouse without expecting anything specific in return and without putting any condition on your companion in exchange for the gift of your love.

INFIDELITY IS A FAILURE OF INTIMACY, NOT SEX

Affairs have little to do with sex, even though sex is often involved. *An affair is a betrayal of intimacy—any type of intimacy—in which you give some part of yourself (emotionally, psychologically, spiritually, or physically) to someone other than the person you promised to give it to.* In contrast, a relationship is the fundamental environment for getting your needs met.

What do you think the likelihood of an affair might be if both people feel safe and certain of each other's love; experience a variety of positive interactions; do fun and interesting things together; know they are crazy about, value, and respect each other; consistently feel connected and loved emotionally and sexually by one another; grow together; and have shared values, backed by activities that help them live out those values? Duh! Sort of sounds silly when you ask!

An affair doesn't happen in this type of relationship unless a deeper problem such as sexual addiction or philandering lurks in the unfaithful spouse. An affair like this is an animal of a very different kind; however, a circumstance such as this is only true in a minority of cases.

At a basic level, infidelity is the failure of a relationship to meet the needs of its participants. Affairs are about getting a need met somewhere other than the primary relationship because of a breakdown in that relationship. Affairs rarely happen in relationships designed around the needs, goals, aspirations, and the abiding friendship of a healthy connection.

AN AFFAIR IS *ALWAYS* A TOXIC CHOICE AMIDST NUMEROUS HEALTHY OPTIONS

An affair is a choice. An affair has nothing to do with whether we think our partner has failed to meet our needs or how stressful or difficult our partner is to live with. It has everything to do with our ability to understand our needs and take responsibility for creating the conditions inside our relationship to satisfy those needs.

There is no excuse for choosing an affair as a substitute for being who we really are in a relationship. The lack of authenticity inside our relationship and the missing conversations we allow to exist there combine to create the source of deception that leads to an affair. That source is the place where we convince ourselves it's easier to lie than it is to tell the truth—the grandest of all lies!

The antidote to infidelity is always authentic transparency. If we intend to honor our partner and create the conditions in our relationship for our needs to be met, we must resolve to tell the complete truth by being courageous, vulnerable, open, and fully honest. (Go to www.prevent-a-divorce.com for additional resources.)

CONTENTMENT IS ABOUT ALIGNMENT, NOT ACQUISITION

When I (Jay) was a young boy surviving a dysfunctional home, I became obsessed with a question many of us ponder: what makes people successful and how do they drive performance to achieve it?

What I didn't know or appreciate was that this question is actually quite dangerous. If, like me, you pursue success as an end in itself and fail to appreciate the nuances the drive to succeed often originate from, you can miss seeing what success is robbing you of during the pursuit.

Most of my life has been a quest to find the answer to this question. Interestingly, my greatest "success" has come from my most profound failures, not my achievements. A few years ago my life was very different from what it is today. The affair I justified being in because "I was successful and deserved to be happy" ended, and with it, the fantasy of "true love" I was chasing. The businesses I spent years developing at any cost were fledgling because, without integrity, nothing works out. I moved from a million-dollar home to a 600-square-foot dive, was estranged from my children, and lost the respect of everyone important to me. At one point, I seriously questioned if life was worth living.

Then something happened—I gave up knowing everything, and Julie, the woman I divorced to find myself, became my greatest teacher. She taught me the true meaning of success. Here's what I learned: (1) to succeed is to love; (2) most of us really don't know how to succeed; and (3) succeeding is about asking the right questions; it's not about having enough status or things, finding the right person to love us, or getting from others what we think we must have to be happy.

Fulfillment is never about acquiring things, status, certainty, or significance. Fulfillment can only happen when we grow sufficiently enough to live from our core (those values and beliefs that give texture, substance, and meaning to our life) and we then contribute from a life that is bearing fruit in alignment with that core.

Ultimately, success is measured by the quality of our relationships, not the robustness of our portfolio. Yeah, I know, pithy—but it's really true. Trust me on that one. What I now know about success is that our wounds (and we all have them) are both the *reason* for success and the *cause* of new problems if we are unconscious of the risks. And despite being a licensed clinician, I was unconscious and sleep-walking through life. How about you?

Pain gave me the gift of hunger to push myself further than many and achieve more than most. However, in the long run, I learned that whenever I tried to transcend a wound and use it as success fuel, I paid a hefty price: the seeds of incompletion and void I left behind always returned in another form at another time.

What we disown, owns us. That which we are unconscious of, can destroy our life, and with it, anything deemed successful. All the success in the world couldn't fill me up in the areas I was asking it to. When we coach people today, the most important question we ask them determines whether they will achieve real success. That question is, "Who do you need to become to have the love and relationship you say you want?"

When I (Jay) failed in life, I wasn't asking this question. I was petty and small, and I complained that the world and the people in it were not cooperating with my agenda or being responsive enough to my needs. That single flaw of not asking myself who I needed to become caused me the near loss of everything important to me. It cost me "success"—that is, until I realized what success really was and how to achieve it.

The idea behind this success principle is simple but not easy to apply: "be *at cause for* designing your life" (own and assume responsibility for all aspects of your life), and if the circumstances aren't cooperating, then change them by choosing who you must become, what state you must operate from, what standards you will hold yourself to, and what beliefs, attitudes, and actions you will embody until you've attained what you're after. Contentment is about aligning your life and relationship with what is most important and means the most to you.

Here's why that is true: It's not by "achieving success" or getting what you myopically chase after that you become successful. Rather, it is by "becoming the type of person" who actually succeeds in loving another human being and by living life consistent with your core values that you are transformed. In other words, it is not in *doing* great things, but in *becoming* a great person that you find meaning, experience fulfillment, transcend self-imposed limitations, and rise above your human nature to encounter true success.

We know a lot of very smart and talented people who are not very successful, and for that matter, aren't too happy or fulfilled either. Why? It's all about relationship. The ability to connect authentically with another is the most essential component of success in business and life, yet most treat it as an afterthought instead of the fundamental truth that it is.

FEELINGS SHOULD BE LISTENED TO, NOT ACTED FROM

When we ignore a wound, we stop thinking about what's right or wrong and become morally bankrupt, and we focus instead on surviving. When we are trying to survive something, we can only see our own needs, wants, feelings, perceptions, and experiences. We are myopic, a type of self-induced narcissism that lulls us into unilateral action. Because at that point we only consider what is in our best interest and have no regard for the way our actions impact those around us, our instincts, not our values, call the shots.

The decision to commit infidelity is a slippery slope fueled by romantic illusions. Those of us who choose infidelity have "ineffective state management" at our core, which means we fail to manage our emotions effectively. Feelings are important, but not that important. Tony and Sage Robbins taught us a powerful life principle that we now live by: there are no good or bad people or problems, only resourceful or "un-resourceful" states. Learning how to recognize and control the two transforms our life and relationships into whatever we choose them to be.

The true hypocrisy within the psychology of the unfaithful (which accounts for the infidelity itself) is this: unfaithful partners claim there's a need not being met in the primary relationship, but they do not show up "clean" for what they claim to want there. That choice alone actually causes the very conditions of *de-vitalization, loneliness, and soul death* they are pursuing an affair to remedy!

Here's the anatomy of infidelity in a nutshell:

- You check out emotionally and leave the primary relationship long before the stage is set to justify choosing an affair.

- You fully contribute to, yet don't take responsibility for, not getting your own needs met by physically, emotionally, and psychologically distancing yourself from your partner. This distancing ensues from the emotional cascade to cut yourself off from your spouse.

- You then falsely conclude, "We must be incompatible. The relationship just doesn't work for me anymore. We've lost our passion and that loving feeling. I'm not appreciated or pursued. My needs are not met, and my partner doesn't seem to care."

- You say, "I have to do something to survive this existence; an affair seems to fit the bill."

- It worsens as the "we just don't have that loving feeling anymore" argument and the "I found my soul mate" rationalization become the perfect storm for making the decision to engage in an affair as a maladaptive solution to soul death.

Here's how it works:

- If you're the unfaithful, you get to denigrate what is often a fragile and vulnerable relationship (the one you are in) in need of immediate repair, while you delude yourself into thinking there is actually a legitimate and real alternative (your affair partner) that you *must* have to feel alive again.

- You pursue your "soul mate" as if that person had the power to make you alive again. (Not!) After all, you *deserve* to feel good since the primary relationship is so unfulfilling.

- In your pursuit of illusory intimacy, you are not remotely available for your primary partner, yet you complain about and blame your partner for not giving you enough time and not fulfilling you. Pretty nasty stuff!

Here's the bottom line: Affair relationships—while replete with erotic excitement, novelty, passion, and the promise of something you've come to believe is unique and attainable only from within the context of the illicit relationship—ARE NOT REAL. Although the feelings experienced in an affair *are very real*, they are inherently untrustworthy, for they are the prized possessions of an intoxicated state.

Your feelings are your feelings, and are therefore valid; they're just not reliable in this context. Affair "love" isn't love at all. It originates from an *illusion*, the fantasy of merging with another person who has the unique ability to "see me for who I really am," someone who will "love me perfectly" as no one ever has before. The problem with an affair is that you get a false positive from it because the relationship has never been tested in the light of day—*reality*. Anytime it's up against reality, the affair comes out the winner.

Affairs are courtships on adrenaline and steroids. Fueled by the deep-seated disappointments of relationship failures, affairs denote serious deficits in personal development. In the vulnerable context of an affair, you use the *experience* (the intoxication of the affair encounter) in the form of an *object* (the person you "love" and delude yourself into believing is the missing piece for a hole in your soul—or what you euphemistically confuse as your "soul mate").

So you make a sexual, emotional, or psychological encounter mean something it doesn't (we promise you, it's really chemical reactions blowing up in your brain—dopamine and oxytocin to be exact!), believe your own lies to justify it, and then feel compelled to make huge changes in your life to legitimize this new movie script that has you as its central character. The problem with the life-size drama you've just created is that it comes at a huge cost to the entire cast and crew.

Feelings should be honored by listening to them and sharing them honestly—not by acting from them, especially when fantasy and illusion are involved. Bringing your feelings to one another in raw, uncensored self-expression is the best way to affair-proof your relationship and add to the vibrant intimacy between you.

SOUL MATES AREN'T FOUND—
THEY'RE CREATED

Most of us believe the main problem with love lies in "finding the *right* person" who will love us and meet our needs. What we miss in this approach to love is that it is self-absorbed—the opposite of what true love requires.

True love has nothing to do with finding the right person to love us; it's about *becoming* the right person, someone who is capable of loving. In this sense, true love is far more than a collection of feelings that allow us to act in loving ways; rather, it is a defiant resolve to DO loving acts, and it stems from a commitment to invest energy into our partner and our relationship. When we walk in this type of love, we contribute to our spouse no matter what we feel like or what circumstances we find ourselves in, simply because living this way is the standard for our life.

So, when our partner says to us, "I love you, but I'm not in love with you," what they are really saying is that they don't have a clue about what love means. What they are trying to say is that they feel "concern and care for" us but they're "not turned on by" us or "excited," or they've allowed their passion to die. They understand the language of feelings but not the requirements of love. Concern and excitement can be pleasant feelings, but they don't equate to love. Here's what does!

Love is not a feeling we "get" from being with the right person; it's the feelings that come "from" what we DO to love another person over time and across different life experiences. Love is something we DO, a choice to act, not something we feel. We don't fall in love and then act; we DO love and then feel it. Love is not an emotion; it is a series of states we embody and act upon that are contingent upon our standards: we make the commitment to love unconditionally and to live by a set of commitments grounded in values that will contribute to our partner.

You see, we don't "fall in love" if we want love to last. True love is never about "falling" into anything; that type of love is based on fleeting emotional states that change like the seasons. True love is always about choosing to *become* a person capable of loving another. To reiterate, real love is never about finding the right person; it's about *becoming* the right person capable of love.

Soul mates are not found; they are always created through an encounter in which two people decide to be *present* with one another in such a way that the possibility of being more known to oneself and each other exists. Self can only be fully known through effective human contact with another.

True love requires a *connection* where intimacy can be created. We create intimacy by the quality of *presence* we bring to our partner during shared moments. Although acting in loving ways is critically important, intimacy that originates from true love demands something more of us. It asks us to move beyond "doing the right things" and to become a person who *consistently* acts from love (versus one who reverts to acting from ego, which is feelings-driven, self-protective, and self-serving in that it always seeks to gain something from the exchange).

Just so we are clear, the pursuit of a soul mate as justification for choosing to have an affair is a desperate attempt to find what is incomplete and missing in us. It is a plea for connection, wholeness, and self-validation. It is the experience of feeling alive by using another human being and the fantasy that we are generating as a conduit for a type of legitimacy that no human being can ever actually deliver on, because no relationship possesses what only we can provide for ourselves.

Essentially, when we have an affair, we have *a legitimate need we are trying to fulfill through an illegitimate means that will NEVER WORK*. It's no accident that affair partners who marry divorce at a rate of over 80 percent!

The pursuit of a soul mate is dangerous business because it is predicated on the most fundamental and illegitimate form of deception known to mankind— the *illusion of intimacy* in the form of an *experience* that cannot compete with *reality* (fantasies always win the competition over the demands of reality). An affair is destined to fail once reality catches up with the delusion the fantasy is built upon. (For more information on this topic and others related to it, go to www.prevent-a-divorce.com and sign up for our free E-zine, *The 7 Secrets of Love and Relationship Design*.)

BE THE CHANGE IN YOUR RELATIONSHIP

Have you ever wondered why some people succeed in marriage and others do not? Is there something that the successful ones do that the others don't which makes the difference between getting the results they are after?

We learned many powerful lessons on our path to healing and recovery. One of the more important ones was this: change of any kind begins when one person makes a single decision to "be the change in the relationship" he wants.

Applying this strategy means you *never* wait for people to change or conditions to improve *before* YOU CHOOSE to do something different. Rather, you decide what you want and why it is important to you, and then you take massive action in the direction of making that happen regardless of whether your partner or the conditions cooperate.

In the process of finalizing our divorce and dividing the assets, I (Jay) was surprised by a love I never knew existed even though I lived right next to it for over ten years. Julie loved me unconditionally in spite of my failings, and through her insistence not to let my terrible choices define her, I was touched by her love in ways that escaped me during our marriage.

The pure clarity and piercing nature of Julie's love (separate from any obligation to do so), along with the affirmation she received from numerous other successful men who courted her after our divorce, rendered my stories about her as a gold-digging opportunist obsolete. Her rock-solid integrity and steadfast love broke me, and I could not deny their power. Her consistent behavior humbled me to the point that I had to search my soul, which led me to a transformation that continues to this day.

I have truly been transformed—all because the woman I chose to have an affair on and divorce *refused to let my actions define her love for me and took an absolute stand for true love despite what I chose to do at that time.*

So the essential question to ask yourself if you want to have an outstanding relationship is not, "Have I chosen the wrong partner?" or "Did I miss my soul mate and my one chance at true love?" but rather, *"Who must I become to have what I say I want in my relationship?"*

Choose to live each day "from a love" that is consistent with your core values and highest standards. Do not live from your feelings, your partner's actions, the wrong decisions you've made, or circumstances you find yourself in. Things will not change in your relationship until YOU change. One individual CAN change an entire relationship, and our story is a powerful testimony of that fact. Love can triumph over anything and should never be underestimated for the potent force that it is.

Typically, if your relationship is in serious trouble and you're at an impasse, the ambivalent or involved spouse will not change until he has a compelling reason to. This is not the time to stand on faulty notions of who's right or wrong, or who deserves to be treated fairly. There is no fairness in infidelity, and true love isn't concerned with being right or being treated fairly; true love seeks integrity, truth, and connection—even if it involves divorce. It's time to love defiantly and be unstoppable by choosing to "be the change" you want to happen in your relationship.

Remember, the power of love lies not in the experience of being loved, despite how wonderful that is; the power of love lies in how we are changed when we truly love another, because it demands that we evolve in ways we wouldn't have, had we not taken the risk or demonstrated the courage to truly love another as that person asked to be loved.

HEALING AND REDESIGN ARE BOTH NECESSARY, BUT DIFFERENT

What does it take to heal a relationship following infidelity? Are there any keys to success that could make the difference between healing and redesigning a relationship or not? In our work with couples struggling with the aftermath of an affair, there is a common question we at Surprised by Love receive. Couples ask with complete sincerity,

"Is it really possible to heal and recover from the affair?"

Our answer to them is always the same: "It depends."

We have found that there are specific requirements for successful recovery, and they have nothing to do with the way you feel, the history of your relationship, or the degree of trauma your circumstances present. Full recovery depends on whether the betrayed and the unfaithful spouses are both willing to make the following three commitments together:

1. **Put the marriage first.**
2. **Do the work.**
3. **Evolve as an individual.**

Healing from an affair and designing a new relationship are equally possible if your approach is right. In fact, we believe they are both not only possible, but also that an affair, if leveraged effectively, can become an unprecedented *opportunity*. Although the opportunity is an extraordinarily painful one, it can bring you and your relationship to a level of fulfillment not experienced prior to the affair. We are married today after an affair *and* divorce because of this truth.

Marriages don't end because of affairs. Marriages end because of the way people deal with the aftermath of the affairs. Divorces don't happen because of marital problems such as infidelity. They happen because people do not effectively *repair* the parts of the relationship that are damaged from it, and they adopt attitudes, behaviors, and faulty assumptions that are toxic and corrosive to what is left of a very vulnerable relationship.

Healing and *relationship design* are two distinct tasks required of couples following an affair. However, they can only occur if *both* people are actively involved in the healing and redesign process. If not, this "opportunity" will not be realized.

Healing requires that the sanctity of the primary relationship be restored; the trauma of the affair be honored, acknowledged, and authentically empathized;

support be given to the betrayed spouse; and boundaries be put in place to protect the fragile relationship.

Relationship design requires that both partners understand the role they played in contributing to the affair and the conditions in the relationship that allowed the affair. The two parties must also be open to learning new strategies and skills for relating effectively to each other. In addition, the spouses must design a new relationship blueprint together and commit to live by it. Finally, they must honor their commitment as they bring the blueprint to life.

THE AFFAIR IS A TRAUMATIC EVENT, NOT A DEFINING ONE

Commitment #1: Put the Marriage First

The first commitment in healing from the aftermath of an affair is to restore the *sanctity* of your relationship. You achieve this step by making the relationship THE priority—putting your partner, the needs and interests of your partner, and the needs of the relationship above anything that might potentially compete with their wellbeing. In other words, everything else in life takes second place to the marriage and its interests.

Healing from the affair does not begin until the sanctity of the marriage is restored through a commitment to exclusivity with your spouse and breaking off all contact with the affair partner. Ties to anything else that competes with the relationship for number-one priority must also be severed because you cannot live in two worlds. Healing requires that both spouses be brought completely into one world—the primary relationship.

In fact, trying to heal or reconcile without this commitment will make your relationship more vulnerable to irreparable damage. If the unfaithful partner refuses to practice this principle, the betrayed spouse will rightly feel the negative effects of that insensitivity and selfishness, which will result in more pain.

The adage "talk is cheap" could never be truer than it is in affair recovery. Following the revelation of the affair, **putting the marriage first** achieves a critical task: *it makes the relationship safe again from outside threats.* It also repairs the friendship, trust, and respect that were devastated by the infidelity. You invest in what you value, and people in relationships only feel valued when both partners make *time* for the relationship, invest *energy* into it, and give one another the *attention* that meets their needs. This is how you begin to practice the principle of putting the marriage first.

Putting the marriage first is a *choice*. It has nothing to do with how you *feel* about the relationship or what circumstances surrounded or led up to the affair. We often hear people say things like, "There's been too much damage done," "I will never be able to forgive or let go of what has happened," "I don't feel the desire to...," "I just am not motivated to...," or "I don't feel like doing what it will take to change this."

This principle, which is the beginning of healing and recovery, has *nothing to do with how you feel*. Frankly, your feelings lie and are inherently unstable. They are a terrible barometer for what is actually possible for your marriage (it's likely not in great shape; otherwise the affair might not have happened), and listening to your feelings may be part of the reason why you ended up here in the first place.

Putting the marriage first is about doing the right thing for yourself, your partner, and your family. Sometimes doing the right thing doesn't feel good, but it's still the right thing to do. Making these choices is the first step to regaining the trust that will begin to create safety in your relationship once again.

Here's what **putting the marriage first** looks like:

- **Stop the affair now and break off all contact.** *Together*, with your betrayed spouse, contact the affair partner and tell the person that the relationship is over, you are not available now or in the future to resume it, and you request that the person not contact you ever again because you have chosen to reconcile your marriage. Together, we (Julie and Jay) wrote a joint letter, went to the post office, and sent it certified mail. The solidarity of our effort was a pivotal point in our healing.

- **Allow access to the things your partner needs to feel safe again.** Examples include cell phone records, email passwords, credit card statements, phone call logs, and travel itineraries. Offer these as a gift without complaint and without making up a story such as, "They're trying to control me and violate my privacy." If there is nothing to hide, there is no reason to deny access. Access rebuilds trust and offers reassurance.

- **Be accountable and completely transparent** regarding *where you are, what you are doing,* and *with whom you are doing it.* Choose to be accountable for your time and schedule. Offer the information *before* your partner asks, and we promise that shortly thereafter the questions will stop. They will be replaced by trust and a sense of safety you have built by choosing to embrace accountability.

- **Close all exists**. Any friendship, male or female, or any activity that doesn't include your partner is a threat to the primary healing and redesign of your marriage—especially if you are getting your needs met through a friendship in a way that causes you to rely on that connection. Change the structure of those friendships, take a break from them, or terminate them altogether. You have a responsibility to bring your needs to the primary relationship; otherwise, you are continuing a form of infidelity.

- **Stop listening to bad advice**. While many people around you often have good intentions, they offer bad advice. It's bad because it's biased in the direction of protecting *you* according to their version of self-protection, which in many instances can be destructive to a failing marriage ravaged by infidelity. Limit your circle of support to a small group of friends who are loyal to your marriage (not just to you) and to credentialed professionals who have experience in working with couples dealing with infidelity.

- **Change jobs and/or your schedule**. Corporate dating, which is endorsed by the business community, is the scene in which men and women who travel the country or the world, work in intimate situations with company-paid happy hours. Many affairs that happen in the marketplace are due to a lack of sufficient *time, attention, and energy* paid to the primary relationship. Careers and job-related commitments frequently take priority over everything else in life.

Recovery and relationship redesign take a lot of *time*, even more *energy,* and consistent *attention* to the needs of each partner. This is gut-check time, and if your career is interfering with your marriage, it's time to ask yourself whether or not it's worth it. Providing for a family and being successful can happen in many ways. Choose ways that do not undermine **putting your marriage first.** Nothing else should come before the primary relationship, and both of you should feel that the other is going the extra mile to ensure that the marriage is the top priority.

THE BEST DEFENSE AGAINST INFIDELITY IS TO HAVE A LOVE AFFAIR WITH YOUR SPOUSE!

Commitment #2: Do the Work

Love is both an *art* and a *science,* and most of us don't do either very well. Fundamentally, an affair is a maladaptive way of trying to meet a need outside of your primary relationship because something is missing in you and/or the relationship. That missing component contributes to your choice to have an affair. We believe infidelity is more a failure of intimacy than it is a failure of character and that unfaithfulness always suggests core needs have gone unmet. This condition creates a void within that leads to the choice to seek fulfillment through a surrogate encounter.

An essential part of healing and redesigning a marriage following an affair is learning *how to love* each other in new ways. These should be changes that allow both of you to have your needs met. Such changes will inspire you to invest your *time, energy, and attention* into your primary relationship, which will make it affair-proof.

There are two essential parts in **doing the work** of learning to love your partner. Mastery of each is a requirement for healing and knowing how to love in ways that endure. *Love is both an art* (being) *and a science* (doing). **Doing the work** asks you to *be someone* who creates a culture for love to exist and *do things* that make love occur.

It is an *art* to bring "who you are" and what you give of yourself to another human being through courage, vulnerability, humility, patience, generosity, forgiveness, kindness, caring, longsuffering, joy, goodness, gentleness, perseverance, diligence, self-control, faithfulness, and being "big," or growing up. These attributes entail the "being" part of love.

It is a *science* to have the skills to develop and sustain friendship (the core of an effective marriage), nurture an emotional bank account, turn toward instead of away from your partner, express fondness and admiration regardless of state or circumstance, effectively communicate, listen empathically, attune to each other's feelings and needs, not be defensive, manage conflict and differences, collaborate to support one another's goals, and create shared meaning for those goals.

Together, the *art* and *science* of love make a relationship successful.

Here is what **doing the work** looks like:

- **Complete the "healing tasks" of recovery.** Healing from infidelity has specific tasks that must be completed for a couple to *heal* and *redesign* their relationship. (For more information on the "Curriculum for Affair Recovery" and the "Healing Tasks Model" please go to **www.drjayandjulie.com**.) We respect that there are many approaches to affair recovery, but we highly recommend that whatever you decide to do, you commit to completing the work involved in the recovery and redesign process.

- **Be coachable.** Find a licensed professional who is experienced in working with couples recovering from infidelity, and/or find other couples who have succeeded in transforming their lives after an affair. Then, be open to their guidance, counsel, and influence. Give up thinking that you "already know" everything, because once you know something, learning stops. Let those who have experience, knowledge, and training instruct you on how to approach successful healing and recovery.

- **Learn from others' successes.** Look for and spend time with good role models who are examples of successful marriages and fulfilling relationships. They offer a warehouse of needed wisdom that can inspire you to bring the best you have to your partner and often shorten your learning curve in designing a relationship that really works. Granted, these couples are a rarity today, but they DO exist. Find them and pursue them as mentor couples.

- **Restore your friendship.** Friendship is the core and foundation of a long-lasting, successful relationship. Restoring your friendship after an affair is also one of the early tasks of healing. In Commitment #1, Put the Marriage First, we identified three requirements for making the relationship a priority: *time, energy, and attention*. Interestingly, those three things are the same specific requirements for what it takes to restore your friendship.

A GREAT MARRIAGE IS POSSIBLE AFTER THE AFFAIR—SO WHAT ARE YOU WAITING FOR?

Commitment #3: Evolve as an Individual

Relationships are not for the faint of heart. In fact, to create a great relationship will be the most challenging and fulfilling task of your life. The truth is that most of us are "love ignorant." We incorrectly think that the fundamental problem in a relationship lies in finding the right person to love us instead of *becoming the right person capable of loving another person maturely.* Very different programs!

It's time to stop blaming your partner and your relationship, which you contributed to creating, and grow up. It's time to look deeply at yourself, your attitudes, your personality, your emotional and relationship skills or lack thereof, and your baggage and unfinished business from the family you grew up in. Take full responsibility for all of it, especially how you were impacted and shaped by those influences. Until you make the decision to own all of it, understand it, and mature and evolve beyond your wounds, habits, self-destructive patterns, and immaturity, all of your relationships will be unfulfilling and will likely fail. We all learned how to love from what we saw modeled in the families we grew up in, and for many, that learning did not teach us everything we needed to know to be successful in love and relationships.

My (Jay's) affair was the biggest failure and greatest opportunity of my life. I grew up because of it. It was compelling, for it confronted me with a basic choice: destroy a family and create a legacy of divorce and failed relationships or evolve as a person, a man, a father, and a husband by owning my life and dealing with my issues. This second option involved my taking full responsibility for learning the life lessons I had run from for years.

It was a crossroad in my life, and I had one chance to either get it right or lose everything valuable and precious to me. I knew Julie would not have waited around forever while I figured myself out because, being the incredible woman that she is, she had plenty of options. I chose to evolve and therefore change my legacy and that of our entire family.

You can't have what you are not available for or don't show up to participate in. Many an unfaithful spouse laments the misery and lack of fulfillment in the primary relationship and uses that complaint as justification for getting needs met through an affair. Ironically, the unfaithful spouse invests more energy in the pursuit of an affair partner and chasing a fantasy than into creating love with the betrayed spouse. The unfaithful partner then compares the crumbling primary relationship to a mythical one (affairs are not real relationships because they are based on deception) and wonders why his needs are never met in the marriage he is choosing to leave behind. Such is the insanity of affair psychology!

Unless you choose to be *vulnerable* (able to expose inner feelings and thoughts) and *transparent* (completely honest and authentic), and until you *connect without conditions* (become undefended, open, and kind; interested in your partner; and willing to give of yourself to gain intimacy), you will not succeed in a relationship—and you most certainly will not be able to heal and redesign a marriage following an affair.

To practice these "habits of love," you must become more intimate, or acquainted, with yourself. This involves understanding *who you are, how you became that way, the ways you have been hurt by life, and how you protect yourself* in response to pain. Having insight into these aspects of your life will make all the difference in whether you are able to take responsibility for your decisions and change the things within you that make or break a relationship. Getting to know yourself in this way requires that you make the commitment to **evolve as an individual,** a prerequisite for healing after the affair and designing a new relationship beyond it.

- Here's what **evolving as an individual** looks like: **Become love literate**. Bookstores and libraries offer an abundance of good information on how to evolve as a person who can love and be successful in relationships. Given such easy access to excellent resources on every aspect of personal development, we have no excuse for being ignorant about love or being emotionally unintelligent. Go to your local bookstore or library and select no less than *five* books on topics of personal growth that will contribute to your process of evolving—then read them daily!

- **Listen to the wisdom of others.** Every day, we listen to speakers on all aspects of individual and relationship development. We even listen to those we don't like because we can learn from them. If you're traveling by plane or driving, always have something with you that challenges your thinking or contributes to the knowledge base from which you continue to evolve.

- **Attend workshops and personal-development seminars.** During our healing process, we spent an entire year traveling around the country and working with a variety of experts who each contributed something essential to our recovery.

Today, we continue to attend coaching and counseling sessions, trainings, and workshops, both for our relationship and for our work as professionals. *In advance*, we *schedule* these activities for the entire year, which ensures that we do not "get too busy" to honor this commitment that has made such a huge difference in how fast we have been able to heal and redesign our relationship. Additionally, we are a part of a network of experts who contribute value to us personally and professionally.

- **Join a support group.** Having an accessible structure for support when you need it is an essential part of evolving as an individual. Most of us are under-resourced and under-supported for what life requires of us. The issue of support is key to personal evolution, and the world is full of these groups if you commit to finding them. Google can be your best friend in finding such resources right in your own neighborhood.

- **Commit to a spiritual community.** Putting your life and its purpose into a larger context than yourself is essential to discovering meaning and fulfillment. Affair recovery is tough work and is emotionally demanding. Whatever your spiritual tradition is, connect to it. Cultivating a relationship with God, as you understand God, can offer you context, strength, hope, and the virtues you will need to mature and grow as a person. Spiritual growth and contribution are essential to evolving as a person and to living, loving, and giving.

- **Go to therapy.** Choose a wise guide who is a licensed professional, understands and has experience with infidelity, and is pro-marriage. Therapy is a form of self-care and an expression of nurturance. The purpose of therapy is to achieve self-reflection and enhanced awareness, which will enable you to make the choices required of you during your evolution as an individual. Today, I (Jay) have an ongoing individual commitment to a sage therapist who is smarter than I am and who keeps me acquainted with the parts of myself that I'm responsible for managing. These are the same parts that were responsible for my choice to have an affair, even though I didn't know or understand it at the time. Now I do.

- **Get a coach.** A good life coach or relationship coach is able to hear beneath the surface, problem-solve with you and your spouse, and move you toward future action. Sorting through the individual and relationship issues following an affair can be overwhelming, and having professional help from a licensed and certified professional is important to **evolving as an individual** and growing as a couple.

We have an ongoing commitment to meet twice monthly with a relationship coach who is also a licensed psychologist. This commitment keeps us in the right conversations at the right times and in the right ways to continue evolving as a couple.

- **Stop listening to bad advice**. While many people around you often have good intentions, they offer bad advice. It's bad because it's biased in the direction of protecting *you* according to their version of self-protection, which in many instances can be destructive to a failing marriage ravaged by infidelity. Limit your circle of support to a small group of friends who are loyal to your marriage (not just to you) and to credentialed professionals who have experience in working with couples dealing with infidelity.

- **Invest in a mentor relationship.** Having informal friendships with people for their wisdom and counsel is a hallmark of the highly evolved. As people, we need to mentor as much as we benefit from being mentored. So if you don't have a mentoring friend, ask someone at your workplace, school, synagogue, church, mosque, or support group who has wisdom and life experience that can benefit you. Marty Feldman, my (Jay's) first-grade guidance counselor, has been my lifelong mentor. I call Marty once a month to hear myself speak and benefit from his wisdom and knowledge of me. I also make a commitment to having breakfast or lunch with a small group of mentors—friends whom I trust and who know me well—and I ask their opinions about all aspects of life. We evolve more quickly by being with people who are willing to share their wisdom and experiences with us.

CONCLUSIONS

You must learn one thing. The world was made to be free in. Give up all the other worlds except the one to which you belong. Sometimes it takes darkness and the sweet confinement of your aloneness to learn anything or anyone that does not bring you alive is too small for you.

—David Whyte*

Life is short, and love is an initiation to living life with more vitality and robustness than is ever possible before we choose to love. Loving, or more importantly, the process of becoming a person capable of loving, is not for the faint of heart. But we were not designed for mediocrity, so we are well able to become who we need to be. We were, in fact, designed to be outstanding in every way, and relationships offer that opportunity to us, for they invite, then provoke us to become more than who we are within our self-imposed limitations (those stories, limiting beliefs, and false conclusions that consciously or subconsciously determine our destinies).

We were indeed "surprised by love"—in all its power, contradiction, tragedy, and hope for triumph over prior experience and failures.

Thank you for sharing our journey with us. We would be honored to contribute to making a difference in your life, and we look forward to meeting you in the future.

To love and success within it, always,

Jay and Julie

---

* David Whyte, *The House of Belonging*, "Sweet Darkness" (Langley, Washington: Many Rivers Press, 2006), 26.

About Jay and Julie

Dr. Jay Kent-Ferraro, PhD, MBA

A LEADER AND RECOGNIZED AUTHORITY in optimal performance coaching and professional development, Dr. Jay Kent-Ferraro brings an extensive background of human performance expertise. With over two decades of real-life experience as a licensed clinician, organizational consultant, certified coach, trainer, author, and speaker (husband and dad to five kids too!), Dr. Jay utilizes proven technologies that get results!

Dr. Jay grew up in Brooklyn, New York, where he received his greatest education through learning about the resiliency of the human spirit and its most valuable gift, the freedom to choose and generate possibility in the face of life's challenges! From Brooklyn, he went on to pursue a career as a psychologist. He completed degree programs in clinical, counseling, and organizational psychology at American Psychological Association-approved (APA-approved) training institutions.

Dr. Jay received post-doctoral training at the prestigious Gestalt Institute of Cleveland, with a specialty in working with small groups and intimate systems. He completed an APA-approved internship with specialties in family psychiatry at the Children's Medical Center. He earned the designation of Nationally Certified Psychologist, is a Licensed Professional Counselor, and Certified Corporate Coach & Trainer. Chosen as a Diplomate of the American Psychotherapy Association and Board Certified in Professional Counseling, Dr. Jay serves on several national boards that promote wellness and enhanced human performance in corporate America and is a sought-after trainer and consultant to organizations around the country. With the added degree of Master of Business Administration (MBA), Dr. Jay offers a unique blend of credentials and experience to his consultancy, and is therefore widely recognized as an expert who possesses sound business acumen in interpersonal technologies. (Please call 877.944.7025 or go to www.drjayferraro.com for more information.)

In addition to founding Empowerment Technologies, an executive coaching, training, and consultation firm that specializes in emotional-intelligence consultancy, Dr. Jay is a frequently featured radio and TV guest who deals in particular with personal- and professional-development topics. He hosted KOTV's noon show, *Life-Designs*, in which he presented the latest in breakthrough technologies for living powerfully both personally and professionally.

He and his wife Julie are authors of the provocative tell-all book ***Surprised By Love: One Couple's Journey from Infidelity to True Love***. As a result of this powerful story of hope, transformation, and reconciliation following an affair, Dr. Jay now has the rare and unique privilege to work alongside Julie as they join their talents through their international company, **Surprised by Love**, to offer transformational seminars, keynote presentations, and consulting and coaching for couples committed to redesigning their relationships.

JULIE KENT-FERRARO

A PERFORMER SINCE AGE FOUR, Julie Kent-Ferraro is no stranger to the stage or camera. With "quadruple-threat" training in vocal music, dance, acting, and public speaking, Julie has performed in live theater, print, commercials, and motion pictures. She has worked with Coke, Safeway, Otasco, and Sonic, as well as many of the country's top modeling agencies.

From 1984 to 1986, Julie was the hostess of *KTUL Kid Times*, a children's educational talk show that aired on local ABC network affiliates. Awarded the Kathleen Turner Scholarship, Julie attended Southwest Missouri State University, where she pursued a degree in musical theatre. She was afterward employed as a featured entertainer by the Walt Disney Company in Orlando, Florida, while she attended the renowned Disney University. In Nashville, Julie recorded her own demo crossover-country album entitled *Borrowed Time*, and she also shared the stage with a diverse group of celebrities such as Brooks & Dunn, Frankie Avalon, and "Weird Al" Yankovic. Julie has held four titles in the Miss Oklahoma organization and was a finalist in 1995. Curious about the other side of the performing business, Julie worked in sales and marketing for a Fox affiliate, a position she calls an "invaluable experience."

After marrying Dr. Jay in 1997, Julie decided to use her skills by building confidence and excellence through the performing arts in what she believes is "our greatest natural resource—our youth." She spent nearly a decade as a vocal performance coach at a private performing school, where she instilled in her students a love of the arts and a distinct appreciation for hard work.

"I'm proud to have had students who performed from Los Angeles to New York and won numerous awards," said Julie. "One of my craziest honors was when I helped a student compose the 'Oscar Mayer Jingle of the Year!'"

As a volunteer for the Miss America Organization, Julie served as the executive director of the Miss Tulsa State Fair Pageant. She holds an impressive track record: most titleholders who won under Julie's leadership went on to place in the top three at the state competition.

In 2006, Julie experienced her own nightmares becoming reality when she simultaneously faced a diagnosis of lymphoma and infidelity within her marriage. Her strength, determination, and love for her family prevailed, and she is now proud to call herself a cancer AND infidelity survivor. Today, Julie is a sought-after speaker by many family, spiritual, and women's organizations. Having been personally trained by Drs. John and Julie Gottman at the Gottman Institute in Seattle, Washington, she also is an affair-recovery coach to couples healing from infidelity. Her most cherished role, however, is being a wife to Jay and a mother to their four beautiful children.

RELATIONSHIP RESOURCES FOR COUPLES

THE SURPRISED BY LOVE™ MISSION

THE TRAUMA OF AN affair and other severe relationship challenges create both pain and opportunity. *Pain* is the result of the betrayal of trust and the violation of what is sacred in a committed relationship. Beyond the pain, however, lies the *opportunity* for deeper intimacy, evolving as a person, and a relationship that is fulfilling and conducive to true love.

SBL's mission is to *humanize infidelity* by explaining why it happens and how to heal from it. We offer transformational experiences that transcend excuses and invite individuals and couples to design new possibilities that did not exist before. Through our professional services, we offer our clients a supportive context for discovering "what they must do" and "who they have to become" to create new relationships regardless of current circumstances.

We use our personal experience and professional training to consult, coach, and equip participants with the strategies, skills, and methods they need to transform their relationships. In addition, we work with couples committed to redesigning their marriage after infidelity and other relationship challenges.

Our passion is to empower people with hope and solutions for discovering new choices that will foster understanding and inspire committed action to heal and transform their relationships.

Our work is based on the belief that IT IS POSSIBLE to create a more fulfilling and mature relationship after the trauma of an affair. This possibility for a newly designed relationship is the hope you need to redesign your marriage.

If not now, when?

A great marriage is possible following an affair. What are you waiting for?

Please call **877.944.7025**, or go to **www.drjayandjulie.com** to find out more!

PROGRAMS AND SERVICES FOR COUPLES

SEMINAR PROGRAMS

T*he Curriculum for Affair Recovery*™ is our unique research-guided healing-and-recovery system for every step of the process. Divided into carefully structured phases, the SBL approach offers focused, outcome-oriented options based on where a couple is in the recovery process.

The Healing Tasks Model™ is the healing-and-recovery template drawn from years of research on infidelity, trauma recovery, and marriage and family therapy in conjunction with the Gottman Institute of Seattle Washington. By using this innovative approach to recovery, we ensure that the appropriate tasks of healing are addressed at the proper time to provide couples with skills, strategies, principles, and relationship-empowerment techniques for designing the relationship of the couples' choosing.

The Advanced Course Programs™ provides couples with ongoing relationship-design opportunities and focuses on issues such as rebuilding trust, learning how to forgive and move beyond the past, and discovering advanced communication techniques to continue building relationships following healing and recovery work. These seminars give couples a variety of specific topic-options to invest in and build a relationship of their dreams!

Please go to the Services section at **www.drjayandjulie.com** for complete details.

INTENSIVE COACHING PROGRAMS

SBL offers a wide variety of coaching programs that include individual and couple's coaching, affair-recovery coaching, life coaching, and executive coaching services. In addition, Jay and Julie offer marathon intensive coaching for couples who desire a customized option. We design a multi-day intervention plan to jumpstart a recovery process, do intense work in a concentrated period of time, and make substantial progress in ongoing relationship work, crisis-intervention situations, or for those couples who place a premium on their privacy and efficient use of time.

Please see our Web site at **www.drjayandjulie.com** or call us directly at **877.944.7025** for a free, confidential consultation to determine if an intensive coaching program is right for you and your relationship.

KEYNOTE PRESENTATIONS

For your special event, SBL offers a wide variety of customized, keynote presentations dealing with family life, marital and relationship issues, infidelity and affair recovery, communication, conflict resolution, forgiveness, and designing healthy relationships. We work with religious groups and organizations, corporations, social-service agencies, professional organizations, clinician groups, continuing-education events, and conference planners to design a presentation that will be inspirational and substantive in content, as well as entertaining to participants.

Please contact us directly at **877.944.7025** to speak with an SBL representative to assist in designing a plan for your next event.

CORPORATE CONSULTATION

In addition to corporate seminars and keynote events on relationship and family-oriented topics, SBL provides corporate consultation for organizations (1) that are interested in designing either pro-family work cultures which promote healthy boundaries in workplace relationships or work-life balance programs, and/or (2) that require specialty consultation for issues related to sex in the workplace.

Dr. Jay Kent-Ferraro is a nationally recognized expert in optimal-performance coaching and is an executive coach to senior leaders in top Fortune 500 companies around the world. He speaks to and consults with organizations and their leadership teams internationally and can bring his unique brand of emotionally intelligent leadership programs and optimal-relationship coaching to empower your leadership teams to perform more effectively.

CLINICAL TRAINING SEMINARS FOR PROFESSIONALS

Dr. Jay and Julie Kent-Ferraro received advanced training in marriage and family therapy approaches at the world-renowned Gottman Institute in Seattle, Washington, where they were personally trained by Drs. John and Julie Gottman. With their extensive experience in working with couples recovering from infidelity and other serious relationship challenges, Dr. Jay and Julie provide mental health clinicians a wealth of knowledge, insight, and information through professional development seminar programs. The Kent-Ferraros offer keynote presentations and entire seminar programs, as well as advanced supervision for clinicians interested in working effectively with affair recovery clients.

Please contact us at **877.944.7025** for specific information on our *Organizational Development Programs* and *Clinical Training Seminars* or to arrange a no-obligation consultation with Dr. Jay Kent-Ferraro.